On Form

ON FORM

Mike Brearley

Little, Brown

LITTLE, BROWN

First published in Great Britain in 2017 by Little, Brown

1 3 5 7 9 10 8 6 4 2

A CIP catalogue record for this book
is available from the British Library.

ISBN 978-1-4087-0735-7 (hardback)
ISBN 978-1-4087-0734-0 (trade paperback)

Typeset in Electra LT Std by SX Composing DTP, Rayleigh, Essex
Printed and bound in Great Britain by Clays Ltd, St Ives plc

Papers used by Little, Brown are from well-managed forests
and other responsible sources.

Little, Brown
An imprint of
Little, Brown Book Group
Carmelite House
50 Victoria Embankment
London EC4Y 0DZ

An Hachette UK Company
www.hachette.co.uk

www.littlebrown.co.uk

For

Luka, Alia and Maia

CONTENTS

NOTE AT THE START

While the fore-note to some novels states that any resemblance to living people is accidental, my problem here is in undoing resemblances to real people – that is, to patients. There are a few such vignettes. In some cases I have conflated two or more patients. In all cases I have disguised the material so that no one who is not the patient(s) would recognise him or her from the description. If a patient does, or think they do, I hope they will feel that I am making a useful point, that they are fairly and sympathetically represented, and that they are well-enough disguised.

Second, the vexed issue of 'he', 'she', 'they', or 'he or she'. The last of these choices ('he or she'. as even in the sentences above) strikes me as impossibly clumsy. 'They' is possible occasionally (also as above) but the grammarian in me dislikes the switch to the plural. Using 'she' and 'he' in a random way is confusing, and also leads curious readers to infer significance when none is present (or at least, intended). As for 'she', I find that too redolent of political correctness, to my ear also over-careful. But I am aware that some will find my use of 'he' for 'he or she', like the use of 'man' to mean 'mankind', or the description of God as 'He', objectionable. I apologise to those of you in advance. One has to do one or the other. To my mind, 'he' is the least of the evils.

PART I: IN AND OUT OF FORM

1

GETTING OUT OF BED
ON THE WRONG SIDE

The wind bloweth where it listeth, and thou hearest the sound thereof, but canst not tell whence it cometh, and whither it goeth: so is every one that is born of the Spirit.

John 3.8

As a classroom teacher for forty years, how could it be that I was teaching well one day and badly the next? In tune one minute, edgy the next? Optimistic one term, low and deflated another? How can one hold on to what is good and what works?

Jonathan Smith

———

As a young adult, I was a friend's weekend house-guest. I was enamoured by the whole, perfect family – warm, funny, frank, intelligent, committed to worthwhile causes and careers. For a while I was the only guest, and was blissfully happy. The house was capacious, the beautiful garden secluded, running down to a quiet stretch of the River Severn, the late-summer weather serene. I remember exciting, erotically charged but also innocent games in the hot sun.

At one point we played pitch-and-putt golf at a nearby course. A novice at golf, I kept hitting the ball straight, onto the green, mood and play in total accord. Halfway through the round, however, other guests joined the party. They were noisy, exuberant and (to my mind) intrusive. I was no longer the centre of attention. Suddenly ejected from, or ejecting myself from, my Garden of Eden, I felt excluded and jealous. The feelings grew more complicated, self-awareness degenerating into self-consciousness about being so childish and petulant. The more I understood what this decline was down to, the less I was able to cope. On top of my resentment, directed both towards those who had usurped me and those whose attention had turned elsewhere, I became moodily self-loathing.

In my golf, too, I collapsed: the ball started to fly off in hectic and drastic slices and hooks. I instantly became an inferior player. Now I could do no right. Socially, psychologically, even physically, I had lost form.

Irritation

Years later, reading Tolstoy's *Anna Karenina*, I was reminded of this convulsive decline when Konstantin Levin, the gentleman-farmer whom we will meet again when he joins his peasants in cutting hay, goes on a dismal shooting expedition with his vain house-guest, the fashionable young socialite, Vasenka Veslovsky. Also on the expedition is Levin's brother-in-law, Stiva Oblonsky. Veslovsky, wearing clothes that are all too new, overrides Levin's proposal to delay shooting until they get to a bigger marsh, thus forcing him to forgo the first foray, since the space is too narrow for three men. Veslovsky then fails to engage the safety catch of his gun, which goes off in the carriage. While Levin takes his turn to go into the marsh, Veslovsky foolishly drives the carriage into the mud, from which the coachman and Levin have to labour to extricate it. To make up for his faux pas, Veslovsky next insists on driving. He overworks the horses, one of which goes lame as a result.

Levin's mounting irritation and resentment lead him to shoot badly – so badly, and in such a negative mood, that his dog Laska gives up on him, and only pretends to hunt for a snipe that he actually has managed to kill.

Early next morning, at dawn, Levin goes off shooting by himself. Now he recovers his usual form. But when after three hours he gets back, hungry for breakfast, he discovers that his companions have eaten all the food. Finally, when they get home, he is further enraged by the young man's renewed flirting with his wife. Tolstoy describes one of these shifts in Levin's feelings:

> Again, as on the previous occasion, he suddenly, without the least interval, felt thrown from the height of happiness, peace, and dignity into an abyss of despair, malevolence, and degradation. Again, everyone and everything became revolting to him.

I know such states, and the startlingly negative impact they have on our form. Instead of our anger remaining focused, our gloomy feelings embrace the whole world, including ourselves. And we cannot shoot straight.

In Trim

So what is it to be on form?

Aspects of form and the loss of it apply to every area of life that calls for skill and freedom. The notion applies most naturally to practical and bodily skills that demand a sound technique. It applies also to activities, many of them mundane, that are primarily mental and emotional: conversing, teaching, doing the crossword, telling a joke or arguing a point, writing. Good form ranges from predictable and reliable steadiness to innovative insights that change a whole field of enquiry. And even in routine activities, form is enhanced by a creative, playful approach to the task, as when parents get a toddler to eat by helicoptering spoonfuls into his mouth.

The former England cricketer Tony Greig told me once about one of his eight Test centuries, I think his first, at Bombay in 1973. Chasing India's total of 448, England were struggling at 79 for four when he came in to bat. Greig and Keith Fletcher added 254 runs for the fifth wicket, and Greig was eventually dismissed for 148. While playing, he was, he said, 'perfectly relaxed, and perfectly concentrated'. His state of mind was attuned to the task, to the opposition, and to his own strengths and weaknesses. It was not a flamboyant innings. He played calmly, from his own centre. He was not rattled by occasional errors or by being beaten by the bowler, nor was he elated by his own perfectly timed boundaries.

Greig's account seems to me to represent the essence of good form: relaxed without being loose, concentrated without tension: nothing extraneous, but poised, the innings lastingly special because of this inner state and its happy conjunction with outer performance. It may well have been an experience of the sublime, of being 'in the zone'.

Teams, like individuals, can be on or off form. When on form, they are creative, efficient, coordinated. They are not dominated by selfish individualism, nor has individual flair been suppressed. The team's morale is properly positive, neither complacent nor rent with excessive rivalry and doubt. Though its members are not always in emotional harmony with each other, they share a common purpose and are able to set aside differences on the field of play. The team is bigger than the individuals; a new entity is created, the team itself, which can be on form when some of its components are not. A climbing team goes at the speed of its slowest member, helping him through, making the best of the situation.

Form is at times a matter of mutual benign influence. As Malcolm Gladwell puts it, the unspoken rule of joint improvisation is that neither participant refuses what the other initiates. You run with what your collaborator proposes, and you need to have confidence that he will run with you. In his child consultations, the paediatrician and psychoanalyst Donald Winnicott would invite the child to make a picture, a 'squiggle', with him. After a first mark had been made by the child or by himself, they would take it in turns, till a whole drawing emerged in which it was not easy to remember, nor even relevant, who had done what. Through this shared, innovative activity, the therapeutic couple might arrive at insights into what at that time was blocking the child's development, which might then be freed up.

Recognising Form

We recognise form when we see it. Not infallibly, of course, but most often correctly. Trainers know when a horse is in fine fettle, sailors when their ship is in trim. There are times when the external and internal winds blow moderately, there is neither a gale nor the stagnation of a flat calm; the boat is sailing well, making optimal use of the conditions. Ship's captain and novelist Joseph Conrad went so far as to say: 'The ship, our ship, the ship we serve, is the moral symbol of our life.'

Fans become restless when their tennis hero or their football team is tentative, off form. The same goes for audiences hearing their favourite violinist, opera singer or orchestra. They

may be worried or angry. However they react, they are sure that what they see is loss of form.

So much for the view from outside. From the inside, we may think we're on form when we aren't, or vice versa. Failing to see the rolled eyes and the fixed smiles, we assume our jokes are amusing and our stories absorbing to the audience around the dinner table. Conversely, we write ourselves off too quickly, making no allowances for the difficulty of challenge or conditions.

But normally we know well enough. We are at ease. There is rhythm, timing, placement, poise. Footwork or fingerwork is sure. Perception and motor skills are realistic and allied with each other. We are clear in our thinking, knowing our way around, yet open to the new. We are spontaneous without going wild; we monitor ourselves without putting a spanner in our works. Risk-taking and caution are in balance. Technique, with its assurance of repeatability and accuracy, is secure enough, and so is attitude – we are not frantic or uptight. In cricket, the batsman is not unduly anxious about losing his wicket; the bowler feels lively in his run-up and action. When stretched we don't panic or become too discombobulated (or not for too long). We are resilient. In-form craftsmen characteristically grow in confidence as they warm to the task. The whole business, whatever it is, does not feel too much like an unwelcome demand for work; we are not 'laboured'.

In his short novel *A Month in the Country*, J. L. Carr describes solid good form:

> You know how it is when a tricky job is going well because you're doing things the way they should be done, when you're working in rhythm and feel a reassuring confidence that everything's unravelling naturally and all will be right in the end. That's about it: I knew what I was doing – it's really what being professional means.

My wife, a silversmith, describes raising a panel of silver to make a vase or a jug. At times, she says, 'the perfectly balanced hammer *feels* perfectly balanced. You find yourself hitting the silver in just the right way. There are no extraneous marks.

You don't hit your thumb. Your left hand holding the silver doesn't hurt from the jarring. It's a wonderful feeling.'

As a psychoanalyst, I am sometimes able to listen more or less simultaneously at different levels to the overt story, to how it is told, to subliminal messages or attitudes. I may then be able to respond to patients with freedom and clarity. Ideas come to me, but they are not set in stone. I can see the wood for the trees, and the trees for the wood. Psychoanalysts have to experience suffering along with their patients, both in sharing what the latter consciously feel, and in feeling what they cannot own, and thus disown by putting outside themselves and attributing to others. Too much ease in my work might result from having missed or refused such projections and difficulties; so we might properly be suspicious if we are too comfortable. But when patients test and challenge me forcefully, I struggle through, open to the disruption, but either not destabilised by it or able to recover quickly enough. (But the on-form analyst may not always be appreciated by the patient.)

As captain of a cricket team, too, I had to respond to pressures: from the opposition, from my own sometimes disgruntled or distressed team members, perhaps from the crowd and the press. As captain of England, I was the recipient of many people's projections; some of their complaints or admiration were earned and appropriate, others were the result of a propensity to find heroes and villains.

Form is not a matter of a moment. It takes time to assess. Nor is it a matter of total ease. We have to struggle through hard times, not all of them down to our own shortcomings. Form is sometimes a matter of solidity and imperviousness, like a great oak in a storm; at other times it is more aptly pictured as a capacity to bend and sway before the wind like the bamboo that survives the hurricane because of its flexibility.

Loss of form is equally evident. If decline is prolonged, we become anxious. Is this it? Is it terminal? We have no guarantee that it will return. Yet for us to change in a substantial way, we often have to suffer a crisis or a setback. It is through failure, or illness, or even breakdown, that we come to see how wrong things are, and how urgently we need serious self-examination, support or treatment. We may need to get on terms with our neurotic selves. At the political and social level, too, it may only be through crisis that underlying problems and the need for change are clearly enough recognised.

Ups and Downs

In all human endeavours, we are often too anxious, but sometimes not anxious enough. We are too narrow in our expectations of ourselves, or over-ambitious, dangerously so at times. In one telling of the legend, Daedalus, the Athenian craftsman who built the labyrinth for King Minos of Crete, was himself imprisoned by Minos for showing Ariadne how to evade the Minotaur and emerge from the labyrinth by using a ball of string. To achieve his own escape, and that of his son, Icarus, Daedalus fabricated wings of feathers and wax. He warned the youth neither to fly too low, where the humidity would clog his wings and cause him to sink heavily into the sea, nor to fly too close to the sun, where the heat would melt the wax. He warned, in other words, against risking both too little and too much, against mania and depression. Icarus, elated by his ability to fly, soared higher and higher – and plummeted to his doom.

To retain form, or recover it, we have to allow and sometimes seek help or guidance. When lost it is good to ask the way or consult a map. Temperaments vary in how far we need to have a plan spelled out in advance. Some are keener on working things out abstractly, from general principles; others, like the Inuit, like illiterate craftsmen, know by the feel of things where they are and which way to go. Legal submissions refer to principles of law, but there is also case-by-case argument.

Form for me is a different matter from form for you. As the old Yorkshire saying has it, 'It takes all sorts'. We have to find a style of working that suits ourselves. We also, as teams and as individuals, need to give house-room to a range of different qualities. My form on Wednesday will be different from my form on Thursday, changing as it must with varying challenges and moods. My later style as batsman or psychoanalyst is different from what it was earlier. We may in our own small ways be drawn more to the classical or to the romantic. From the age of seven, my own cricketing hero was the orthodox Middlesex opening batsman, Jack Robertson, rather than the dashing romantic stars in the same team, Denis Compton or Bill Edrich. There are different forms of form.

Moreover, how we formulate to ourselves what the key issues are makes a difference to the kind of form we aim at. The presenting problem in someone seeking help may disguise hidden, underlying issues. Psychotherapists may rightly suspect that somatic pain, say, covers deeper emotional anxiety; in a family, a child's hyperactivity may express something of the parents' or the whole family's unhappiness or conflict. Puzzling changes in social and political attitudes – for instance a popular shift to the right combined with widespread conviction that social difficulties in the country are a result of excessive immigration – may have their roots in a deep sense of neglect by the powers-that-be.

There is, however, no simple narrative logic to this book. It is certainly not *Tips for Being on Form in Ten Easy Chapters*. Form is an elastic concept, even slippery. It spreads out into creativity and change of heart at one end, while loss of it descends into breakdown at the other. In between are all the varied ways we find or lose form in the whole gamut of skill-requiring activities of life. Writing the book has taken me down alleys I had never thought of in this connection. For instance, I hadn't imagined going into disruptions of form so extreme as hardly to be called being 'out of form' at all – Othello's collapse, say. And at the other end of the spectrum, I am surprised at how much I am inclined to refer to enhancements of form so close to transformations as to hardly be called form either – Tolstoy's recovery of faith, for example, and his revelation of its meaning. Writing the book has made me think.

In this process I have gone through all sorts of moods and levels of form myself. At dark moments, for consolation, I remember how the great work of philosophy, *A Treatise of Human Nature*, by a hero of mine, David Hume, 'fell still-born from the press'.

We tend to personify form, or 'Form'. Like 'Lady Luck', she may be more like a solid friend than a lover. These deities have power over us, just as Death or Disease seek us out, ineluctable. But form is *not* simply in the lap of the gods – it is not, or not simply, a matter of which side of the bed we got out of that morning. So: how far can we control our form? Can we harness it, make it work for us, or is it a wild horse, never to be tamed?

2

ZEN AND THE ART OF BATTING

Physician, heal thyself.

Luke 4.23

Sometimes we shouldn't make sophisticated arguments about the uncertainties of this course of action or that; we should simply do what is right.

Alan Paton

A psychoanalyst is walking along a hospital corridor. A medical colleague is walking in the opposite direction. They haven't seen each other for a while. The medic says, 'Hi, how are things?' The analyst replies: 'You're well, how am I?'

Some are better at helping others, even at knowing them, than they are themselves. John Arlott, the cricket writer and broadcaster, once wrote a piece about me with the headline 'Physician, heal thyself'. The advice was, and is, apposite. Not all that long ago a colleague, referring to my work as a psychoanalyst, asked me when I was going to start captaining myself.

I am more willing to admit to failings in cricket than in other areas of my life. My batting record in Test cricket was poor (though I found myself using the anodyne word 'modest' to myself), and I still at times replay moments of bad thinking which led to unnecessary dismissals. I also recognise and regret failings of character which were at the root of my repeated errors. I am not deluded into thinking I might have been high in the echelons of batting history. But I could have (that is, I might have, had I been a better, or bigger, person) been more successful than I was.

In the 1976–7 series in India, we played the fifth Test in Bombay. India won the toss and scored 338. We started batting in mid-afternoon on the second day. By the close, we were 99 for no wicket, of which I was 68 not out. I had played with greater freedom than in any previous Test innings, or indeed would do in any subsequent one. The next day, unfortunately for me, was a rest day. So I had a long time to contemplate my continuing innings. That evening I was invited to dinner by someone I hardly knew. I sought and was given assurance that dinner would not be late and I could get back for my sleep and for the early departure to the ground. (Test matches on the short Indian winter days started at ten o'clock.) In the event, we stood around for several hours in a hot room, crowded with smokers, drinking whisky (in my case, sipping weak whisky) and inhaling smoke. Dinner was not served until 10.30. I grew tired, bored, allergic, frustrated and hungry. I gulped down my food and got a taxi back to the hotel. I felt depressed and angry. But why did I stay? Why not leave at eight and get a meal at the hotel? Why did I feel I had some obligation to people who wanted me as a minor trophy at their social gathering? What feebleness of ambition! What reluctance to offend! When I batted the next day, some freshness was lacking. India bowled with more defensive fields. I struggled to 91, and then got out. I never scored a Test century.

(Having scored my first County Championship century – 173 not out – against Glamorgan in 1974, I followed this in the next match with 163 not out against Yorkshire.)

When I walked onto the big stage of Test cricket I was often too tense, and made mistakes that I would not have made when facing similar bowling in county cricket. I remember a conversation with Mike Gatting, who captained Middlesex and England after me. At Lord's in 1984 he had been out lbw to Malcolm Marshall, the great West Indian fast bowler, twice in the match, each time without playing a stroke. He was, he told me, 'just trying to be careful'. The anxiety of the occasion and his sense of responsibility had led him to be over-conscious of the bowler's capabilities. Warning himself of what *might* come at him, he neglected to focus on what *did*. I am reminded of the paradoxical remark of the old Nottinghamshire and England batsman, George Gunn: 'The trouble with most batsmen is that they pay too much attention to the bowling, instead of going with the tide.'

Gatting admitted he was paying the wrong kind of attention to the bowler, telling himself: '"We must see Marshall off, I mustn't play at a wide one, I must watch out for his outswing". You would have thought that I would have been wiser second innings, but it was coming to the end of the day, the old mind-set returned, and I was more concerned about leaving the ball than playing it.' Facing the same undeviating deliveries in a county match, he would have played them comfortably with the middle of his bat rather than the middle of his pad.

Here are some of my moments of foolishness. In the matches leading up to the first Test in India in December 1976, at Delhi, I had been in the form of my life. I had started the tour with a score of 206 at Poona, and had made runs and batted well regularly since then. I felt in fine fettle as I went out to open the batting with Dennis Amiss, after Tony Greig had won an important toss. The pitch was flat, hard and dry. The day was dreamily hazy, with that veiled sunlight so common on winter mornings in northern India. The crowd, smaller than at most Indian Test grounds in those days, but still substantial, felt mistily distant, almost unreal. After two or three overs, a large yellow-and-brown butterfly settled by the stumps at the non-striker's end, basking. I could attend to the butterfly and to the bowling with equally detached interest.

India's bowling strength in that era was mostly in their spinners. They had one quickish bowler, Karsan Ghavri. Though we had doubts about the legality of his action when he bowled a bouncer, Ghavri was not someone whose pace would make one apprehensive; after all, we had just been playing against the West Indies, whose fast bowlers were in a different league of speed and hostility. After a few overs, in which I scored four comfortable singles, Ghavri bowled me a short ball, perhaps a bouncer. I went to hook it. It was on me more quickly than I expected, and went off my gloves to backward square leg for another single. I was then uncertain – should I attempt to hook or not? To my shame, instead of quietly deciding not to hook for the time being, while the ball was new and likely to zip off the pitch, I momentarily lost my nerve.

When I next faced Ghavri, having pushed the ball in a controlled way towards mid-off, I set off for a foolish single. Brijesh Patel, an excellent cover fielder, swooped to his right, picked up one-handed and threw down the one stump he could see at the bowler's end. I was run out, less than half an hour into the match. A dreadful mistake, which arose out of my anxiety and my wish to get to the other end. Not noble, not clever. It was less a matter of fear than of uncertainty. I had been courageous enough against West Indians Andy Roberts and Michael Holding the previous summer – in fact one main reason I had been picked for England in the first place was that I batted for three hours against them when they bowled faster than anything I had ever previously faced in the first innings of the MCC v. West Indies match at Lord's.

At Delhi, we were soon five down for 125, but Amiss and Alan Knott took us to a respectable score of 381. We then bowled India out twice, for 122 and 234, to gain a remarkable win. John Lever, who had also scored 53, took ten wickets in the match, swinging the ball beautifully. But for me personally, this moment of madness spoiled my whole tour. I had only this one innings in Delhi (we won by an innings); I failed in the next Test match at Calcutta (also batting once, except for a few balls in the second innings, when I was not out). And in the third Test at Madras (now Chennai), I was caught and bowled for 59 off a rebound from the head of short square leg. Not until that last Test, at Bombay, did I play with the fluency that I might have developed over the whole series. Greig told me later he could have cried when I ran myself out at Delhi. So could I.

Another moment. England v. Australia at Headingley, 1977. This was the match that won us the series 3–0 and the Ashes with it. It was the occasion of Geoffrey Boycott's hundredth century – and, less memorably to everyone else, of my dismissal to the second ball of the innings, bowled by Jeff Thomson. It was full of length, and swinging away. I played a horrible shot, reaching for it outside off-stump. I hit the ground with my bat, missed the ball and was given out caught behind, the umpire confusing the sound of bat on ground with that of bat on ball.

The problem was what was going on inside my head. Someone had recommended to me *Zen in the Art of Archery*, by Eugen Herrigel, a book that 'brought Zen to Europe after the War'. I was unable to sleep the night before, and had read a couple of chapters of the book in the middle of the night. It is a measure of my stupidity that, instead of taking seriously the years of discipline that go into making someone a master of archery or any other physical skill, or indeed of any transformation in mind-set, I carried out onto the pitch that morning a vague ideal of some sort of Zen-like calm, of not letting my conscious mind interfere in automatic mind-body processing. My mind (or my body-mind), left to its confused self, processed things badly. Once again, a mental flaw had disastrous results; I cringe at it forty years on. Thinking, including the thought-imperative, 'don't think', had intruded fatally. I had allowed myself to be seduced by a romanticised version of a state that is arrived at, if at all, through long, disciplined training.

Yet another incident. In a Test match at Lahore in 1978, I middled a cover drive off leg-spinner Abdul Qadir, which unfortunately hit a close fielder, rebounding towards short third man. I looked for a single and was sent back, perhaps belatedly, by my batting partner, Geoffrey Boycott, and was run out. All understandable, no doubt. But what this external account omits is that my eagerness to get the run was in part based on a sense of entitlement, as if the fact that I deserved at least one for this shot, which would have gone for four if it hadn't hit the fielder's leg, was more relevant to right action than where the ball actually went. I was like the car driver who, going through a red light, privately justifies his action to himself on the grounds that if someone in front of him hadn't dithered, he would have got through on green.

I think much of this chapter of accidents reveals a mixture of insecurity, arrogance and naivety. In 1964, at the age of twenty-two, years before these Test appearances, I had been selected as a young hopeful for the last MCC tour of South Africa before the ban on sporting contacts. I am not proud of having gone on the tour, but exposure to the system of apartheid during it, and travelling to all sections of the country for a month afterwards, was an education for me, firming up my belief that it was wrong to play sport against a country where discrimination governed all areas of life, including sport. I met the novelist Alan Paton, author of the definitive novel on South Africa's harsh social realities, *Cry the Beloved Country*, who responded to my concern about the possible disastrous consequences of upheaval, even revolution, in South Africa by telling me that sometimes it is necessary simply to do what is right.

I came to realise that though it was hard to be sure that a sporting boycott would be effective, even in that sports-mad country, it felt intrinsically wrong to carry on sporting contacts, and I spoke out against such tours in 1968 and subsequently.

On that 1964–5 tour, I did well enough in the run-up to the first Test at Durban, averaging over 40, having batted at every position in the top six. We had a strong batting line-up, and it was clearly right that I was not selected for the Test. One day during the match, a man stood behind the nets at the rear of the stadium watching me practise. As I came out, he asked quietly if he might make a comment on my batting. Yes, of course, I said. He suggested that I was holding the bat too tightly, as if my life depended on it. He said I needed to relax my arms and both hands, especially the top hand. I listened politely. And walked away.

At some point I was told that this sallow man who seemed old to me (he was only sixty-four and died of cancer a few weeks later) was none other than Wally Hammond, one of England's most successful batsmen, and one of the greatest stylists of all time. Despite knowing this, I did not properly take on board what he had said. I had the idea that relaxing would mean being loose (as indeed I was in the Zen example years later). I thought I knew better.

It took me a decade to realise the truth of what Hammond had told me. In 1974, Tiger Smith, then in his nineties and nearly blind, watched me score a stiff-upper-lip 74 against Warwickshire at Edgbaston. Remembering the respect that Warwickshire and Somerset all-rounder Tom Cartwright, whom I admired greatly as cricketer and friend, had for Tiger as a coach, which he had told me about when we were team-mates on that South Africa tour ten years before, I asked him for his advice. We were in the players' dining room. Tiger told me to stand facing him with his walking stick as my bat and 'play' a few shots. He then asked, 'Do you think frowning helps you hit the ball harder?' He showed me how tense I was, in face, hands and arms, and I came to see how much easier it is to swing a bat when the body relaxes. Smith's method of coaching at that moment focused not so much on my technical shortcomings, which he might also have prioritised, as on my bodily and emotional state. He made plain to me a basic assumption that had long interfered with my level of skill.

Left to right: Tiger Smith, Wally Hammond and Ian Botham

I needed to have the same message reinforced yet again a few years later, by the great all-rounder, Ian Botham, who showed me how the fingers of his right-hand batting glove were almost unmarked by holding the bat; and he hit the ball hard enough!

I was arrogant not to take any tip from Hammond seriously. I was also insecure, not solidly in my own self. I was both eager to please and unwilling to buckle down in order to reflect on what was said, and work to strengthen my technique.

It is true that coaching was not an activity valued by many cricketers of my generation. There was a pseudo-amateur attitude to coaching and learning that one should learn by apprenticeship, by watching and listening. County coaches tended to lack the confidence to advise or criticise first-team players. For many years, there was widespread scepticism about the potential usefulness of coaching aids that are now taken for granted, like bowling machines and cameras. When, as captain, I tried to persuade Middlesex to get a video camera in the early 1970s, the request was turned down as unnecessary and too expensive.

In 1985, I predicted, 'Twenty years from now cricketers will, I think, regard the present approach to coaching as . . . antiquated.' I was right. Coaching in the broad sense needed to be, and has been, upgraded and updated. By 'broad' I mean to include, within the concept of coaching, mentoring, mental toughening and facilitation. What is often needed is akin to what novelist Pat Barker refers to as resulting from a course run by another fine writer, Angela Carter: 'She did not so much teach me as give me faith in my own voice. The best teaching is to recognise the voice and encourage it, and gently discourage attempts to be someone else, and Angela was a very good teacher.'

Looking back over all those cricket-playing years, I some-times feel that I lacked not only a coach, but also someone to talk robustly to me about my approach to batting. Boycott, the other young hopeful on that tour of South Africa, always had his personal batting mentor, the Yorkshire-born Somerset leg-spinner Johnny Lawrence, with whom he checked in regularly. I, however, would ask for advice only during periods of bad form, and would then move from one well-meaning colleague to another, often bewildered by the conflicting pieces of advice gained from people who, however generous, were not committed to an ongoing process with me, and nor I to them. I failed to make the effort to find a person I could rely on. I might have asked a senior Middlesex player such as off-spinner and all-rounder Fred Titmus. And when I *was* given advice I didn't take it in fully, as I have shown. Perhaps if a more professional system had been in place, I would have made more use of it; but perhaps – more likely – not.

3

ON TO THE COUCH

If we can't control our conscious responses, what chance do we have against the influences we haven't recognized?

Edward St Aubyn

You asked me what I consider essential personal qualities in a future psychoanalyst. The answer is comparatively simple . . . You have to have a great love of the truth, scientific truth as well as personal truth, and you have to place this appreciation of truth higher than any discomfort at meeting unpleasant facts, whether they belong to the world outside or to your own inner person.

Anna Freud

At some point during my time as a student at Cambridge, I joined the Samaritans. I didn't know why. I did know that I was excited by the philosophical teaching and writing of John Wisdom, Professor of Philosophy, who argued that uncovering unconscious ideas and assumptions is an important element in dealing with philosophical perplexity, as of course it is in psychoanalysis. But I had not been conspicuous in help-ing others, nor had I been aware of depression in myself; nor again had I encountered anything labelled depression in my family or surroundings. I would say that my parents, loving and well-meaning as they were, were not alert to difficult emotions.

Looking back, I think I may have had an inkling of such aspects of myself, and joining the Samaritans was a way to gain some sort of contact with them. (When years later I applied to rejoin, in Brent, north London, I was at first turned down, partly because I offered this as one reason for my interest. I think the person interviewing me thought I was self-centred. It was not that I had no wish to help others; rather I was trying to give some sort of account of that wish.) In my telephone work with the Samaritans, I found that people didn't ring off quickly – I could listen to them. I was also puzzled about why they were so despairing, even suicidal. I wanted to understand more.

Years later, my (never-finished) PhD topic, in philosophy, was 'Emotion and Reason: Explanations of Action'. I was trying to find my way into the life of the mind. I had always sensed that there was more to it than I was, in my naivety, aware of. I was uneasy about my father's down-to-earth scepticism about religion. His name was Horace: and when playing Horatio in the school production of *Hamlet*, I was taken by Hamlet's remark: 'There are more things in heaven and earth, Horatio, than are dreamt of in your philosophy.' I was searching for this something more. The thesis remained unfinished, partly because I wasn't a true academic or philosopher, partly because in those days you could get a university teaching job, as I did in 1968 at the University of Newcastle upon Tyne, without a PhD. And the first years of this work left little time for my own writing.

I had played occasional games for Middlesex while at university. During this time Fred Titmus, a fine all-rounder with a sharp sense of humour, who had come up the hard way, learning football, boxing and cricket at a boys' club in King's

Cross, would accost me with questions such as 'What is this thing we're paying for you to do, this philosophy, then?' Partly he was teasing; partly, though, he was curious to know more. Much later, during my last four years captaining Middlesex, I was having psychoanalysis myself five mornings a week before play, sometimes at 6.15 a.m. (thanks to the generosity of my analyst) in order that I could travel to Basingstoke, say, or Chelmsford, for an 11.30 start. Again I found in the dressing room a similar, somewhat defensive, curiosity about this strange commitment. One season – I think it might have been 1981, when I scored a lot of runs early on – Graham Barlow, one of the Middlesex batsmen, said to me: 'Maybe we should all come and lie on your analyst's couch!' Many people, puzzled about what goes on in this strange encounter called psychoanalysis, oscillate between envy, curiosity and ridicule.

But I found the analysis helpful in my role as cricketer and captain. Cricket is a psychological game – a lot goes on in the head, in terms for example of shrewdness, resilience, bluff, individualism and team spirit. And captaining calls for a down-to-earth sense of what makes players tick, both to help get the best out of one's own team and to probe the weaknesses of the opposition. People have asked me if psychology helped me in this role. It did, but the reverse applied equally – cricket helped me to be more psychologically aware.

In 1976, the year I first played for England, I had a preliminary interview for training at the Institute of Psychoanalysis with Anne-Marie Sandler, a prominent analyst, originally from Switzerland. After the interview, she wrote, understandably, that I needed more experience with people who were in psychological trouble before making a full application. Some weeks later, I had a charming second letter from her to the effect that British members of the Admissions Committee had

informed her that captaining a cricket team had more relevance to training to be a psychoanalyst than she had realised.
I could proceed with my application.

Some people believe psychoanalysis has been disproved and
superseded. Is it not as outdated as Mesmerism, or Rosicrucianism,
as dead as the dodo? Has not Freud, like Marx, been discred-
ited as a pseudo-scientist?

Well, no, actually. Five-days-per-week psychoanalysis *is*
under threat, both from less frequent (perhaps once-weekly)
arrangements and from more packaged treatments (such as
cognitive behavioural therapy), just as five-day Test cricket
is challenged by much shorter forms of the game, including
Twenty20 matches – consisting of twenty overs per side – which
are completed in three hours or so. But psychoanalysis is vigorous
still, and has much to offer to a world that too readily accepts
simple accounts of the mind, and yearns for quick solutions.
And in therapy as in cricket, the shorter game relies for some
of its depth and appeal on the long version. Psychoanalysis
incorporates an overall attitude and philosophy of life, a set of
interlocking ideas that cover not only pathology but also many
aspects of ordinary healthy living. It offers a thoroughgoing
picture of human beings: filled with inner voices, the mind is
largely unconscious, deep and conflicted; we are ambivalent
between love and hate as we are between dependence and
independence. This is a rich and nuanced view of life as
involving struggle; we have to do justice to both selfishness and
altruism, to meanness and generosity. Psychoanalysis offers
both a tragic and an ironic view of life.

Form for the Psychoanalyst

Let me start with empathy. The analyst steps as it were into
the patient's shoes. In a sense he 'becomes' the patient, like a

Bushman entering the mind-set of a cheetah in order to follow it to its prey (which he can then purloin). For cricketers in general, the need for empathy is subtle – for instance, to support your batting partner, sensing his anxiety or his vulnerability and helping him through; or, as a bowler, to intuit when a batsman is about to take a particular kind of risk. The captain has to be more systematically empathic, entering into the problems of his team members in order to help restore their confidence when they are struggling. Similarly, the parent of a small child 'intuits' or discovers by attentive trial and error what is upsetting her child – is he cold? Or hot? Or hungry? Or lonely? Or in a mess? And the young child intuits what is safe and what is risky largely from its elders. Such empathy is a basic human quality.

Here is a story about sports coaches. A player has fallen into a hole and can't get out. One coach says, 'What you should have done is see the hole, why don't you keep your eyes open?' and wanders off. Another coach looks down sardonically, remarking, 'You won't be able to play in the next match if you're still in a hole!' The third coach is irritated: 'You need to try harder, if you're really serious you wouldn't fall into holes, and if you did, you'd be able to climb out.' The fourth coach, however, jumps in. The player is shocked: 'That's really stupid. Now we're both stuck down here.' 'Yes,' says the coach. 'But I've been here before and I know how to get out.'

We analysts have to get into a hole with our patients. We imaginatively have to gain a sense of their suffering, their temptations, their ways of being. It is true, as the player in the hole says, that we're no use if we are *simply* in the hole with no method or experience of such holes – we also need some idea of how to get out (though our knowledge will rarely be as clear-cut as the story suggests).

Being a psychoanalyst requires empathic judgment, including good guesswork, in deciding when to put into words one's understanding – however partial – and when to stay silent. A colleague told me once: 'One of the most important things my analyst gave me was that she allowed me to be depressed in peace.'

The etymology of the word *understand* seems to me relevant. We have to stand there, supportive of the patient, attentive to him. Under-standing is not only an intellectual process. It includes being open to the unknown and supportive of the patient's predicament. This support may come (partly) through words; at other times it is a matter of availability: being fully present, listening quietly, and sharing the feelings.

A further requirement is courage, allied, as Anna Freud says in the quote at the beginning of the chapter, with love of truth. This can be seen in this example, which shows the impact a patient, Marijke, had on her therapist, Peter, a man who was in analysis with me.

Peter dreamed about the courage he needed in the work with her. Marijke, who had Dutch connections, was a lawyer armed with a powerful intellect. She could be, as he had repeatedly reported, contemptuous of him, and was toying with the idea of stopping her therapy. Peter dreamed:

> He is in a camp, during the Second World War, in East Anglia, opposite Nazi-occupied Holland. He is due to be landed in Holland as part of an expeditionary force. He becomes extremely anxious about whether, if captured and tortured in Holland, he can trust himself not to give information away. He is aware that he needs help in deciding whether it is braver to own up to this, and refuse to be dropped in Holland rather than risk the outcome, or

whether it would be cowardly to pull out of the dangerous expedition. He goes to find a priest, who is with some men kicking a football around. The priest accompanies him to the entrance to his, the priest's hut. The dreamer is struck by how freezing the wind is. He thinks that a screen of glass has been put across to shield them from the wind.

My patient and I came to see the dream as expressing Peter's anxieties in relation to his 'Dutch' patient, who was represented by the potential Nazi captor and torturer. The dream expressed his self-doubt in the face of her tormenting contempt, along with his need for someone to help him, the priest-analyst-footballer (myself). Peter's question was: did he have the inner resources to trust himself to go on an analytic expedition into territory under the control of the Nazis – that is, into areas of the patient and her analysis in which cruelty predominated? Would it be more honest, as well as safer, for him either to give up the whole enterprise and allow the analysis with her to end, or, less drastically, to steer clear of attempts to confront the torture to which he would be exposed if he risked being dropped into that territory? As I knew, he was indeed tempted to appease her and avoid the whole issue. But he was also afraid that staying away from the torture would be a cowardly stance, an evasion of his duty. Would he be letting his patient down? As to the screen from the wind, I understood it as the priest/analyst's effort to provide a space for thought despite the chilling situation. (I leave aside further questions about my patient's own possible cruelty, and his fears of all these emotions and behaviours being actualised in the relationship with me, his analyst.)

We psychoanalysts are sometimes inclined to veer away from facing and finding ways to confront the primitive force of our patients' love, hate and cruelty. We are also tempted to hide from our fear, hatred and desire; perhaps from our own areas of madness. I felt that this dream was a healing dream, in that it laid out with clarity an underlying anxiety that inhibited Peter in his work with this troubling, tormenting patient. It allowed him to see how much her contempt was affecting him, and how much he needed help with that scenario. The dream, along with our work on it, enabled Peter to be more courageous and frank with his patient about her cruelty.

James Strachey, who translated the works of Freud, argued that often what we should interpret is that which we find most difficult to say. This view does not imply that we should rush in to confront the patient without thought of his sensitivities or his capacity to tolerate knowing his own emotions and motives. We have to work hard to find ways of making our point palatable to the patient. But Strachey was right: the analyst, like the patient, needs courage, and tolerance of uncertainty.

And What About the Patient?

Psychoanalysts and patients alike are fortunate to have the encouragement to be honest – something that the theory and practice of our discipline offer both as an aim and an ideal. Truth – I don't mean absolute truth – if it can be borne, is food for thought. And we have the further encouragement that when we do face an uncomfortable truth we are already part of the way to psychic change of a probably helpful kind. A patient said to me once that when she started her analysis she was simply depressed; now, after some years of work together, she was able to 'walk round her depression'. She could see its contours. The depression was no longer felt to be all there was; she now had some awareness that there were boundaries and limits to it. Indeed her 'walking around' the depression modified the depression itself.

But there is something odd about applying the notion of being on form to patients. After all, their task is to gain some access to the unconscious patterns or moulds that shape their lives, often in limiting or distorting ways. By their nature, such patterns cannot be revealed and worked through without discomfort, disruption and acting out. When a patient associates freely, as he is explicitly or implicitly encouraged to do, his fluency, which looks like a sign of good form, may need to be interrupted. The patient whose talk flows on without a pause might feel that he is on form, whereas the analyst rightly suspects him of (unconsciously) slipping away from uncomfortable feelings, or perhaps being over-pleased with his own productions. The process of analysis is a mixture of playfulness and struggle, of spontaneity and disruption. It involves hard reflection.

Free associations sometimes come to a halt suddenly. Freud suggested that one reason for blockages in the patient's associating is the intrusion of disturbing feelings or thoughts relating to the analyst. Such sudden silences, lapses into incoherence, or palpable unease, may indicate embarrassment or arousal at, say, a mocking or sexually explicit thought about the analyst, which may be unconscious. A patient of mine had been speaking articulately and in an engaged way about her family situation. Suddenly she became hesitant, stumbling for words. Curious about what had prompted the shift, I asked her what, if anything, had crossed her mind at that moment. She realised to her surprise that she was picturing a severe, bewigged judge. I gathered that she had been abruptly stopped in her tracks by the fear of me, now experienced as a merciless figure of authority. I had ceased to be a friendly listener.

Patients vary greatly in their freedom to speak, and each patient is less or more free at different times, often alternating frequently within a single session. They vary too in the degree to which their speech is authentic: sometimes their presentation seems natural and without calculation; at other times they may be appeasing, or cut off, or go over things in a particularly obsessive or manic way. Or perhaps they indulge in some sort of acting, for example when trying excessively hard to entertain or impress the analyst. In such cases, the analyst may focus more on the tone of the patient's words and what that conveys than on the detailed content. The form of a patient has to do with genuinely free association, but this is different from getting stuck on autopilot.

One aspect of the courage required by the patient is highlighted by Freud:

> [The patient] must find the courage to direct his attention
> to the phenomena of his illness. His illness itself must no
> longer seem to him contemptible, but must become an
> enemy worthy of his mettle, a piece of his personality, which

has solid grounds for its existence, and out of which things of value for his future life have to be derived. If this new attitude towards the illness intensifies the conflicts . . . one can easily console the patient by pointing out that these are only necessary and temporary aggravations and that one cannot overcome an enemy who is absent and not within range.

PART II: IN THE ZONE

4

A KIND OF RAPTURE

The spirit of the Lord is upon me.

J. L. Carr

You're making that white ball dance.

Ronnie O'Sullivan

When you track an animal you must become the animal. When the springbok heart beats in your ribs, you see through its eyes. Tracking is like dancing.

Karuha

———

For me as a cricket captain, there were, occasionally, passages of play when everything seemed to come together, the world falling in with my thinking. Clive Rice, the South Africa and Nottinghamshire all-rounder, was an accomplished, force-ful batsman, who liked to stand tall and hit the ball through cover off the back foot. In the first innings of a match against Middlesex in 1982, he had played himself in and was looking to be more aggressive. I sensed there was a chance of a ball from our young fast bowler, Norman Cowans, bouncing higher than Rice would anticipate, in which case there might be a thick out-side edge. And here I felt my way into Rice's body and the shape of the ambitious shot I imagined him playing. I pictured the ball flying to a deep wide slip, perhaps 25 yards back. I rehearsed this scenario again to myself, and, acting on the hunch, put Clive Radley in that unorthodox position. Shortly afterwards the ball went straight to him at a nice catching height.

Something similar happened in the second innings, this time on the leg side. Once again I 'shaped' myself, within my own mind and with my body, into the body state of the stroke I imagined him playing, this time a wristy flick to the leg-side – and on the basis of this I placed an unorthodox, deep-ish, short leg. Again, the ploy worked perfectly. Rice thought there was something magical about this captaincy; in fact it was a mixture of a sensory and bodily intuition laced with luck. I was 'in the zone'.

'In the zone' is a modern, maybe modish, term for an ecstatic state where everything flows smoothly. To be in this magical area, where there is little sense of effort, is a more seductive aspiration than simply being 'on form'. One is raised beyond the prosaic or the everyday to an orgasmic or spiritual level. It is more like being in love than being friends. We are tempted to use words like 'inspired' or 'blessed' for such exceptional states of mind. We long for them. We remember them. They may become benchmarks for why we do the things we do. Whether applied to individual sportsmen or to teams, style and beauty come into it, a free-flowing, graceful elegance of timing and placement that expresses an inner state of being. (I am reminded of St Augustine's definition of sacrament as 'an outward and visible sign of an inward and invisible grace'.)

A genius is one who inhabits such states more naturally than others. In cricket, I think of West Indian all-rounder Gary Sobers, named 'the King', the 'Four-in-one' by his compatriots, probably the greatest all-round cricketer ever, a man whose

every move on the field spoke of ease and spontaneity. His play expressed delight and freedom, and evoked the same in the spectator. Even his walk was languidly elegant. We are less inclined to attribute 'being in the zone' to a 'grafter', slang for a workaday player whose effort shows all the time, however good his form.

When we are 'in the zone' the world appears to cooperate with us, to be in harmony with us and we with it. Even the opposition seem to exist as opportunities for us to display our true skill. (The Australian batsman Ian Chappell, asked what spinners were for, once said, 'to get you from sixty to a hundred as quickly as possible'.) Collectively, a whole team feels itself 'as one'. By contrast, being merely on form may involve more struggle and willpower. There is something of the contrast between play and work here. Novelist J. L. Carr compares the natural grace of his character Caroline Driffield with that of Herbert Sutcliffe, a distinguished Yorkshire and England cricketer (Oldroyd and Sutcliffe opened the batting for Yorkshire through the 1920s and early 1930s):

It boils down to this. She had style. You either have it or you haven't. That's all there is to it; it's beyond doubt. Herbert Sutcliffe had it: Edgar Oldroyd, for all his runs in the scorebooks, didn't . . . It's like that man in the Old Testament, who says casually, 'The Spirit of the Lord is upon me.'

Until the Animals in the Safari Park Come Home

There is another stream of meaning in 'the zone', less to do with grace than with tranquillity. This kind of in-the-zone batsman is not fazed by aggression, or by sniping from the opposition or crowd, or indeed by the total lack of crowd or atmosphere (as in recent Test matches in the UAE and elsewhere, played in almost empty stadiums). Of modern English batsmen, Alastair Cook most conveys this sense of unruffled assurance; like his predecessors as opening batsmen, Geoffrey Boycott and Michael Atherton, he is in his natural habitat at the crease, effectively oblivious to provocations. Opponents don't bother to sledge him; they save their breath.

At Johannesburg in 1995 Atherton batted for ten hours and forty-three minutes, scoring 185 not out, to save the second Test match against South Africa. The journalist Scyld Berry interviewed him when he came off the field at the end of his marathon innings. Atherton was, he writes, 'quiet . . . not visibly tired at all, far from drained, just serenely calm . . . He looked as though he could have gone back out to the middle, taken guard again and batted until the animals in the safari park came home.' In this state, losing a partner was no cause for disturbance: he had been 'too far above the battle to notice, too inwardly certain of success to think for one moment of failure'. It was a 'trance-like state', rarely to be recaptured. Fear of failure would, Berry continues, have interrupted the 'blessed state'. So too, I suggest, might recklessness or complacency. Atherton achieved that perfect balance in which timidity and hubris are equally out of the question.

Small children have this quality when absorbed. I like the story told by the educationalist Kenneth Robinson of a six-year-old who was asked by her teacher what she was doing. 'I'm drawing a picture of God,' she said.

'But,' said the teacher, 'no one knows what God looks like.' Quick as a flash the girl replied: 'They will in a minute.'

Out of Nowhere

The zone state of mind may occasionally transport the creative writer. Here is novelist Don DeLillo:

> There's a zone I aspire to. Finding it is another question. It's a state of automatic writing, and it represents the paradox that's at the center of a writer's consciousness – this writer's anyway. First you look for discipline and control. You want to exercise your will, bend the language your way, bend the world your way. You want to control the flow of impulses, images, words, faces, ideas. But there's a higher place, a secret aspiration. You want to let go. You want to lose yourself in language, become a carrier or messenger. The best moments involve a loss of control. It's a kind of rapture, and it can happen with words and phrases fairly often – completely surprising combinations that make a higher kind of sense, that come to you out of nowhere. But rarely for extended periods, for paragraphs and pages – I think poets must have more access to this state than novelists do. In [my novel] *End Zone*, a number of characters play a game of touch football in a snowstorm. There's nothing rapturous or magical about the writing. The writing is

simple. But I wrote the passage, maybe five or six pages, in a state of pure momentum, without the slightest pause or deliberation.

A 'secret aspiration', a 'letting go', 'out of nowhere': these phrases convey the sense of being seized, of rapture. We are for a moment angels, messengers of God; or, like Mary, we receive an annunciation, becoming the vessel for a force bigger than ourselves that uses us for its benign purposes.

Like Atherton, we feel a sense of stillness and alertness, one that may be enhanced by having (out)-faced danger. Climber Andy Kirkpatrick, reflecting on his solo ascent of Reticent Wall on Yosemite's mightiest wall, El Capitan, one of climbing's technically hardest routes, said on a radio programme: 'You confront how mortal you are. If you can push though that, you get to this amazing tranquil place.'

Time seems to slow down or stand still. Absorbed in the moment, we feel freed from everything insignificant and petty, from the shackles and complexities of our own personality and of a flustered everyday life, from extraneous thinking. There is a feeling of acute well-being, of luminosity. Pioneer aviator Charles Lindbergh expresses such all-embracing openness: 'These minute details in my cockpit. The grandeur of the world outside. The nearness of death. The longness of life.'

Exaltation

Experiences of being in the zone may, unlike being on form, be momentary. I remember a catch I took in a match for Middlesex against Essex at Southend, probably in 1980. I was fielding at slip. The ball ballooned up over the wicket-keeper's head towards the sight-screen. Running back at full tilt to get to where the ball would drop, I was aware of being utterly, even aggressively, confident that I would make it. In the event I dived full length and caught the ball inches from the ground. Briefly, I had that exalted sense of acting with total conviction in exactly the right way, of everything being in place. Such conviction may be illusory – belief may falter in the face of a recalcitrant world and a flawed self. (A friend recalls an experience that started like mine, but led to treatment in A&E for a squashed middle finger, still a misshapen reminder fifty years on.)

In *Burmese Days*, George Orwell sums up this aspect of being in the zone when he writes about an exciting excursion. John Flory takes the beautiful Elizabeth Lackersteen shooting. When she kills her second bird, 'it was one of those shots where there is no aiming, no consciousness of the gun in one's hand, when one's mind seems to fly behind the charge and drive it to the mark. She knew the bird was doomed even before she pulled the trigger.'

Overcoming Duality

Ronnie O'Sullivan is snooker's occasionally wayward genius. He has been world champion five times. He holds the world record for the largest number of maximum (147-point) breaks in competitions – thirteen – one of them achieved in an incredibly quick five minutes twenty seconds. In an interview in the *New Yorker*, writer Sam Knight found that O'Sullivan 'spends a lot of time thinking about the white ball'.

> He has come to believe that the quality of initial contact between his cue-tip and the sphere – the momentary grip, the transfer of energy and intent – is what decides everything else. If the white responds, he will not lose. 'You're using your hands. You're creating. You're making

that white ball dance.' O'Sullivan feels the connection instantaneously. 'It's invisible, but it's night and day to me,' he said. 'I know I'm playing a different game from what they're playing.'

This 'night and day' difference lies, then, in the intimacy of the connection between his mind-state and the material ball out there in the world. The everyday duality between the self and the world, between mind and matter, feels in such moments as though it is transcended.

Psychoanalyst Donald Winnicott asks himself what allows the child to feel fully alive and engaged, what gives him, and later the adult he becomes, the secure sense of *being in* the world. Winnicott's answer is that the infant has been given a necessary illusion that his desires move the world. He wants milk and, lo and behold, milk is on offer. He feels lonely, and his mother or carer hugs him, intuiting his need. Gradually, of course, the growing child has to learn that he is not omnipotent. But for the older child, and the adult he becomes, to be at home in the world, not alienated or cut off, this initial sense of connectedness-via-agency is vital. The schizoid person, by contrast, feels as though there is a barrier, sometimes represented as a sheet of glass, between him and the world. O'Sullivan, it seems, discovers in his play a heightened experience of this intimate belonging, with his 'transfer of energy and intent . . . making the white ball dance'. For him, being in the zone is a regaining of intimate connection with, and traction on, the world outside.

Captain as Bushman

San hunters, also known as Bushmen, pursue on foot animals that run much faster than humans. These hunters have been

filmed in the Kalahari following the tracks of kudu in the dry, stony ground, 'becoming' the deer, using this bodily identification to find and move on from the faint footprints. They literally 'shape' themselves into the deer's way of moving, taking a few flickering, deer-like steps, and by this means find its actual course, picking up its trail again from the next visible footprint a few yards further on.

Karuha is one of the 'running hunters'. Through the hottest part of the day, he runs down some kudu. He 'no longer follows the tracks, but runs where they will run. He twists back where they will twist back. He runs among the thorns to chase them out of the shade. He does not slow down. He thinks of his family who must eat meat.'

Karuha himself says afterwards, 'When I was running I was really a kudu. It is a long time since I felt like this. You know how hard kudu is working when you feel it in your body. You have taken kudu into your own mind. As it tires you become strong, you have taken its strength into your body.'

After more than four hours one kudu is at last exhausted, and Karuha is able to get close enough to kill the animal with his spears. The method is an example of the tortoise and the hare. It is also an example of successfully entering both the mindset and the body-set of one's prey.

The same is true with other animals. Karuha also says, of hunting a porcupine: 'When you follow the prints you see in your mind how the porcupine thinks. Every animal is like this; you jump when the track shows it jumps. When the springbok heart beats in your ribs, you see through its eyes. You must know the ways of the animal to hunt it.'

As a cricket captain one may become a San to the opposition. One may also do something similar for one's team-mates, entering their mindsets, but with a different purpose – to gain their support rather than to defeat them.

> You learn the ways of the birds that come on the wind to you. They whisper to you 'the rain is coming' . . . My father's tracks have long since been washed away. He taught me. Even now when I am hunting I'm singing his song, I'm dancing his dance. Dance is talking to god. Our god Bihisabolo put us here. He brings us the animals.

More generally, hunter-gatherers have rituals to ensure that they can reach this kind of mental place reliably, and to remarkable depths. The Dunne-Za of northern British Columbia, for example, dream of fusion with each individual animal they hope to hunt. Similarly the San do a trance dance, where the hunters circle a fire and dance for long periods, until they transform themselves into the animals they need to know.

Becoming the Other

To our modern 'scientific' minds, becoming the other may seem airy-fairy, fringing on the esoteric or the paranormal. On the contrary, I suggest it is one of our most basic capacities.

The small child not only perceives the mother's feeling, he instinctively shares it. This is the basis of early animal and human learning. We take in and reproduce emotional reactions that are necessary for survival – the small creature learns what is to be feared, what not, what is to be explored or eaten, what left alone.

Psychoanalyst Joseph Sandler reminds us that as adults too we may at times be caught up in another's experience as if it were our own. He recounts walking along the edge of the pavement on a crowded street in London when 'suddenly a man who was walking a yard or two in front of me slipped off the edge. I immediately righted myself, just as if I were about to stumble into the street' – as if it were *he*, Sandler, who was the person slipping. Sandler suggests that sympathy of this kind is the cement that binds human (and perhaps animal) societies together.

As a small child, my granddaughter Alia entered into the bodies and attitudes of animals of all kinds. This process was, and is, part of her appreciation of their qualities and their ways of being, and enters into her drawing of them. When I asked her once if the dog-noises she was making in the back of the car were her toy dog speaking to her, she told me scornfully, 'No, Mike, I was *being* the dog. Don't you understand, that's the point of toys, you bring them alive.'

Children play anywhere; but they also create sacred spaces for play, rather as sportsmen have their own 'field' of play, their space-time frame. For Alia, from the age of two and a half to around five, and me, a room that was not used when I was seeing patients downstairs functioned in this way. The room was named The – or, to be more phonetically accurate, 'Ya' – Beach, since it started as a place we went to for pretend-swimming and for sea-related play. Quickly such activities

44

expanded into any sort of play – we, especially she, became tigers, dogs, unicorns, dragons, sharks; doctors and patients, teachers and students, plane or bus travellers; monsters, zombies, princesses and princes. She would 'tell' (or invent) dreams. There were games in which points were scored for impersonating baby elephants or zombies. This set-apart space had different rules from other spaces. Her parents were not invited (though if she fell and knocked herself she would run to one of them for comfort). On occasion, when he felt at a loose end, her older brother was admitted, but usually as a brother only. When I was away, the room became, boringly, merely a 'room with two sofas' – not Ya Beach at all.

In this space, magical transformations were routine: a dog could become a dragon could become a baby dinosaur could become a prince or a princess. The world was created by her – occasionally I would make a semi-serious protest, asking, 'Today, am I allowed to *be* the dog' – or dragon, or whatever – 'and do what *I* want, or do I have to be just what you make me?' She would usually insist with a triumphant grin that I had to say and do just what she told me.

The image of a special space is central to C. S. Lewis's *The Lion, the Witch and the Wardrobe.* The children go through the wardrobe in the spare room into the parallel universe of Narnia, ruled by the White Witch, who keeps the land frozen. She has usurped the rightful king, Aslan the lion, who is 'on the move again'. It is the world of the imagination, which can itself become frozen as one grows up. As with Ya Beach and the sofas, the wardrobe could be at one moment a portal to a magical world, at other times a mere cupboard.

Sport, psychoanalysis and theatre all have their sacred areas. The consulting room and stage are separated off from the rest of life, set aside for serious play of different kinds, with different rules, permissions and duties than in everyday life; for illusion, too, through which a person can over time become more himself, a team can become a real team. This potential is due in part to the relative safety of these boundaried spaces, each permitting in its own ways a frankness and freeplay of emotional expression that go beyond what is normally permitted in ordinary social, more or less civilised, life; the behaviour released rarely tips over into physical violence or actual seduction. In these physical settings, a significant element of the setting – beyond the physical – is provided by the minds, attitudes and culture of the host – the analyst, me in Ya Beach, the writer and director of the play, the artist.

Theatre directors and artists not only have boundaries, they also play with them. Performances where the actors enter through the audience, or interact with them, make the division less absolute. There are vivid paintings by Howard Hodgkin that spill over onto their bright-coloured frames, so that they are ambiguously both framed *and* unframed pictures. Such less sharply framed 'productions', like exceptions to the 'rules' of poetic scansion, depend for their effect on the ordinary use of a frame.

These literal frames have a parallel in virtual frames – that is, invisibly bounded personal and social spaces where different 'rules' control or at least influence the interactions that take place within them. Hodgkin, for instance, was like all of us born into a certain artistic culture; he was taught and became familiar with particular styles of painting. He developed his own style against the background of paradigms of what was felt to constitute good or great art. The poet who writes a sonnet or a haiku willingly constrains himself or herself into sonnet or haiku form, and into the atmospheres of writing in those traditions. Interacting with the form and its history opens up new possibilities. We may be freed to be ourselves in relating to, and playing with, constrictions that evoke a particular attentiveness and focus.

The quality of imagining one's way into another's mindset is also of value to grown-ups in everyday life. Abraham Lincoln, according to his biographer Doris Kearns Goodwin, 'possessed extraordinary empathy – the gift or curse of putting himself in the place of another, to experience what they were feeling, to understand their motives and desires'. For Lincoln, she suggests, this sensibility was a source of pain, a result of 'changing places in fancy with the sufferer . . . [It was also] an enormous asset to his political career. Listening to colleagues at a Whig Party caucus, [he would] cast off his shawl, rise from his chair, and say: "From your talk, I gather the Democrats will do so and so . . . I should do so and so to checkmate them."'

'Gift or curse'? Rapture segues not only into the potentially unbearable pain of shared suffering, but also into dangerous mania.

5

WHO CLEANS UP AFTER THE PARTY?

Closer and closer to perfection.

Ayrton Senna

I felt I could almost pass through them physically . . . A strange feeling of invincibility.

Pelé

Flow is like a mad party – it goes on till all hours and somebody must clear up afterwards.

Hilary Mantel

––––––––––

After practising in 1988 for the Monaco Grand Prix, racing driver Ayrton Senna said:

Some moments when I'm driving detach me completely from anything else. Suddenly I was two seconds faster than anyone . . . I was driving in a different dimension, like in a tunnel well beyond my conscious understanding. I never really reached that feeling again. I had reached such a high level of concentration it was as if the car and I had become one.

But, in the immediate aftermath of this experience:

> Suddenly it was as if I woke up and realised I had been on a
> different level of consciousness. I was shocked, went straight
> back to the pits and didn't drive any more that day. Faster
> and faster, closer to perfection. But also more vulnerable,
> with much less safety margin.

Before the 1958 World Cup in Sweden, Brazilian footballers were put through psychological tests to assess their mental
strength. The great Pelé, then only seventeen years old, was
written off as 'obviously infantile'. He was deemed to lack the
necessary fighting spirit; he 'did not', the report stated, 'possess the sense of responsibility necessary for a team game'. Pelé
was omitted from the opening two group matches. Selected
for the crucial quarter-final against Wales, he scored the only
goal, and then, in the semi-final, a second-half hat-trick against

France. In his autobiography Pelé writes about the final, against Sweden:

> I felt a strange calmness I hadn't experienced in any other games. It was a type of euphoria; I felt I could run all day without tiring, that I could dribble through any of their team or all of them, that I could almost pass through them physically. I felt I could not be hurt. It was . . . a very strange feeling of invincibility.

Brazil won 5–2 after being a goal down. Pelé scored two of the goals, making his personal tally six in three matches. At the end of the match, he is said to have fainted. Brazil also won the next World Cup, in Chile four years later. In the same book, Pelé writes about the 1966 tournament:

> In the run-up to the 1966 World Cup in England everyone was still obsessing about our victories in 1958 and 1962. *Everyone* – supporters, journalists, managers, players even – was still talking about the titles Brazil had won in Sweden and Chile. We were thinking about the possibilities of being *thrice* champions now, and of winning the Jules Rimet trophy for good . . . As far as the directors were concerned, we were just going over there to fetch the cup, take it around to show the other countries, and then bring it home. But our preparations were not planned with the same humility as in 1958 and 1962. We were already starting to lose the title before we even set foot in England.

Conversely, dubious motives may at times be inspirational. Paranoia is not to be generally recommended, but it has its uses. In cricket's Twenty20 World Cup, held in India in 2016, the winners, West Indies, were clearly well-motivated and well-led. After their surprise victory in the final, the players spoke out about the sources of their success. What was crucial, they said, was the group's unanimity and solidarity against a hostile world. According to Darren Sammy, the captain, 'When you see these fifteen men playing out there with hunger and passion, it all stems from what has been boiling inside' – a boiling anger, that is, against 'disrespect', first from the Cricket Board, with whom the players had been at odds for some time, secondly from some journalists. In the build-up to the tournament, one presenter had dismissed the team's chances on the grounds that they were 'short of brains' (he later apologised unreservedly for his 'throw-away phrase', and for having been 'pretty damn lazy').

On 1 May 1994, Senna was killed at Imola, hitting the wall at Tamburello while going at 130 mph. There is no straightforward account of his state of mind leading up to that lap, or to the race itself. But there had been two terrible accidents on the circuit in the previous two days, including one in which his friend Roland Ratzenberger died. Some suggest that Senna did not want to race that next day. But if his misgivings about safety on the course intensified as a result of these accidents, the demands of competition, the fact that he was without points in the two previous Grands Prix – all this meant that withdrawing was out of the question.

No one knows why he failed to take that corner. Was it a steering problem in the car? Or mechanical errors on the part of the engineering team? Had the chassis hit the tarmac on the bumpy bend and caused the car to behave skittishly? Was Senna less able in the technically more sophisticated Williams car to overcome its shortcomings by sheer brilliance? Or, in upping his speed over the previous lap or two, had he got into a dangerously over-confident mindset? No one knows. But we know, as Senna himself knew, at times at least, that 'close to perfection' is also 'close to vulnerability'.

Psychoanalyst and composer Francis Grier wrote about the wishful thinking that makes zone experiences alluring: 'Wouldn't it be wonderful if one could just drink a magic potion which would automatically get one "in the zone"?' But, as he went on to suggest, 'If we cock a snook at reality, reality has a habit of thumbing its nose at us.'

Success readily goes to our heads. We are tempted to puff ourselves up, and to slip over into a dangerously euphoric, even manic state. And the joy of flow-states easily lends itself to self-deception. A story is told about Cardinal Hume, when he was head of the Roman Catholic Church in England. At an ecclesiastical drinks party, a colleague was telling him about his recently published book. A third person entered, and praised the book fulsomely. When he moved on, the Cardinal said to the author, 'Enjoy, but don't inhale.'

We may be enamoured by the trappings of flamboyant style. In *The Mirror of the Sea*, Joseph Conrad writes about a usually cautious ship-master who, succumbing once in his career to an uncharacteristic impulse to show off, courts disaster.

There were masters whose very art consisted in avoiding every conceivable [difficult] situation. It is needless to say that they never did great things in their craft; but they were not to be despised for that. They were modest; they understood their limitations . . . One of these last I remember . . . Only once did he attempt a stroke of audacity, one early morning, with a steady breeze, entering a crowded roadstead. But he was not genuine in this display, which might have been art . . . He hankered after the *meretricious glory of a showy performance* . . . It would have been a fine performance if it had come off, but it did not. Through a touch of self-seeking, that modest artist of solid merit became untrue to his temperament. It was not for him art for art's sake: it was art for his own sake; and a dismal failure was the penalty he paid for that greatest of sins.

And Conrad ends this passage:

Of all the living creatures upon land and sea, it is ships alone that cannot be taken in by barren pretences, that will not put up with bad art from their masters.

Cricketer Keith Fletcher, as captain of Essex, would criticise extravagant or showy performances by his batsmen in similar, though blunter, terms: 'Glory shots again,' he'd say. The real motivation for the batsmen's apparent selflessness was not the good of the team, but to look good by making things happen quickly and gloriously. They eschewed the more prolonged ordeal of cautious consolidation, and the risk of their teammates' criticism if they scored too slowly.

To save ourselves the effort and sometimes the agony of self-mastery in a recalcitrant world, and to avoid the discomfort of taking care, or of acknowledging our ignorance about the best course of action, we leap blithely over these difficulties. There is a slender margin between being in the zone in a creative and constructive way, and on the other side slipping into arrogance, omnipotence and obliviousness to risk. Losing the capacity to stand aside and watch with a professional's eye may be suicidal.

Mutual Illusions: Banking's Objects of Phantasy

States of exaltation often involve others. The term *folie à deux*, invented by nineteenth-century French psychiatrists, means 'madness shared by two', a delusional belief passed back and forth between two people. These collusions may end up as collisions.

A couple may, for instance, delude each other and themselves into a mutual fantasy of being in love. T. S. Eliot's marriage to the vivacious, highly strung Vivienne Haigh-Wood in 1915 (also described as a *maladie* à *deux*) 'cut through all his problems at a single stroke', Eliot's biographer, Robert Crawford, writes. 'Or so it seemed at the time. Years later, after bitter experience, [Eliot] re-described the situation: "I came to persuade myself that I was in love with her simply because I wanted to burn my boats to commit myself to staying in England".'

Eliot convinced himself, then, that he was in love with Vivienne (see woman in white, below) in order to rule out returning home to America to be a professor of philosophy at Harvard. When he wrote these words, almost half a century later, he knew it had been a mistake: 'To her, the marriage brought no happiness.' It tipped Eliot himself towards a breakdown.

The disaster, however, had its benefits: 'To me it brought the state of mind out of which came *The Waste Land*.' While he was recovering, he finished the poem, which was published in 1922, a few months after James Joyce's *Ulysses*, and a few months before the English translation of Proust appeared. Perhaps, then, it was for him a productive delusion, however tragic in other ways. Some people have to break down if they are to break through.

Like Grand Prix drivers, World Cup footballers and poets in love, speculators in financial markets can live close to the edge, gambling for high stakes. The word 'phantasy' is used in psychoanalysis to mean unconscious imagining. Psychoanalyst David Tuckett coined the term 'phantastic objects' to describe the kinds of projects that became rampant in the financial world in the years leading up to the banking catastrophe of 2008. He was referring to the schemes (including those known as 'derivatives') that some investors imagined would satisfy their deep desires for huge profits without compromising security – schemes with which they fell in love. But these obscure objects of desire, like some romantic partners, proved harder to control than predicted.

Banks over-extended themselves. Mervyn King, a former Governor of the Bank of England, describes this as a 'lapse into hubris':

> The balance sheets of too many banks were an accident waiting to happen . . . Levels of leverage were on such a scale that they could not resist even the slightest tremor to confidence about the uncertain value of bank assets. For all the clever innovation in the world of finance, to transform risky assets into riskless liabilities is indeed a form of alchemy . . .

What's more,

> Derivatives also allowed a stream of expected future profits, which might or might not be realised, to be capitalised into current values and show up in trading profits, so permitting large bonuses to be paid today out of highly uncertain future prospects.

It was not that the promotion of these complicated but ill-backed derivatives was, as a rule, a conscious deception on the part of bankers and others. No doubt there was the occasional crook; more often, people were self-deceived. Many invested their own money in the schemes. Nor was the behaviour 'inconceivable stupidity'. Rather, financial investors were trapped by 'the prisoner's dilemma', a term that refers to the inherent difficulty of finding a way to cooperative solutions when individual self-interest is at stake:

> If before the crisis banks had exited the riskier types of lending, stopped buying complex derivative instruments and reduced their leverage, they would, in the short term, have earned lower profits than their competitors. The Chief Executive would likely have lost his job, and other staff defected to banks willing to take risks and pay higher bonuses.

King quotes Chuck Prince, the CEO of Citigroup (at the time the biggest bank in the world), saying before the crisis: '"As long as the music is playing, you've got to get up and dance. We're still dancing" . . . As individuals, they naturally responded to the incentives they faced.'

Psychologically the situation was, at a group level, similar to what Ayrton Senna noticed in himself: 'faster and faster . . . but also more and more vulnerable, with much less safety margin', or Pelé's 'strange feeling of invincibility'. The phantasmagorical structures of greater and greater cunning and complexity were piled higher and higher on the flimsy base of the assumption that the future could be predicted and controlled.

Investment bankers and others split off from awareness the need for sober assessment of risk, and ordinary self-doubt, with the result that no evidence was allowed to count against their convictions. In fact, King suggests, it was (and is) more likely to be the case that shares go up or down according to chance or unforeseeable factors than according to anyone's rules or systems. Yet the radical uncertainty of the market, as of many other kinds of futures, was denied, and people were fired with 'passionate intensity'. When confidence started to dissipate and panic set in, there was a collapse not of single individuals or companies, but of the whole financial and banking system.

The Cleft Stick

Psychoanalysts, too, if not alert to the dangers of overconfidence, may not only become complacent and miss new, less comfortable elements in the next phase of work, they may also be pulled into a *folie à deux* with the patient, and be deceived about their joint achievements. Perhaps the analyst has the idea that he alone can rescue a particular patient, which leads him to exalt himself and his work, and feel entitled to break limits and rules because his relationship with the patient is so special. Psychoanalyst Tom Main, who was also in his role as psychiatrist the director of the Cassel Hospital (originally set up for victims of shell shock after the First World War, and now a mental health hospital) in the 1950s and 60s, writes about such a scenario, where a group of 'special' patients in the hospital split the staff into two groups: on one side, a few exceptional individuals who alone were, in their own estimation, sensitive enough to understand these highly sensitive patients, and on the other the majority, who disagreed with these special and exceptional arrangements amounting to rule breaking. This can be a seductive situation for the 'special' therapist.

Folies à *deux* also happen between family members, particularly in the wake of traumas. A couple lost their daughter, Bridget, in a car accident. Bridget was twenty-four, married with a three-year-old son. The dead woman's mother, Anne, became utterly devoted to her son-in-law, Dermot, and to this grandson, wishing to rescue them from their grief and devastation. Her passion for and preferential treatment of these bereaved members of the family led her to exclude or undervalue her husband and her other daughters and their families. Anne explained that she and Dermot had a unique understanding, fostered during their joint vigil at Bridget's bedside. I came to the idea that Anne had in her unconscious mind *become* Bridget, so that Dermot had become for Anne – if unconsciously – her husband/lover. She appeared to offer him every possible solace. She entered into his lifestyle and his tastes in music, and joined him in his use of drugs. She had become, it seems, a different person in the company of Dermot, more animated and uninhibited than with her own husband. Thus, Anne could feel that Bridget had not really died, and did not have to be mourned fully. She did mourn her daughter, but she also compensated for her grief by means of this high-minded, ardent relationship with her bereaved son-in-law.

As her analyst, I was in a position similar to her husband's, taken for granted but not of much consequence. She had a dream of driving a car, and holding hands with a young man with curly hair sitting next to her, while there was in the back seat a shadowy and perhaps dangerous figure. I interpreted this as her excitement at driving ahead with the son-in-law, while I, like her husband, was demoted to the back seat. She didn't find this easy to take in, and became sleepy, once again avoiding being awake to difficult feelings. Dermot and she, holding hands together in a state of ardent selflessness, were living in the fast lane, risking a crash or at least an outburst from the husband or analyst in the back seat.

In 1988 Senna was able, despite his exalted and euphoric state, to see quickly enough its dangers. He was able, on that occasion at least, to avoid the lure of mania and the danger of a potential crash. For such reasons, I am with Cardinal Hume. I am more comfortable with the aspiration to 'being on form' than with the exciting siren-call of 'the zone'.

The Goose

I don't want to be too prescriptive here. I'm not saying there is no room for excitement in sport or in our relationships. We need it, and it fills our lives. There is something lacking in those who inhibit all enthusiasm, or who are unable to enter into intensely passionate states.

As a bowler, Bob Willis went into a private world – a zone – that seemed cut off from reality. He would pound in at high speed, arms and legs pumping. We called him 'Goose', so frenetic were his preparations for take-off. Running alongside him as he strode off to fine leg at the end of an over, trying to keep up with his giant strides, I felt as if I was knocking on the closed door of a windowless house, shouting 'Is anyone in?' But Bob valued my attempts to gain access; he heard and needed the encouragement and the suggestions: 'Keep running in', 'You look good', 'Perhaps a yard fuller for your stock ball?', 'What about trying a yorker?'.

The trance served him well. For one thing, it protected him from feeling tired. Bob's special zone, with its own atmosphere and character, enabled him to concentrate solely on the task in hand. He was in a heightened state, as if communing with his hero, Bob Dylan.

There are two paradoxes about being in the zone. One is that, despite the risk of having our wings melted by the sun and plunging into the sea, we *may*, in our zone, like Willis, be intensely, automatically, in touch with what the situation calls for. There is something of the animal in the uncomplicated sharpness of attuned antennae.

The second paradox is the importance of a sort of inspired madness in many exceptional achievers, people who create new paradigms of theory or practice, in art, in science or in everyday activities, including sport and psychoanalysis. It is not after all so long ago, in the larger arc of human life, that it would have been absurd and irreverent to have the idea that the world was not flat. It clearly was, and anyone who suggested otherwise was mad and dangerous!

6

DISENCUMBERING
CONSCIOUSNESS

It is necessary to disencumber consciousness of the burden of thought by learning a skill.

Wilfred Bion

The brush must draw by itself. This cannot happen if one does not practice constantly. But neither can it happen if one makes an effort.

Alan W. Watts

———

Babies become toddlers by learning to walk. How does this happen? Walking is instinctive, but – unlike new-born foals, however wobbly on their legs – humans do not do it from the start.

Very gradually, babies gain control of parts of their bodies. They lift up their heads to look around. They reach for their feet, or for their mother's hair. Wanting to get somewhere under their own steam, they pull themselves along on their tummies. Some crawl. Balance is improved by reaching for things from a sitting position, or rolling a ball back and forth with an adult. Parents give ongoing encouragement to these efforts. After some months, children begin pulling themselves up, holding on to chair arms, adults' legs, hands reached out to them. When they stand, they want to move, to be like grown-ups and older siblings. Grown-ups hold their hands, leading them, helping them to fall without hurting themselves.

At last the momentous development – the child's first unaided steps. He can now aim for something and sometimes get there. Then the parental task is to make spaces safe enough for exploratory walking – clearing the decks, removing cords on which the child might trip, or sharp edges, providing staging posts for the new toddler to hold on to.

Achievements like walking become increasingly effortless. Wilfred Bion, a creative and influential postwar British psycho-analyst, puts this kind of transition with customary terseness: 'It is necessary to disencumber consciousness of the burden of thought by learning a skill.'

Bion is referring to the necessity for continuous screening out of many sensations, emotions and thoughts, freeing one-self of the unnecessary and burdensome clobber of conscious effort and awareness of detail. We have to forget, ignore, suppress, repress. Were we not to do so, we would be oppressed and overwhelmed by the sheer number of phenomena vying for attention, like a man who told me that he felt as if his mind was filled with a flock of sheep all trying to get through a gate at once. 'What happens next?' I asked. 'I go blank,' he replied.

'If we had a keen vision and feeling of all ordinary human life,' George Eliot wrote in *Middlemarch*, 'it would be like hearing the grass grow and the squirrel's heartbeat, and we should die of that roar which lies on the other side of silence. As it is, the quickest of us walk about well wadded with stupidity' – wadded, that is, with a stupidity that is essential to wisdom and sanity. We learn to enhance and trust what has been called 'muscle memory' or, more scientifically, 'procedural memory' – the capacity to store knowledge of how to do things, especially motor skills.

The ancient Chinese philosophical tradition of Taoism makes a parallel point about virtue. The best butcher in the village has been chopping meat for so long that he doesn't need to pause and consider where the next slice should fall. Instead – *chop-chop-chop-chop*! – he instantly and precisely cuts the meat by force of habit. If he stopped to think about what he does, that perfect efficiency would be lost. Living well is being the butcher – rarely having to stop and think, yet taking the right course. Virtue is a matter of effortless action – intuitive, instinctive, almost second nature.

In the familiar process of learning primary skills, there is no emphasis on what the child *can't* do. The adult's tone is not admonitory. No blame attaches to falling. In fact, falling is part of the process. It has been estimated that toddlers practise walking for a thousand hours before becoming fairly stable. They must fall thousands of times.

Furthermore, it is not by breaking the process down into parts, and teaching in an 'analytic' way that success is achieved. Children learn instinctively, that is, from the nature of their bodies and their potential, and from observing and 'becoming' others. Nor do we teach the young child to learn from general principles. Contrast how 'naturally' we imbibe the grammar of our native tongue with the painstaking learning of subjunctive clauses in Latin at a 'Grammar' school in Shakespeare's day, or for that matter sixty years ago.

This imbibing method is not an unmixed blessing. Without being given any specific instruction, my four-year-old son, getting interested in cricket, started to bat like me, with a high, exaggerated backlift. More beneficially, he modelled his bowling on the idiosyncratic approach and fine, high action of my colleague at Middlesex, South African bowler Vintcent van der Bijl.

The art of coaching, and of teaching, includes finding a balance between making the learner conscious of details of technique and giving him or her the chance to inhabit a style or way of being without too much focus on the segments of an action.

There is a paradox or tension here. On one hand, it is, as Bion says, natural and vital that we 'disencumber' consciousness. Imagine what would happen to the centipede if it tried to work out the movements of each leg one at a time! I have seen cricket coaches come down the net after each delivery to give a young batsman a new piece of advice. On the other hand, much excellent teaching and coaching, whether in sport, psychoanalysis or other fields of activity, *is* a matter of making the learner aware of details, whether physical (he must bend his front leg when playing a forward defensive shot) or mental (he needs to take up his patient's contempt, which he has missed or ignored). How, then, does scrutiny not interfere with George Eliot's 'stupidity'? Are we not 're-encumbering' consciousness when we teach in such ways?

Trying Too Hard

Timothy Gallwey has written a series of books in which he looks at the inner games that go on alongside our outer game-playing. In his first book, *The Inner Game of Tennis*, he described the state we aim at, in tennis as in other activities of life: 'the kind of spontaneous performance which occurs only when the mind is calm and seems at one with the body . . . All that is needed is to *unlearn* those habits which interfere with (the unconscious mind) and then to just *let it happen*.'

Having realised how technical instruction can inhibit the tennis learner, he decided to introduce a beginner, Paul, who had never before held a racquet, with as few instructions as possible. To keep Paul's mind uncluttered, he explained,

> I was going to skip entirely my usual explanations to beginning players . . . Instead, I was going to hit ten forehands myself, and I wanted him to watch carefully, *not* thinking about what I was doing, but simply trying to grasp a *visual image* of the forehand. He was to repeat the image in his mind several times and then just let his body imitate.

What Gallwey learned from this experiment was that, without any specific instruction, Paul absorbed and reproduced every detail, *except* the one – to do with moving his feet – that he gave himself and *tried* to remember. This was the only area where he failed completely! When Gallwey's novice pupil, rather than focusing on technical details, 'became' his teacher, absorbing, in an overall visual way, the embodiment of the forehand, the ability, including the technique, came naturally.

Gallwey goes on to posit two selves, a 'teller' (Self 1) and a 'doer' (Self 2). He asks his reader to 'imagine that instead of being two parts of the same person, [the two selves] are separate persons'. What often happens is that the 'teller' characteristically harasses, scolds and despises the 'doer', attitudes that are bound to put the latter off. We often 'try too hard', he says, clenching our muscles to do what Self 1 tells us to do, while perhaps secretly rebelling against this domination. (I agree, though sometimes Self 1 helps rather than hinders Self 2.)

Likewise, in *Thinking, Fast and Slow*, the psychologist Daniel Kahneman describes two types of thinking: System 1 thinking and System 2 thinking. The former is involuntary, quick and intuitive; the latter effortful and deliberately chosen. Kahneman speaks of the two systems as two agents within the self, sometimes in harmony, sometimes at odds with each other. He refers to psychodramas between the two characters

in their internal dialogue. I too believe it is helpful to think in terms of different kinds of agents and thinkers within the self – often more than two – each having its own point of view, its own agendas, aims and defences.

The form we long for may be obstructed both by technical and by emotional factors. We may be pushed out of our comfort zone by technical challenges – a piece of piano music near or beyond the limits of our ability, calling for arduous practice – and/or by our consciousness of inordinate risk – we are playing at the Royal Albert Hall, with a prestigious orchestra, in front of a large audience and the leading critics. In sport, big matches provide both sorts of challenge; it is why Test matches bear that name.

Matthew Syed, a former table tennis international, comments in a similar vein on the distinction between walking along a narrow path in an everyday context (where System 1 thinking is natural and adequate for us) and on the other hand walking along the same path with a 1,000-foot precipice on either side. In the latter case we find ourselves in System 2 thinking whether we like it or not. Suddenly we have to 'think about how we are moving our feet, the angle of our tread, the precise footfall on the path. And this is when we are most likely to fall' – a situation similar to being so anxious about saying precisely the correct words that, instead of just saying them, we *try* to say them, and become tongue-tied.

Premeditation – The Graveyard

The disencumbering of consciousness needs to occur not only in early childhood, but beyond. Indeed it is at its peak with the highest-level practitioners of any skill. It takes a top cricketer, for example, to enter such a state, whereas a lesser player is more likely to be thrown off track if he falls into automatism, like me with the fragment of Zen at Headingley. A jazz player emphasised to me the formality of jazz as an art form; the player has to have internalised a practical knowledge of structure before he can play with proper freedom his brilliant and spontaneous eight- or sixteen-bar improvisations.

Donald Winnicott offers an analogy from music for his work as a child psychiatrist:

> The only companion I have in exploring the unknown territory of the new case is the theory that I carry around with me, [which] has become part of me, [so] that I do not even have to think about it in a deliberate way. This is the theory of the emotional development of the individual . . . One could compare my position to that of a cellist who slogs away at technique and then actually becomes able to play music *taking the technique for granted.*

At times I too am open to what patients bring and to their impact on me, without too much straining to make sense of their state. I feel steady in my analytic orientation. I feel little or no desire or expectation for the patient to behave in a particular way – either of which orientations would tend to restrict my ability to pick up on something new or different from what I have grown used to. I am alert to hints of unconscious thought. As Freud wrote, 'To put it in a formula: [the analyst] must turn his own unconscious like a receptive organ towards the transmitting unconscious of the patient. He must adjust himself to the patient as a telephone receiver is adjusted to the transmitting microphone.'

Being on form in my work, I might approach Freud's aspiration for the analyst, that he should 'avoid inclination or expectation', or Bion's later version of this precept, that he should be 'without memory or desire'. This advice, or ideal, is remarkably similar to that offered to cricketers by Greg Chappell when he refers to 'that graveyard of batting, premeditation'.

Chappell, previously one of Australia's best batsmen, and since then a leading coach, argues that a batsman

> needs to get away from thinking about technique or any of the other things that interfere with watching the ball and just responding to what he sees . . . In performance the conscious mind must be kept occupied so as not to interfere with the subconscious mind doing its job . . . The conscious mind can be involved with the big picture stuff such as strategy, but once the bowler approaches, one must trust the subconscious and the years of training to do the rest . . . Premeditation is the graveyard of batsmen.

Chappell continues with some more general remarks about life:

> The best coaching is where one sets up the environment to allow the players to develop this instinctive style rather than trying to 'teach' the game academically . . . I think that the key to all good performers is trust in their ability. Fear is the biggest inhibitor for most people. By putting the focus on the process one can overcome fear of the outcome and move on with life.

Neither Bion nor Chappell ignores the need for a long and exacting training and apprenticeship in their fields. We have seen how learning to walk or play jazz requires practice and support. But the best outcome of such intense training is a sound and trusted technique, and a deepening familiarity with the tasks involved. Ultimately, we have to be willing to cast ourselves adrift, without a script or a textbook or a coaching manual, trusting ourselves, our training and our experience. Such a state is an ideal rarely achieved, and has all the risks of an ideal. Without effort and struggle we will never be proficient enough to let go of control with any chance of success. In top form, however, relaxed in our concentration, there is little strain, and the brush does, as the philosopher Alan Watts put it, (almost) 'draw by itself'.

PART III: TECHNIQUE AND CHARACTER

7

PRACTISING YOUR SCALES

*A player may be perfect in technique, and yet have neither soul
nor intelligence.*

George Grove

Our beginnings never know our ends.

Harold Pinter

———

A boy in my class at school had no ball sense whatever, but he
used to stay out on the rugby field after practice as the darkness
drew in, trying to achieve a drop goal from 10 yards. He was
uncoordinated – only rarely could he kick the ball cleanly on
the half-volley. He might miss it altogether, or it would bounce
off his shin, and it almost never went between the posts. Yet his
efforts were extraordinary, and to me touching.

Technique is a *sine qua non*, integral to form. It is in essence
a method that has proved reliable and fruitful. A sound basic
technique means that the activity in question becomes 'second
nature', so that the percentages are favourable. It enables
a batsman, for instance, to have a good chance of hitting
the ball, and (unless he deliberately lofts it) of keeping it on the
ground to avoid being caught. The title of the autobiography

71

of Surrey and England cricketer Ken Barrington was *Playing it Straight,* and a 'straight bat' – a phrase that has gained moral connotations – means that the bat stays on the line of the ball for longer than when one plays with a 'cross bat'. In any complicated process or skill, it is by means of a good technique that the broad range of components come together. For the cricketer, again: head, feet, knees, hands, wrists, eyes and body weight all need to be coordinated for correct technique.

One may be in the zone for a moment, achieving in a single stroke perfection of timing and placement. I remember opening the batting for Middlesex against Northants at Lord's in the 1960s. I faced the first over from David Larter, a giant of a fast bowler. The sun was out, the pitch benign. Early in the over, I played a cover-drive with minimal use of the feet. I timed the ball perfectly, and it bounced back off the front of the Grandstand. A zone moment – but unreliable: a couple of balls later, I missed a straight ball and was bowled for four. My memory of the intense pleasure of that stroke is eclipsed by a sense of shame at the looseness of my play. It was a flash in the pan, not a harbinger of form.

Conversely, a series of low scores does not of itself mean one is out of form. Barrington, who first played for England in 1955, was one of our best postwar batsmen. Rugged and strong, he was a great scrapper, who gave up his earlier flamboyance in favour of a more tenacious, more cautious, style. He was capable of disarming and winning round crowds who barracked him; when he was being peppered by hostile fast bowling, he would march over towards the loudest critics and histrionically pretend to offer them his bat. At dead moments in Test matches, he impersonated W. G. Grace at the crease, with the characteristic cocked front toe, and the jerky movements of the early film footage – but his bat would still come down dead straight; behind the comic was the straight man, in front of him the straight bat. Later he became a much-loved manager of England touring teams, prone to malapropisms ('if you pitch it there you'll get him in two-man's land'), or sayings that became clichés ('on this pitch, book in for bed and break-fast'), usually followed by his self-effacing chuckle.

There was in 1960 a patch in the career of this most relia-ble of batsmen when he was dismissed quickly four times in a row for a total of one run. Barrington was out for 0 in the sec-ond innings against Somerset at the Oval, followed by a pair in the Bank Holiday match against Sussex at Hove. In the first innings of the next match at Trent Bridge he scored 1. A fan commiserated over his 'lack of form'.

'How can I be out of form?' he retorted. 'I've only faced nine balls all week!'

Form is not simply a matter of tangible or measurable suc-cess. What form we are in takes time to assess. One swallow does not make a summer, nor do a couple of fieldfares signify winter. On occasion it takes a fine, in-form batsman to be good enough to get out to an excellent, near-unplayable ball. And it is a mark of the player who makes the most of his ability that he hangs in, struggles through, when stretched to the limit. Form is partly a matter of recovering from patches of difficulty, and learning from them. When conditions favour the bowler, when the opposition is on top and making life difficult, the batsman manages to hold in mind the memory of his earlier fluency. He does not become defeatist or pessimistic. The same is true in all walks of life.

Technique can often be worked on in a detailed way, in a space separate from that of the task as a whole, as when a bats-man practises a particular stroke in the nets, or a pianist his scales. The aim is to make certain habits automatic, so that the knowledge is *grooved* in the body – or in the body-mind – and needs little conscious effort – an apt metaphor, since once the groove is created, there is a natural tendency to stay in the path it creates. (Though of course we may get stuck in it.)

Performers are constantly monitoring their technique and adjusting it, often in small ways. A batsman may find that his right foot moves slightly back towards the leg side in facing quicker bowlers, so that he is coming across the ball towards the off side, and risks being caught off the outside edge. He adjusts so that his back foot goes back and across, thus making sure his head is over the line of the ball on off-stump. But over-correction of one fault leads to another – he falls over to the off side, moving his head too far outside the line of the ball and losing his firm balance. Then he is liable to miss the ball that comes in from the off. But adjust we must, and do, often more or less automatically, without conscious deliberation.

Poor technique lets you down, limiting your potential. In sport, high-quality opponents 'read' you, and play on your weaknesses. And the more difficult the challenge, the more inclined a player is to rush and stumble. He reverts to old errors. This may simply be a matter of having learned a faulty technique, or having failed to put in the work needed to establish a sounder one. Or the default position may be a kind of addiction, offering easy gratification – my flowery, flashing cover drive against Larter, risky as it was, being more gratifying than the safer, straighter drive, with proper footwork, towards mid-off. Like the addict we regress to our drug when over-confident, disappointed or up against it. It is difficult to break bad habits.

The basic rules of good technique apply to all. But each of us has also to develop our own individual technique, what really suits us, depending on our physique and personal ability, our predilection and style. For some this will entail a more risky, more adventurous approach than for others. But even the dourest players have their expansive moments, and the most charismatic and innovative of batsmen will do many basic things in an orthodox fashion. Kevin Pietersen, the star batsman of recent English cricket, played strokes and innings that no one else of his day could, but nevertheless had a standard grip and stance, played most strokes with a straight bat, lining the ball up, and watching it onto the bat. However unconventional his house, it was not built upon sand.

Technique is like a secure base from which one may make excursions. It is like the safe proximity of the mother for the growing child. Technique is the basis of solid plans, although one may also, on occasion, throw these over in favour of a hunch. Former England captain Len Hutton said that 'you can have all the plans in the world, but once you get onto the field they go out of the window'. I would say: yes, but also, no. A captain does need the flexibility and the readiness to trust his gut feelings (well trained, we hope) in response to the reality of the immediate situation. But the pre-formed plan may need to take precedence, or be stuck to for sufficient time. Lack of immediate success does not mean that it is not still the best possible plan for the situation.

Hard Work and Practice

Only by purposeful practice, training and hard work can we as sportsmen, psychoanalysts and other skilled practitioners establish the groundwork which will enable us to find form more or less reliably.

In 1964 I played with Fred Titmus in a match for MCC against a South African A side at Benoni. On the first day, he bowled forty-one overs, taking four wickets for 145 runs. Several catches were dropped off his bowling. Next morning, he was out on the practice ground with a bag of balls, bowling without a batsman. He laid stumps flat on the pitch to mark the areas where he wanted to land the ball. He bowled several overs. I asked him what, after his long bowl the day before, he was trying to do. He said, 'I've got to let it go right at my end. If I can do that with confidence, then I can start thinking how to deal with a batsman who does something different at the other end.'

Titmus knew it was up to him how the ball left his hand. What the batsman did with it was another matter. He was talking about what *he* could control. This kind of hard work in mastering a craft provides a solid foundation for more subtle variations, for being ready to adapt to the individual or idiosyncratic qualities in the pitch or the batsman, and for the possibility of transformations into heightened states of mind and body.

Purposive Practice

Practice itself must be meaningful and focused. We waste time if we merely go through the motions. In cricket, for example, practising on unsuitable pitches does little for either bowlers or batsmen. The former can't bowl flat out, for fear of injuring themselves as a result of poor footholds, or the batsman if the pitch is too unreliable. The latter can't bat properly, as orthodox shots are unproductive and there is too much risk of injury. Both lose energy and confidence. All are liable to get into bad habits. Much of the cricket practice I was involved in was of poor quality. Net pitches were often badly worn or uneven; bowling machines or video machines – both crucial assets now taken for granted by professionals – were as I've said rarely available. Like many others, I failed to formulate with sufficient clarity the areas I needed to work on, or to make overall appraisals of my technique and approach, both of which might have helped clarify what coaching would have been most appropriate. I was not always clear about the best timing for a radical change in technique: it is usually a mistake to attempt such changes when big matches are imminent, or when on tour, as they are bound to have unknown consequences, which need to be worked through away from the big stage.

Training should, as a rule, be realistic. Having nets against schoolboys bowling spinners or medium pace is no preparation for a Test match against a side full of fast bowlers. A batsman needs to face at least some bowling of the kind he will encounter in the middle, and in conditions that are relevant. Often the main bowlers in your squad differ from the batsmen in the kinds of practice they need. (Bowling machines are invaluable, as are 'throw-downs' – using a kind of mini-catapult – from 15 yards.)

Coaches and mentors themselves have to be creative and willing to improvise. It is important too that coach and player commit to each other. Neil Burns, a professional cricketer for various counties in the 1980s and 90s, described conducting a whole-day session with an international batsman (I will call him 'Jim'), preparing him for an upcoming tour.

Burns had Jim hitting plenty of balls; running up and down the pitch for ones, twos and threes, wearing his protective gear all day. He subjected him to different rhythms of bowling to simulate different intensities, and to get him ready for the whole range of bowlers he would be facing – all this interspersed with periods of waiting. The aim was to test and strengthen Jim's physical, mental and emotional stamina in preparation for batting for long periods, whatever the state of the game. Burns writes:

> I try to disrupt his rhythm with extreme pace by the bowl-
> ing machine from 17 yards. This simulation of aggressive
> bowling produces in Jim a state of combative defence, in
> which he is at the same time geared up to counter-attack by

playing pull and hook shots. The downside is that he tends to lose his flowing offside driving capacity, something he is best able to realise against less hostile bowling. So I intersperse with such spells periods when in alternate overs the machine delivers slow bowling to tempt him out of the resultant committed defence and feeling of entrenchment.

Burns also coaches Ray, a slow bowler. One day, to heighten his kinaesthetic experience of bowling, he had him bowl blindfolded. After bowling some balls into the side netting, Ray then decided not to merely 'put it there', not, that is, to try merely to make the ball land in a certain area; instead he resolved to be energetic in his bowling action, pivoting over the braced front leg, using his body, and really spinning the ball. The resulting deliveries were much more accurate and well directed. Despite being blindfolded, he even bowled some 'magic' balls.

On another day Burns got Ray to bowl for two and a half hours to a right-hand and a left-hand batsman. In the gaps after each six balls – between 'overs' as it were – Burns encouraged him to find his 'calm, still place', but also to be more 'on the boil' at the start of the next over, rather than (as he tends to do) ease in slowly and perform with less intensity at the beginning of an over.

This attitude to preparation reminds me of military training. The prospect of entering combat, especially for the first time, is terrifying. In a wartime edition of 1943, *Life* magazine's 'Life Report' conceded that everyone goes into battle scared. 'But encounters with the enemy are most terrifying when they are unfamiliar . . . so that any action [that is] so drilled in that it is mechanical helps when you are scared.' For the recruit not to be totally overwhelmed by the 'fog' of actual war, he needs to have gone through simulated violence and real hardship

in the war games that are part of his training. These realistic 'games' test strength of mind as well as physical fitness.
Participants are required to think for themselves, to work out,
for example, the best route and tempo for a march across harsh
terrain against the clock. They learn to take responsibility for
their own actions. Things can go wrong; but it is arguable
that, in the long run, making the training as lifelike as possible reduces casualties in actual war situations. Such activities
are in one sense the converse of square-bashing, in which no
individual initiative is called for, simply endurance – no doubt,
both forms of training are necessary.

On a less extreme note, theatre director Joan Littlewood
used unconventional rehearsal methods at the Theatre Royal,
Stratford. She was convinced that the main aim was for the actors
to play scenes with 'physical truth'; to do this in the early rehearsals, they needed to know only in rough outline what a scene
was about. In 1958, she directed the first production of Shelagh
Delaney's A *Taste of Honey*. The play starts with the mother,
Helen (played by Avis Bunnage), and daughter Jo (Frances Cuka)
coming on with suitcases. Cuka remembers Littlewood saying:

> 'Well, we've got to get this first scene right . . . these suitcases
> haven't got anything in them!' and she put stage weights
> in them, she put God knows what in them . . . and then
> she made us go round and round the stage, with Murray
> [Melvin, who played the part of Geoffrey] being the bus
> conductor who wouldn't let us on – 'not with that suitcase
> you're not getting on', until Avis and I were at daggers drawn,
> and we're not speaking to him, and we're about to kill Joan,
> and then she said 'Right! Start the play' . . . You never forgot
> the frustration and hatred.

Only through arduous training, Littlewood maintained, can actors enter into and express their characters' arduous feelings.

Technique but No Soul: The Cookie Cutter

Obviously, however, technique is not enough. When we say of a sportsman or musician that he 'has a good technique, but . . .' what sort of comment might complete the sentence?

The qualification normally alludes to some shortcoming in personal qualities – *but* he lacks confidence, conviction or courage. He lacks heart, perhaps, or passion. His play doesn't catch fire. Or the point may be that he lacks judgment or shrewdness, that he can play all the strokes or notes correctly but seems unable to apply this proficiency in particular practical contexts. 'A player may be perfect in technique, and yet have neither soul nor intelligence,' as the musicologist George Grove put it.

Diligence and talent together are not enough. China correspondent Joseph Kahn and culture editor Daniel J. Watkin comment in the *New York Times*: '[Western] classical music,

Chinese critics say, is still treated too often like a technology that can be mastered with the right combination of capital, labour and quality control. But,' they argue, 'a combination of technique, culture and creativity [is] needed to create music that sounds spontaneous, sensitive and rich in emotion – not wooden and shaped by a cookie cutter.'

Sometimes an earnest diligence comes from our internal authority function, the part of the self called by Freud the 'superego', which at times behaves like a martinet, harsh and even paralysing, stifling life and growth, rigidly shaping performances like a cookie-cutter.

Technique then becomes a master rather than a slave, an end rather than a means or mode. The poet W. H. Auden alludes to 'goodness carefully worn, for atonement or for luck'; careful, careworn, over-polite 'goodness' is one source of falsity in the self, an ingrained conformity that betrays an inability to access our own desires and convictions. Technique is enlisted to obey or appease the superego's voice. This takes precedence over enjoyment, spontaneity and full engagement with the living of life. Auden urges us to counter this oppression by valuing the instinctive life of animals: 'On each beast and bird that moves, turn an envious look'. We need passion and discipline in equal measure.

Tricky Technique

Technique may also be used trickily, to seduce, manipulate or even brainwash. There is nothing wrong with persuasion, of course. The question is: how low will someone stoop to gain the day? Politicians may use rhetorical techniques to 'play' their audience, to win them over, regardless of truth, probability or relevance. At the crudest level, there are those who give voice and respectability to base views that have become morally unacceptable in public life, and win support by subtle scapegoating and tuning in to grievances. *Animal Farm*, George Orwell's novel of 1945, is a parodic storehouse of the kinds of rhetorical devices used by disreputable politicians and governments: 'Four legs good, two legs bad', later smoothly distorted into 'Four legs good, two legs better', and 'All animals are equal', metamorphosing into 'All animals are equal, but some are more equal than others.' Classicist Mary Beard makes a further point: rhetoric may be not so much manipulative as bland, descending to the mere recital of slogans and one-liners. Party machines, she suggests, are too risk-averse to countenance real speech.

If technique encroaches upon love or friendship, we suspect that calculation has seedily overruled sincerity. We sense that a person behaving in such a way is playing a part rather than being himself. For instance, I heard once of a woman writing a love letter that included a long unattributed quote from Emily Brontë's novel *Wuthering Heights* – an attempt to create a seductively romantic atmosphere. Sometimes, too, a stereotyped professionalism is, or comes across as, inauthentic. In selecting students for training in psychoanalysis, we try to distinguish between those who have the makings of a devotion to the subject and the process, and those who hanker after the accolade, such as it is, of the title, becoming, perhaps, pompous and over-clever in their application.

Whatever our talent, and whatever grasp of technique we have achieved, there are, as Grove has described, other qualities that have to be learned or developed if we are to improve at any activity where form is a factor. Graham Gooch, recently England's batting coach, used to say that he didn't coach batting, he coached *run-making*. I like this distinction, one that Gooch himself learned, as part of the 'principles of batsmanship', from his mentor, Ken Barrington. Top players do at times have technical issues for which ordinary coaching is relevant.

But it is more often a priority for them, as Gooch says, to learn different kinds of lessons – how to build an innings and change gears, say, or to gain the application to turn good scores into huge scores, or to know when to dig in. We often need to improve our practical and emotional intelligence or 'nous'; not to panic when in bad form, nor to become careless when in the zone. Then there is the business of 'reading' the game – when to take risks, and what are the safest and most productive risks at any moment. Are we able to learn from both failure and success? Do we make the best of our ability and technique? Joe Root, England's star young batsman, and now captain, learns from his mistakes, and by nature always seems to play according to the demands of the situation. This is what we mean by 'sporting intelligence'. It has little to do with intellectual knowledge or capacity, much more to do with common sense and a shrewd, constructive attitude.

Top cricketers may need, too, to expand their repertoires. With Gooch's advice, Alastair Cook, England's most successful opening batsman, learned to play the slog-sweep in one-day cricket, a shot that forces the opposition to put a fielder at deep mid-wicket, thus giving scoring opportunities in another area of the field.

In 1976, at the beginning of England's tour of India, Derek Underwood and I found ourselves having lunch together in Bombay. We 'talked shop' for two hours, especially about his craft – slow, or in his case slow-medium-left-arm bowling. I talked about how I tried to play him, he about what he least, and most, liked to see in a batsman. We discussed the strengths and weaknesses of different approaches. We talked about the speed he bowled best at. I recalled my unproductive suggestion to him some years before, in Pakistan, that he should try bowling more slowly on those flat pitches. We discussed field- settings. Already an experienced Test bowler, Derek was conservative; he didn't like to give away runs, nor did he like having his field changed more than necessary. I wondered aloud with him about the circumstances in which bowling over the wicket to right-hand batsmen might be worth a try as a variation, especially when the pitch was worn around leg stump as a result of the follow-throughs of right-arm seam bowlers bowling from the other end. We went into detail about the fields he might have for such a line of attack.

Some of Underwood's reluctance was overcome. And the conversation paid dividends a few months later, in the Test match at Old Trafford, when I talked him into bowling this way in Australia's second innings, reminding him with diagrams on the back of an envelope of the field placings we had discussed. He took three crucial wickets with this mode of attack, ending with a match-winning six for 66. Never before, he told me to my surprise, had he talked in as much depth about bowling as we had done that afternoon in Bombay.

Art v. Craft, Gardening v. Carpentry

It is not always easy to discriminate sharply between technical difficulties and emotional ones. If I give up too quickly on how to operate the strange washing machine in a holiday apartment, is this because of my technical shortcomings, or because I refuse to use my practical intelligence? Do I need technical advice and practical help, or a tough challenge to my passivity and impatience? And since the latter, if successful, results in better functioning, would not this capacity become part of my technique in dealing with technical matters? As I see it, the term 'technique' pulls in two directions. One is towards procedures, rules, calculation, even mechanics or technology. The other is towards attitude, orientation – towards overall personality.

It is true that different skills call for differing degrees of technical – as opposed to emotional – knowledge in their application. The philosopher R. C. Collingwood discusses the role of technique in relation to craft and art. He differentiates two ways of thinking that reflect the two kinds of skill I have been describing. One form of activity (which he calls craft) calls for technique in the sense of the Greek root, *technê* (τέχνη), as a means to a clearly distinct, pre-planned end, while another form of making, called by him 'art' or 'art proper', requires not *techne*, but instead what he refers to as 'imaginative expression'. The craftsman's ultimate end, he argues, like the orator's, is to create a state of mind in the customer. The artist, by contrast, has no such end in view. Much of what passes for art, he says, and much of what aestheticians and philosophers have taken for art, is in fact pseudo-art; it degenerates into magic or amusement, which are degraded or corrupted versions of art; they are, that is, in his terms, craft.

The essence of art proper, for Collingwood, is the expression of emotion by means of the imagination, an activity akin to the serious play of children. Imagination is to be contrasted with wish-fulfilment, where one *conjures up* a gratifying feeling. 'What the artist wants to say becomes clear only as the poem takes shape in his mind or the clay in his fingers,' he writes. 'Expression is an activity of which there can be no technique.' He adds a comment on truthfulness: 'If art means the expression of emotion, the artist as such must be absolutely candid.'

Collingwood speaks of the artist extricating himself in his artistic work from a helpless and oppressed condition of perturbation and unconsciousness, and moving to a state of clarity and consciousness. Means-to-an-end technology or technique are not applicable here, Collingwood suggests. One does not know in advance what the end will be. Moreover, the relation to the hearer or recipient of the work is also different, less calculated, without templates for the psychological end-product.

This point is amplified by psychologist Alison Gopnik in her book on education and being a parent, *The Gardener and the Carpenter*. She too makes use of the distinction between means-to-end approaches and more expressive thinking. Gopnik argues that 'parenting [is] a curious thing that happened to mothers and fathers and children in the late twentieth century – and that this cultural trend makes the task like that of a carpenter'. You are, it is true, called on to pay some attention to the kind of material you are working with, but 'essentially your job is to shape that material into a final product that will fit the scheme you had in mind to begin with'. By contrast, '[real] caring for children is like tending a garden, and being a parent is like being a gardener'. When we garden, 'we create a protected and nurturing space for plants to flourish . . . The glory of a meadow is its messiness . . . there is no guarantee that any individual plant will become the tallest, or fairest, or most long-blooming'.

We can't *make* children learn, Gopnik says, but we can *let* them learn. Instead of bringing up children being 'an act of spontaneous and loving care, [it] became a management plan': we have come to believe that as parents or educators our task is to turn blocks of wood into pre-designed products. Such an approach is taken for granted in many self-help books on topics such as bringing up children, or how to be on form. Gopnik sees this as missing the essences of the process.

In his Nobel Lecture, 'Art, Truth and Politics', playwright Harold Pinter writes about the origins of his plays:

> I have often been asked how my plays come about. I cannot say . . . Most of the plays are engendered by a line, a word

or an image. I shall give examples of two lines which came right out of the blue into my head, followed by an image, followed by me . . . The first line of *The Homecoming* is 'What have you done with the scissors?' The first line of *Old Times* is 'Dark' . . . In each case I found myself compelled to pursue the matter . . . Our beginnings never know our ends.

8

'YOU IDIOT, RAGS!' –
TALKING TO ONESELF

How can you hit and think at the same time?

Yogi Berra

The analyst's emotional response to his patient within the analytic situation represents one of the most important tools for his work.

Paula Heimann

I am a pessimist because of intelligence, an optimist because of will.

Antonio Gramsci

What goes on in the mind of a batsman during an innings? The most notable attempt I know to give such an account is Dudley Doust's reconstruction of Derek Randall's match-saving – and in the end match-winning – innings of 150 for England against Australia in the fourth Test at Sydney in 1979. Doust interviewed Randall at length, and also spoke to the five Australians who had bowled at him during what was then the slowest century (411 minutes) in the long history of Test cricket between the two countries.

Sport is about much more than passages of relaxed, flowing concentration. Randall was never, even at his best, a paragon of calm. And this innings was not a thing of beauty. But it was a thing of character, and of eccentricity. Moreover, one of his tasks on this particular occasion was to refrain from doing what was 'natural' for him.

Was he on form during that innings? I would hesitate to say so, though he did through strenuous effort win through to being, in a self-disciplined fashion, in better form as he went on (until fatigue led to carelessness towards the end). His self-regulation, though stern, was informed by enthusiasm and hope. Maybe it stands as an example of how few general rules there are for achievement in sport and elsewhere.

The innings was magnificent in its effort and endurance. One reason was that twice already in the series, including in the first innings of this match, Randall had been caught for 0, hooking. Second, the weather conditions were the hottest I remember in my (pre-global-warming) cricketing experience; by the time he batted in that second innings, the temperature was consistently above 100 degrees Fahrenheit, with hardly any breeze. In those days no extra drinks were rushed out onto the field at every opportunity. One's tongue rapidly came to feel like sandpaper in the mouth. Of course, such conditions were even worse for the bowlers. Moreover, Australia's best bowler, Rodney Hogg, who ended the series with a record-breaking 41 wickets at twelve runs apiece, had a tendency to asthma, and his condition was apparently at its worst in this airless heat. But Randall's too was a huge feat of endurance, 582 minutes of it in all.

This innings was the fulcrum of the series. After winning the first two Tests, we had just lost the third, at Melbourne. And at one stage in the Sydney match, our main strike bowler, Bob Willis, was off the field sick, and Australia were 126 for one in reply to our meagre first-innings score of 152. We were staring down the barrel. From this position, it was a considerable achievement to restrict Australia to a lead of 142 runs. But seven minutes before lunch on the third day, after just one ball in our second innings, a loosener from Hogg that Geoffrey Boycott missed, Randall was on his way to the crease.

What is most striking about Doust's description is how nervy Randall was. On the pitch, he constantly talked out loud, half to himself, half to the opposition. Mainly, I think, he was boosting and haranguing himself. As Doust put it, 'Randall lives in a world of his own, peopled principally by himself.' Much of the vexation Randall caused the Australians was unconscious, but there is no doubt he did puzzle and irritate them with his jittery mannerisms, his idiosyncratic foot movements, and his constant chattering, which Hogg for one found 'incomprehensible gibberish'. He provoked, took up time, got under their skins.

Randall referred to himself as 'Rags', as he had done since being a ragamuffin playing with bigger boys, when he had learned to pull balls that others would have defended. Now, his first preoccupation was to refrain from being drawn into rash pulls or hooks early on. He had had a lecture from team manager Doug Insole after his first innings duck. Insole reminded him of his responsibility: before he started hooking, he ought to have a long look at the bowling and get the pace of the pitch. 'Another thing; you simply have *got* to learn to play your innings in segments. You have got to be there at lunch. You have got to be there at tea. You have got to be there at the close.' (Willis had said in the dressing room earlier on the tour, about batsmen's carelessness, 'They have to be told,' and Insole told him.)

Randall had at first demurred. 'I've got to get a couple of good shots early on for my confidence,' he said. 'It's the way I play.' But Insole was having none of it. 'If so, maybe you should give some serious thought to the way you play,' he replied sharply. We can't simply, complacently, trust ourselves. At times we have to restrict ourselves deliberately.

(Not that one learns these lessons permanently. The old Adam reasserts itself. Two years later, Derek and I were playing against each other at Nottingham. I stayed overnight with him at his home between the second and third days' play, as he had done the year before with me in London. In the first innings, immune to Insole's advice, hooking his second ball, from young fast bowler Simon Hughes, he had been dismissed for 0, hitting it straight to Phil Edmonds at deepish square leg. Two days later, on our car journey to the match after breakfast, I asked him when he thought we would bowl the bouncer in his forthcoming innings: would it be first ball? Or third? Or perhaps second, as in the first innings? According to plan,

Hughes's second ball was identical to the earlier one. Randall played an identical shot, and deep square leg took an identical catch in the same position.)

In Sydney, Randall had been chastened by Insole's lecture. Fortunately, Hogg was out of sorts, disgusted with the pitch – 'You can't get the ball to lift at this place.' From one end the wind (such as it was) was against him, from the other the slope. And he was aghast at his side's batting performance. 'We had England on toast,' he told Doust. 'And then we screwed up. Some days you feel like bowling and some days you don't. I didn't on that day.'

Randall's monologue would run along these lines: 'Come on, Rags. Get stuck in. Don't take any chances. Get forrard [forward], get *forrard*. Take your time, slow and easy. You *idiot*, Rags. Come on, come on. Come on England.' In the very first over, after getting off the mark with a single, he was provoking Hogg, asking the umpire to 'take a look at Hogg's right forefinger'.

It was discoloured. Hogg's finger was examined. The fast bowler's eyes blazed. 'It's stuff for my blisters,' he cried out. His finger was covered by a mild astringent, potassium permanganate, which is used, quite legally, to dry blisters. But Randall had won a small skirmish, so much so that Hogg stepped over to him and gave him a firm little slap on the jaw.

Randall went on baiting Hogg, and by the same token boosting his own confidence. There was an exchange when Hogg had bowled some no-balls. Randall started scratching at the crease with his studs to mark the line more clearly, making out that the umpire should keep an even sharper eye on the bowler's front foot. His scratching was not likely to mar the bowler's foothold, but that was what Hogg felt in his irritation. '"Stop scratching around where my foot lands!" he shouted. "I'm not scratching around," Randall replied, "I'm showing the umpire where your foot landed." [This interference alone would be sound reason for a pungent response from umpire and opposition.] Hogg was incensed. He swore. "I don't go where a batsman stands and start fiddling around." A ball or two later he indeed "fiddled around" where Randall stood, stomping his boot into the ground, pawing at it like a bull.'

There were further exchanges between the two. Hogg found Randall enigmatic: 'He's always trying to get my goat. He's always saying something stupid.'

In Doust's words, 'At no stage in his batting marathon did Randall believe England might win. He therefore chose to play slowly, using up as much time as possible without arousing the ire of the umpires.' One method was to ask for fly repellent, even though the flies were not bothering him. 'Randall found that the cream carried by [umpire] French was more useful than the spray from [umpire] Bailache's aerosol can. It took longer to apply.'

At one point 'Randall received a full-toss, head-high, from leg-spinner Jim Higgs. "Most times I would have put it away for four, but I was so concerned with not losing my wicket I became over-cautious and played it softly down for a single. If I had gone for it I might have hit it straight down the fielder's throat."'

At the end of the day, after four hours of batting, Randall 'peeled off his sodden gear and slumped onto a bench. Insole came up and offered his hand. Randall took it without a word. He had answered the call for caution.' He continued to do so for another five hours on the fourth day.

Unlike Mike Atherton in Johannesburg or Tony Greig in Bombay, Randall was far from being in the zone. At the start he was not even on form. His head was full of remonstrance and endeavour. The most prominent figure in his world, as Doust says, was the self that exhorted, cajoled and encouraged himself. I think his riling of his opponents was a way both of keeping himself upbeat, and of getting them to feel his confusion or lack of confidence. Perhaps 'the way he played', the compulsion to get going quickly, to feel the confidence from hitting the ball hard with the middle of the bat, was also a counter to his uncertainty.

Randall continued to curb his aggression and to niggle the Australians for much of that fourth day. He added 58 with Graham Gooch, 68 with David Gower, 30 with a cautious Ian Botham (who scored only six in ninety minutes), 40 with Geoff Miller. When he was eventually out, with our score on 292 for six, Randall banged his bat against his pad in annoyance at himself, aware that 'if we lose a couple more wickets the Aussies will be back on top in the morning.' But we knew we now had a chance of a remarkable turnaround.

In fact the last three wickets added a useful 35 runs, and we were able to set Australia a target of 205. We then bowled them out for 111 in 49.2 overs to win by 93 runs. 'Higgs said, generously, "It wasn't really a memorable innings because there weren't many memorable shots. But it was the innings that won England the Ashes." Of the ball that got him out, Hogg said, graciously, "He just missed it. He was as tired as I was."'

During this long innings there was little flow or tranquillity. Randall was constantly making conscious efforts, both by self-exhortation and self-recrimination ('You idiot, Rags'). Yet his self-scrutiny did not dismantle him. He kept his sense of being up for the task.

Boredom in Place of Disappointment

In the autumn of 2012, I was invited to speak at the London School of Economics, alongside two philosophers, on the topic

'In the Zone: spontaneity and mental discipline in sport and beyond'. This was when the seeds of this book were sown. I had long been interested in how we find, or fail to find, form; and how various states of mind, including what was increasingly, if trendily, being referred to as 'being in the zone', enhance or disrupt it.

As we were finishing up at LSE, a man called Tim Newton asked if he might contact me to talk about his own lack of form on the golf course. His interest was in improving his mental preparation and performance. Although he had been playing with a low handicap for some time, he told me, he had always struggled with self-belief, so that he had been outperformed by many who lacked his talent. Now aged thirty-eight, he was committed to a 'broad improvement programme' encompassing coaching, training and, he hoped, some psychological work.

We had an exploratory meeting. I felt it went well. I heard nothing more for two years, when I had a second email from him. Here is part of what he wrote:

> I really enjoyed our meeting, and found it to be very beneficial. You asked several key questions . . . and you also made me more aware of a couple of negative tendencies. Your calling me out for feeling bored during poor performance as a mask for disappointment has been a revelation, and I have worked hard to 'notice' this and turn things around as quickly as possible when it is happening. The concept you suggested of moving away from a feeling that 'nothing I can do is good enough' in much of my life, towards viewing golf as 'my space' to express myself in, and to enjoy performing the thing I am best at, has also been invaluable to me, helping me to relax, and 'allow' performance to happen, and be maintained. You were also clear that any progress would be limited unless I continually worked in parallel on my technique.

I wanted to let you know that I have had a particularly good period of form recently – in terms of both technique and approach – and have achieved the ambition I have had for many years of getting down to scratch. So thank you for helping me break through what has been a significant barrier over a long period of time. As a 'prize' I get to play in the Open Championship Qualifying (tournament) next year.

Tim had clearly been ready to listen and take on board what I said. I was struck by what he remembered about slipping into boredom. My point was that in general one way of dealing with disappointment or frustration with oneself is to become indifferent and passive. I recalled a patient who suddenly felt extremely tired. As far as he could tell, this tiredness was a fact of life, something that simply happened to him. I suggested that it was, rather, a phenomenon that, without deliberate intent, he partly concocted. Like him, Tim had denied the fact that he *minded* being off form. He yawned his disappointment away. We are all more active than we know.

Tim was able to notice the process of evading disappointment *as it happened*. Realising his agency, he was empowered to alter it. He freed himself from his self-protective trap. He became able to tolerate his annoyance with himself, and attend to and wrestle with the task in hand. He no longer felt bored or uninterested.

Here was an example of someone coming to know himself better, and then being prepared to face his damaging mode of being, and struggle with it – leading to a definite improvement in form. Of course we can't know how influential his other activities – being coached, practising, getting fitter – were in his progress. It is enough that the psychological work played a part.

Working on Our Own Feelings

We need to work on our feelings, as Derek Randall and Tim Newton did. Self-scrutiny is vital, though not if it is the kind that demolishes confidence. Just as teams that are on form accommodate and do their best to help off-form members, so this may happen inside the self. Like Randall, we talk to ourselves. We may have a sort of overarching self that tolerates and allows work on the part that is responsible for our being out of sorts. As in teams, much depends on who is (internally) in charge, under whose aegis we are functioning: that of the self-destructive voice, or that of a containing self that can accommodate negativity but not be dictated to by it.

Moreover, one of our main resources in helping *others* is *self*-scrutiny: we can learn a lot about those we come into contact with by reflecting on their impact on ourselves. One of my formative experiences in deciding to apply to train in psychoanalysis came from being a member of a small group of qualified and unqualified nursing staff at the Adolescent Unit of Northgate Clinic, led by psychoanalyst Donald Bird. We started each weekly meeting by considering how a patient had affected us. Bird taught us to notice and then think about what we felt and how we were inclined to act in relation to particular patients, and to regard it as potential evidence of what those patients projected into us. I remember our discussing a boy who tended to get bullied by the other young people in the unit. We came to see how much we too felt irritated by him, and how this was a result of his subtle, unconscious invitation to others to put him down. He had found a way of coping by being a self-righteous victim, as a result feeling and coming across as superior to his attackers – a process that further provoked them (and us). By noticing and then reflecting on our emotional reactions in Dr Bird's group, we arrived at a fuller understanding of the patient, more sympathetic both to him and to his bullying peers.

Crises that arise both as a result of the impact of others and from purely internal sources – as when we have a serious illness – disturb our placidity. They may also offer salutary revelations of neurotic and negative patterns in our way of living. It often takes a wound to our omnipotence to motivate us to realise and then work on these patterns, and in the end to change and grow. For psychoanalysis to be of value, an important factor is that the patient accepts that he really is a patient, that he suffers, that he has some responsibility for this suffering, and that he wants to understand himself better and change.

But *Can* One Hit and Think at the Same Time?

But will not awareness of these patterns interfere with our spontaneous 'going on being'? Does not thinking undo grooving, that basic element of technique and performance? Was Yogi Berra right, that one can't hit and think at the same time?

As Ken Barrington wrote: 'When you're out of form, you're conscious of needing to do things right, you have to think first and act second. To make runs under those conditions is mighty difficult.' We over-think; we are 'sicklied o'er with the pale cast of thought', as Hamlet puts it. We 'try too hard', frowns etched into our foreheads, body and mind tense and over-conscious.

We also at times think unproductively when batting, succumbing, as the Australian philosopher and cricket-lover John Sutton suggested, to 'vainglory . . . a temporary manic narcissism which perseveres, skewing my allowable response repertoire as the next ball arrives and draws me into another flash, a nick, the gut-wrenching lurch, the swamping disbelieving misery, the self-criticism, the rumination'. Or we suddenly have the intrusive idea that the bowler will bowl a short ball; getting into position for this, we miss a straight half-volley.

We know from everyday experience that we need to 'disencumber consciousness': it would be fatal for ordinary activities like walking or riding a bicycle if we needed to work out each movement diligently, separately and in advance. Instead we create trained habits, schemas, that have become natural to us. This 'procedural memory' brings our embedded knowledge and skill with swift adaptability to the particularity of the present. As batsmen, say, we are poised between repetition and improvisation.

But we also know that conscious thought is continually applied to skills. We monitor our ways of going about things. Just as batting partners give each other small nudges and encouragements, so do we converse with ourselves. At times we even scrutinise ourselves, that is, turn an unflinching, questioning eye on our own behaviour and thought processes. Then we are more like a coach proposing radical changes in technique, or a psychoanalyst making a deep interpretation about a picture that 'holds us captive'. Without thought we would never learn from experience, correct faults, make productive adjustments or change deep-rooted patterns. Some grooves become ruts.

So, how is it that thinking does not *always* interfere?

First, we don't (normally) attempt to change everything all at once. Unless we rely on many aspects of our play staying the same while we focus on a particular element, we will confuse ourselves with constant corrections. The great philosopher René Descartes attempted to doubt everything at once. 'If you would be a real seeker after truth,' he wrote, 'it is necessary that at least once in your life you doubt, as far as possible, all things.' This project was *ipso facto* a very different enterprise from ordinary doubt, the latter implicitly contrasting that which is dubious with what is known or at least provisionally taken for granted. When we are lost we are not, generally, lost in relation to everywhere. The art of coaching, as of interpretation, is to pick out what is most crucial and most reparable, what the recipient has a good enough chance of taking on. It is not a matter of overloading him with across-the-board doubts or prescriptions.

Second, our internal dialogues are similar to external ones. The best external 'coach' is able to say just the right amount, at the right time. He does not bombard the struggling player, but gets into the hole with him, though without the latter's helplessness. The learner is assumed to know how to do some things. The *inner* coach or analyst will do well to remember this. He is not helpful if he is a martinet, ridiculing the self and stripping it of all its good qualities, but nor is he helpful if he ignores every problem. Psychoanalyst Marion Milner comments on the role of this judging self in playing table tennis, that the 'internal gesture required' is often to 'stand aside; the arm itself knows what to do'. The whole self knows what to do. What often happens, however, is that the superego, the part of the self that stands over the spontaneous self (including the decision-making, choosing part – called by Freud the 'ego'), gets in the way with its interference and its condemnation. Our superegos are often neither wise nor moderate. And even if they are, it is often hard to take the advice seriously, and at the same time refrain from wheeling it out inappropriately. Just as we need to do with suggestions from other people, we have to take in the advice of our own superego, and then integrate it with our own way of being. It is not a cure-all. But nor is it helpful for the superego to remove itself altogether. If there is no monitoring, we may go so far as to hand over our moral values to someone else, to the state, say, and merely follow orders.

Third, thought is more embodied than we tend to think, and often as automatic as walking. Physical action is purposive movement, that is, movement infused with intentionality, with thought. Thoughtfulness is a process wide-ranging enough to embrace the timing achieved when hooking a fast delivery, and the stern lecture a person gives himself. It may be as natural and as procedural as the action itself. Like the footballer who has just headed a magnificent goal, we may be able to say no more about these practical choices and judgments than the superficial: 'The ball came over, and suddenly it was in the back of the net.' There may be no conscious or unconscious moment of cognition sandwiched between stimulus and response. Sutton quotes French philosopher Maurice Merleau-Ponty: 'We merge into this body, which is better informed than we are about the world.' We rely on embodied thinking and remembering, as well as on verbal nudges. 'Thinking on your feet lies at the heart of batting', as Sutton writes. Sport, one might say, is articulacy in action.

Some people need to be more spontaneous, less cautiously circumspect. Others, who speak and act without reflection, opportunistically saying the first or most rebarbative thing that comes to mind, need to pause for thought. One suit does not fit all.

Without Memory or Desire

Greg Chappell's advocacy for the batsman to 'just respond to what he sees' is not a panacea, nor is Wilfred Bion's ideal state of the mind for a psychoanalyst, namely, to be 'without memory or desire' – to be open, that is, to whatever the patient brings, without effortful remembering or desire for one outcome rather than another – an unqualified aspiration for the psychoanalyst.

We often need to *set ourselves*. A batsman playing in a Twenty20 match has a totally different orientation to the task from someone going in to bat in a Test match. In the former context he is looking to score off every ball; he is constantly aware of the pressure of time and the urgent need to evaluate where his side should be after the next over or two. Chappell calls this pre-planning, rather than 'that graveyard of batting', premeditation. For him it comes into the same category as becoming aware (as part of one's background mental equipment) of where you are likely to score runs off each bowler you face. Perhaps we could call it a hypothetical premeditation, which is, indeed, different from unconditional premeditation. Such planning and pre-figuring – hypothetical premeditation – is a necessary precondition to Chappell's aim that one should be free to respond without fear, trusting one's ability and training.

Being without memory or desire is often a counsel of perfection, aimed at the highly skilled player, and geared to a scenario in which there is unlimited time. Most, perhaps all, batsmen have to do *some* premeditating, if only in ruling out certain options. Even Denis Compton, the mercurial, spontaneous genius of the 1940s and 50s, *set himself* to be on the back foot when facing quick bowlers. Most players *pre-decide* at certain stages of the game whether to go for the hook or, alternatively, to defend or evade the fast, short-pitched ball; they adopt a policy. In shorter games, all players predetermine, or at least have a range of possibilities and priorities in the 'back of their minds'. Sometimes they play pre-planned shots, scooping a delivery over the wicketkeeper's head, for instance, or stepping outside off stump as the bowler lets go of the ball to be in position to play a sweep; premeditating, at least in the hypothetical form: '*if* the ball is outside off stump, say, or on a certain length, I will play that shot'. Sutton suggests that batsmen 'alter the probabilities of attempting certain shots to a certain range of deliveries'.

Similarly, a player, or a whole team, may decide on a policy against a particular bowler. The strategy may be to see him off by resolute defence; or, planning to dent his confidence once and for all, they may opt for out-and-out attack as soon as he comes on to bowl. At the Oval in 2013, Australia, in the person of Shane Watson, demolished the confidence of left-arm spinner Simon Kerrigan within the latter's first few deliveries in Test cricket. It was an agonising spectacle. Kerrigan was taken off after two overs, which cost 28 runs, including six boundaries. His own paralysing anxiety, combined with and intensified by the belligerent batting, made his debut a nightmare. Instantly, he was in the territory of the 'yips' – the disintegration of key motor skills.

It is hard to draw a sharp line between this kind of provisional premeditation – if that indeed is what it was in the Australian team (what Chappell calls the 'big picture stuff, the strategy') – and what he would think of as intrusive premeditation.

There are similarities in psychoanalysis. Once the analyst has arrived at an idea, for instance, he may *consciously* plan (reminding himself of the patient's sensitivities, for example) how best to present it. In my early days as an analyst I had a patient who found fault with a lot of what I suggested. At first I thought her carping was solely in response to my getting things wrong. But I gradually realised that her contrariness got going whenever I came up with an idea that she had not thought of first. I came to see that this reaction was a result of envy, and of the patient's pressing need to be the one who was in the know. I decided that I had to wait for an instance where I was confident that my interpretation was good enough to merit consideration, and then be willing to confront her by interpreting her envious opposition. I resolved to stand firm against the reactions, both head-on and diversionary, that would inevitably follow. At that stage in my career, I had to premeditate the ground on which I was prepared to stand, and gird my loins for the ensuing battle. Later, with more experience, I might have come to such a way of being with less deliberation. But the memory and desire will at times necessarily, constructively, be conscious.

The distinguished psychoanalyst Hanna Segal writes that the analyst who is being idealised by a patient should be 'watchful for the appearance of bad figures in the patient's extra-analytical life, and take every opportunity of interpreting them as split-off bad aspects of himself'. She advocates, in other words, being *on the look-out for* a likely consequence of ideal-isation, namely, denigration, and for its being directed, even diverted, away from the analyst. This is not a state of mind that is without memory or desire.

Simplicity of Approach, Complexity of Understanding

A balance needs to be struck between theoretical complexity on one side, and practical simplicity and good sense on the other. The Italian Marxist theoretician and politician Antonio Gramsci stated, 'I am a pessimist because of intelligence, an optimist because of will.' However unlikely we are, our brain tells us, to achieve an aim, we nevertheless need to act with commitment, even optimism.

In 2010, Australian fast bowler Mitchell Johnson was going through a bad patch. In the first Test against England at Brisbane, he took no wickets for 170 runs and was dropped for the second Test at Adelaide. Only a year before, cricket writer Peter Roebuck, a good judge, had rated him the best fast bowler in the world. He was indeed fast and hostile, and when on form a threat to any batsman. But his shortcomings were well known: he tended to fall away in his action, and, if his tim-ing was only a little awry, with his unusually low arm action he would err in both length and direction.

Johnson used this week away from the limelight to work privately in the nets at Perth with his mentor, Dennis Lillee, one of the great fast bowlers. Lillee came up with a mantra or check-list for Johnson: 'TUFF'. T stood for 'target': 'at the back of your run-up, focus on your target, where you are aiming to pitch the ball'. U was for 'up': 'stand up tall, don't let yourself be dragged down in the search for pace'. The first F was for 'front': 'think of reaching up with that front arm'. And the second F was for 'follow-through': 'after delivery, follow through straighter, towards the batsman, don't fall away'. Here were four things for Johnson to hold in mind, one at each stage of a delivery. Technically and psychologically, the simple mantra helped restore his form.

Johnson, who later became a more consistent scourge of the English team, was transformed. He played a major role in winning the third Test (taking six for 38 and three for 44, as well as scoring 62 in the first innings). Though his performances in the remainder of that series did not quite match this, he was the leading Australian wicket-taker, and five years later reached a milestone of 300 Test wickets.

If a physiologist, or a coach like Lillee, were to *analyse* Johnson's action, he could have referred to many other factors in an account of what he did when bowling at his best or, for that matter, at his worst. But such knowledge is often misused. Indeed, in life in general, in everything we do, we have to disencumber consciousness enough to allow many of the essential elements of our physical and mental activities to take care of themselves. We need to notice when they are askew, but even in questioning and doubting ourselves we should not burden ourselves with over-complicated, over-conscious reminders. It is similarly confusing and counter-productive to have several coaches concurrently, or even shortly after each other:

numerous cooks spoil broths. What Lillee offered his protégé were reminders to correct his personal default tendencies.

Johnson's dramatic change of form was due in large part to this shortlist of Lillee's, along with his working through them with the player. No doubt the impact was also down to the fact that it came from such an admired ex-player. If a man in the street had given him the list, it would not have had the same result.

Complex events have complex causes. We need to clear our practical minds of too much clutter, so as to focus on the next delivery. But we need shrewd tips and nudges (internal and external) to take us forward. Derek Randall's self-scrutiny, prompted by his manager, was fierce but optimistic.

9

'WE LET OUR CRICKET
DO THE TALKING'

If the person is developed, we are likely to lose the player.

Glenn Hoddle

Another bloody four!

Geoffrey Boycott

I attempt to formulate three witticisms [a day].

Kazuo Ishiguro

———————

In sport, as in life, there are thin lines between arrogance and proper pride, between modesty and self-belittling. Glenn Hoddle was a midfielder in the 1986 World Cup football match against Argentina when England were beaten as a result of two goals by Diego Maradona. The second was an individual goal of sheer genius; the first (the 'Hand of God' goal) was punched in with his fist. Hoddle, describing Maradona as the greatest player he has seen, before or since, does not hold this against him, calling it 'instinctive'. Speaking of players who emerge as 'street footballers', Hoddle reckons that we are likely to lose their 'temperament' if they are 'developed' too much.

When Geoffrey Boycott, one of England's best-ever opening batsmen, played an aggressive stroke in the nets, he would taunt the bowler: 'Another bloody four!' His success was partly, I think, based on an urgent drive to reverse his childhood sense of his family's low status. His crowing was part of his gritty temperament.

I agree with Hoddle that one must be careful not to take away someone's 'edge' – his aggression, pride, toughness and resilience. However, I would argue that the 'street' sportsman may have acquired many valuable qualities relevant to survival and success: he knows life is a struggle in which you have to rely largely on yourself, in which you take what you can get and are willing to scrap; in which shrewdness is vital. Hunger for success, which may well grow out of deprivation early on, has a good side to it, as well, potentially, as a bad side. It would certainly be a mistake to try to drill it out of a person in a moral crusade towards humility or modesty. Becoming passive doormats or masochists does not make us better people, let alone better sportspeople (though I am not convinced by Hoddle's claim that Maradona's 'hand of God' goal was excusable on the grounds that it was 'instinctive'. One might as well forgive a footballer for biting an opponent, provided it was spontaneous).

Viv Richards, who came from Antigua, and the West Indies team (which he captained in 50 Tests), dominated the stage of world cricket for almost twenty years from the mid-1970s. Scyld Berry makes a compelling argument that they were in part motivated by a fierce drive to show opponents – particularly the British – that (in the words of Trinidadian Learie Constantine, a West Indian cricketer of an earlier generation) 'they are no better than we'. Given the extent and horror of colonial cruelty, especially in Antigua, which lasted well into the twentieth century (and is also described by Berry), I am struck by how little the fiery attitude of Richards and others flared up into vengefulness, triumphalism or contempt. On the whole, West Indies, when at their peak, said little on the field. 'In our part of the world,' Richards is said to have replied to Merv Hughes, when during one match the Australian fast bowler was sledging him, 'We let our cricket do the talking.'

(Though the story had a sequel. A few balls later, Hughes got Richards out. He sent him on his way with: 'In our part of the world, we say "fuck off".')

The motives that lead to exceptional performance are not always mature, wholesome, polite or even fully authentic. We all have omnipotent and greedy childhood wishes alive in us, or we cover up qualities we don't want to know about. And a sudden irruption of sanity in the shape, say, of unaccustomed humility may ruin form, as Hoddle implies. Some creative people are nervous about psychoanalysis because they fear that it may deprive them of energy and creativity arising from their base or neurotic motives. In my view, it is likely to allow them access to more, not less, of themselves; so that in the long run their work will become deeper.

Threats and Flattery

Influential and powerful people tend to get their own way with the help of intimidation. Some years ago, I worked as a psychological consultant to the board of a large organisation. One of its department heads – I'll call him Robert – was clever, hard-working, innovative and intense. A typical example of his behaviour was to convey to senior management that unless the company promptly and in every detail supported the particular initiative he was advocating, the result would be a catastrophe for the organisation. Robert's assessment and predictions were, in fact, speculative; he asserted them as if they were incontrovertible.

Robert was an energetic propagandist who brought a battery of arguments, ranging from broad principles (with which most people would, in the abstract form in which they were presented, agree) to complex technical and financial data that was hard to follow; the statistics and tables looked objective, but in fact his conclusions were not so simply measurable, nor were the figures as solid as he made out.

Robert warned of the drastic risks involved in delay. He forcibly made it known that he was *the* expert on this situation (which was partly true – he certainly was *an* expert); that he alone had his finger on the pulse of significant figures and groups, and he alone knew how they would react. Robert would wheel in prestigious people to back up his point of view, even if they had no particular expertise in, or knowledge of, the current situation. In his view, the company's position was dire, and this was the fault of the powers-that-be (in other words, of the chief executive and the board). He treated any doubting of his judgment as either naivety or disloyalty and lack of trust: a matter of ignorance or malice. He adroitly combined flattery and menace towards those whose support he sought. If you agreed with him, the message went, you were one of the chosen, one of the in-group. If not, you were beyond the pale. Though he did not consciously intend this, and indeed was surprised when it was pointed out to him, he was skilful in making the chief executive and others feel small, like children. Any uncertainty, lack of confidence, doubt, vulnerability and envy that Robert *himself* might have felt were evacuated into others, who then found themselves filled with anxiety and uncertainty. His personality had a powerful impact on the chief executive and all who had the job of running the organisation. Being the recipient of such projective functioning is one element in what is ordinarily referred to as 'stress'. We tend to believe that thoughts and feelings are private to the person who has them, but often they 'vibrate', creating unease in others. Thoughts and feelings are like perfume, whose origin and nature may also be hard to pinpoint. We think they stay inside, but they don't; they radiate and infuse.

Robert got things done, *and* had a demoralising effect on his colleagues. His form depended largely on his conviction, optimism and ruthlessness. He was a bully, driven by a compulsive need for power.

All this made it extremely difficult to challenge him. To do so risked withering contempt. It was hard to slow him down in order to come to an informed decision. Inevitably, the board struggled to cope with the impact Robert had on them. There were divisions within – some wanted to get rid of him, others were eager not to alienate him. The chief executive suffered from sleepless nights, and was tempted to resign.

In the end, this particular confrontation ended as well as possible. The board and other senior people managed to keep Robert in post, making use of his undoubted skills without being overwhelmed by him. While Robert continued to be a difficult but often productive member of the team, the chief executive's authority grew. Future confrontations were less bitter and less destructive.

More generally, possible outcomes in such a scenario might be divided into three categories, two unsatisfactory, the third more positive.

1. The overall leader takes on the projections of incompetence – that is, they coincide with a part of himself – and collapses. He gives in not because he is persuaded by the arguments, but because he has succumbed to sophisticated bullying. He becomes the helpless child, and is reduced to

being only notionally in charge. This may amount to a kind of breakdown. The provocateur has got under his skin and damaged his self. His own severe or even ego-destructive superego colludes with the attitude conveyed by the projector. This kind of collapse may also happen to the board as a whole. We are all vulnerable to bullying.

2. Alternatively, the difficult manager is got rid of. This outcome may be better than the demolition of a good leader or board. However, it may rest not on rational grounds, but be the result of the board's reciprocal arrogance and disparagement. Rather than becoming impotent, they are inclined towards a retaliatory omnipotence. For these leaders, agreeing with their colleague would be experienced as surrender, and would, they assume, invite further trampling or bullying. The sadism in his arrogance arouses a reactive sadism in the recipients. One problem with such a response is that people are unable to see the good in what the Roberts of this world have to offer. It is possible that here too the chief executive collapses, but in this scenario more from guilt at his own triumphant narcissism, however much that may have been evoked by the manager, than from collapse into helplessness.

3. In general the best scenario is that there is enough strength and clarity in the leadership group for a manager like Robert to be accommodated without submission to his bullying, and enough modesty and realism in the manager for him to modify his stance. His insights and drive can then be utilised for the good of the group, while the leadership retains its proper authority.

Like Maradona, Robert will not become tame. But we need to make the best of his good qualities if we can.

Force Fields

Often we are unaware of the origins of our actions and personalities. For instance, we play roles laid down for us by others or constructed by ourselves. From birth onwards, perhaps even before, we are all thrown into the lives of our families, carers and society. Entering them, our development is moulded. We give up some of our potential in order to find a place in our world. Roles are often like force fields, compelling us like magnets. It takes energy and aggression to refuse or modify them.

Mahatma Gandhi, the leader of the Indian independence movement, was talking of such invisible boundaries and pressures when he wrote: 'I do not want my house to be walled in on all sides . . . I want the cultures of all the lands to be blown about my house as freely as possible. But I refuse to be blown off my feet by any.'

He thus criticises equally the idea of the melting pot (being blown off one's feet by another culture) and the outcome of cultural or racial isolation (a walled-in house).

Existentialist philosopher Jean-Paul Sartre describes a man who puts on a charade of being a waiter. Sartre imagines this role taking over the waiter's life like a parasite within. He argues that such a waiter denies his own freedom, even though his playing the part is a pretence that he himself has chosen (I would say, has *unconsciously* chosen). Sartre calls this phenomenon 'bad faith'. Another of his examples is also located in a café. A couple arrange for their bodies to touch in some way, but then make it appear to have been an accident when in fact it resulted from partially disavowed intentions. They collude in this 'game', each participant behaving on the surface with propriety, disowning dangerous desire. Their mutual behaviour is a shared pretence or act.

We may work hard in the service of bad faith; our unconscious intentions that get things done being in the service of the roles that we have chosen, however much they have also been imposed. Our form may be directed, without our explicit awareness, towards such ends.

For many activities and skills, practice improves performance, even if it doesn't make us perfect. But the very idea of practising jars in some contexts. In Kazuo Ishiguro's novel, *The Remains of the Day*, we are made aware of the awkward formality of the butler, Stevens, the narrator of the story. Here is a man whose dominant unconscious aim has been to limit his personality to his official role. This severe constraint makes him unable, for instance, to respond with authenticity and love to his more spirited colleague, the head of housekeeping, Miss Kenton. Stevens also lacks a sense of humour. He refers to 'witticisms' and 'banter', but views them from the outside, as esoteric phenomena through which people seem to find ease with each other. Like an alien, all he can do is copy and practise: 'I have devised a simple exercise, which I try to perform at least once a day . . . I attempt to formulate three witticisms based on my immediate surroundings at the moment.'

Reading of these earnest efforts, we are saddened. They are simultaneously naive and artful. Practising witticisms strikes one as inauthentic, unlike practising bowling, say, or rehearsing a part in a play, especially as Stevens is unable to find them at all funny. The butler's tragedy is that he cannot live for himself, cannot enjoy things for themselves; all his efforts are directed at the perfecting of his role, an end measured by him in terms of the impression he makes, or imagines he makes, on Mr Farraday, his employer, and on fellow-butlers employed at other houses. Living within invisible walls, he acts in archetypal bad faith.

We create force fields for ourselves. V. S. Naipaul talks about a temptation for him as a writer: 'I could adapt or falsify my experience to make it fit a grand form.' But this would have been a 'falsification', as he says. He had to note and then resist this lure into grandiosity.

Individually and as groups, we also create force fields for others. Victor, a man in his fifties who has achieved much in his area of expertise, where he is efficient and creative, makes in the course of his work presentations to large audiences of students and academics. On these public occasions his appearance has become increasingly dilapidated. He shuffles onto the platform, dressed like a sloppy, or stroppy, student. He seems to be unclear about what he is supposed to do. He underplays the intellectual content of his ideas, resisting interesting comments made by audience members during question time. He makes out that his work has no broader meaning. He invites the audience to feel affectionate towards this version of himself as ineffectual.

Victor's audience is also liable to feel puzzled and critical. We sense that we are enlisted to play parts in his script. For Victor does not strike us an innocent, more as a performer. But why does he invite such complicated but almost scripted responses? I suggest that, in his repudiation of any possible impression of intellectual vigour, he is covering his insecurity by a mask of incompetence.

In 1948, the First Secretary of the Union of Soviet Composers was a composer, Tikhon Nikolayevich Khrennikov. He is described by Julian Barnes as having had 'an average ear for music, but perfect pitch when it came to power'. Force fields compel us both from outside and from inside. They colour our moods and our capacity for authenticity. The 'fields' we convey, correspondingly, invite others into similarly scripted roles and responses.

Frankness is often a relief from pretences and pretensions. Exasperated by the false and earnest intellectualisations of interviewees, the senior tutor of a Cambridge college once asked an applicant if he found rhythm in a matchbox. 'No,' said the young man, honestly, 'I'm afraid I don't.' The tutor replied, 'Thank God for that.'

PART IV: THE TEAM

10

THE MAKING OF A TEAM

The soul of man is a dark vast forest, with wild life in it.

D.H. Lawrence

Simple football is the most beautiful. But playing simple foot-ball is the hardest thing.

Johan Cruyff

A bunch of imbeciles, everything revolves around their own belly buttons.

Raymond Domenech

———————

Most of what is true of individuals applies also to teams.

Like individuals, teams can be on or off form. I remember nothing of a match at Taunton between Somerset and Cambridge University – not the year, not the scores, nor who won or whether I scored runs – except a sunny afternoon session when everyone in our side fielded above himself, diving (in days when diving was not common) to save boundaries, picking up and throwing with aggression and accuracy. My memory is of our being lifted by each other, as if we were, for this couple of hours, a single organism.

As with me and my golf, disturbed by a new batch of arrivals,

phases of immaturity also undermine team form. Teams may be demoralised or over-confident. They may be averse to experiment, or over-excited by it. Teams need to practise and work hard to build a technique, and to make some sequences of play habitual, almost automatic. At the same time, technique is not enough: they also need passion, flair, resilience, shrewdness; as a group, they have to be able to seize a moment or dig in. Teams constantly monitor themselves, not only individually but collectively. Their motives are always a combination of basic group tendencies – paranoid, passive, or manic – and of a more mature ability to learn from experience and face reality.

Like individuals, teams as a whole can be in the zone, 'on the go', and this is one of the reasons that team activities appeal to us. In Tolstoy's *Anna Karenina*, the landowner Konstantin Levin joins the peasants in their hay cutting. They work from dawn to dusk, mowing the field with long scythes in wide rows, each person cutting his own swathe. Tolstoy vividly conveys the joy of this activity, social, humorous, inclusive. Early on, the work becomes harder and harder for Levin, 'until at last the moment came when he felt he had no strength left'. Precisely then, Titus, his mowing master, 'stopped and began whetting his scythe', giving him a breather. The old hands encourage, and banter with, him. They offer practical tips. There is the rhythm of the work, and the satisfying sight of the swathes of cut grass.

> His work was undergoing a change which gave him intense pleasure. While working he sometimes forgot for some minutes what he was about, and felt quite at ease. Then his mowing was nearly as even as that of Titus. But as soon as he began thinking about it, and trying to work better, he at once felt how hard the task was and mowed badly.

Time speeds by, his tiredness hardly noticed:

> The longer Levin went on mowing, the oftener he experienced those moments of oblivion, when his arms no longer seemed to swing the scythe, but the scythe itself his whole body, so conscious and full of life; and as if by magic . . . the work accomplished itself of its own accord. These were blessed moments.

Such moments are possible not only as a result of Levin's capacity to let go conscious control, but also because of his experience of being part of a team that is on form, in good humour, and that welcomes him, respecting the willingness of their eccentric landowner to share their labour and their lunch.

Most of us know what it feels like to be part of such a team or group. These are indeed 'blessed moments', the analogues (in sport, for instance) of being in love, or of those rare conversations which take off: when everyone has a say, differences are allowed, and there is sufficient underlying respect, humour and shared humanity for people to be frank but also willing to learn from each other, taking account of different emphases and points of view. As with individuals, we are inclined to use the word 'inspired' of teams, when each player breathes in the others at their best, each is strengthened by that identification, and each gives off similar vibes. The form of the team is enhanced and expanded. Such experiences, with their whiff of the spiritual, can become benchmarks of excellence and enter the team's collective memory. This team-pleasure shows itself in posture and gait. There is a spring in the step. As the novelist and teacher Jonathan Smith writes: 'Teams keep each other alive. On special days [a team] hums, you feel moments of perfect harmony between your self and your world, and you walk tall.'

One could almost say: a team *is* an individual. Each team has its own character, style, demeanour. It is cohesive or 'in pieces'. It has its characteristic weaknesses or vulnerabilities, as well as its strengths. Qualities and traditions are handed down from one generation to the next. The team is an individual greater than the sum of its parts.

Similarly, the individual is a team, with many of the qualities of teams, a composite. David Waterman, cellist in the Endellion String Quartet, notes a difference between soloists and quartets. While the latter, 'with their natural capacity for diversity, need to strive for unity, solo pianists need to learn to divide themselves . . . sometimes into four or five voices' (especially, I imagine, when playing contrapuntal music, like a Bach fugue). He suggests, plausibly to me, that the quartet has to work harder to achieve balance and unity of tone than the solo pianist, whereas the latter may have to put more effort into making each voice audible and strong. But quartet and pianist alike aim to achieve both overall cohesion and strong discrete voices.

Each of us has different part-selves – whether one thinks in terms of id, superego and ego, or of the child and adolescent within the adult. There is a generous self and a greedy self, there are known and unknown aspects of ourselves. We aim at integration, wholeness. This is achieved not by simple uniformity, but by harmony and honesty of interaction between parts of the self that are at times in tension if not in conflict. We have different voices, moods, value systems, affiliations, identities and agendas. We are passionate selves stirred up by drives and emotions. We act; and we are simultaneously the selves that watch our activities, commenting internally on the scenes, influencing our emotional selves. We are the snaffle and the bit to our own horses. We are, to varying degrees, different selves – even at some moments Jekyll-and-Hydes.

Such brindled variability may be an asset or a burden, an expression of health or of pathology. In a coruscating essay on Benjamin Franklin, D. H. Lawrence ridicules him for reducing us to a domesticated version of humanity:

> Man has a soul, though you can't locate it either in his purse or his pocket-book or his heart or his stomach or his head. The *wholeness* of a man is his soul. Not merely that nice little comfortable bit which Benjamin marks out. It's a queer thing is a man's soul. It is the whole of him. Which means it is the unknown him, as well as the known. It seems to me just funny, professors and Benjamins fixing the functions of the soul. Why, the soul of man is a vast forest, and all Benjamin intended was a neat back garden. And we've all got to fit into his kitchen garden scheme of things. Who knows what will come out of the soul of man? The soul of man is a dark vast forest, with wild life in it. Think of Benjamin fencing it off!

Lawrence sees this 'vast forest' as a source of richness, a reason for celebration, and so do I. For many of us, the experience of psychoanalysis gives house-room and access to this range in an enlivening way. We are more than neat little front gardens.

The Thing He Did Not Want to Want

Our forest may, by contrast, be damagingly split. In his novel *Solar*, Ian McEwan presents his main character, the overweight, alcoholic physicist Michael Beard, arriving back at Heathrow from a trip to Berlin. During the flight he has drunk champagne, a large gin and tonic, and three glasses of Burgundy, and has eaten everything business class has to offer for lunch, all this barely two hours after a meaty German breakfast. Late for his next appointment, and further delayed by immigration, he notices that his footsteps are taking an intermediate path between the direct route towards the station (for the fast train to his appointment) and a devious one via the newspaper stall. He thought he would not succumb, but 'his route was bending this way'.

McEwan refers to the mind as a parliament, a debating chamber, in which 'different factions contend'. The relevant contention here is between Beard's 'old Adam' of greed and his saner sense of duty, restraint and punctuality. Predictably, having bought the newspapers, 'as he handed them across for their bar-codes to be scanned, he saw at the edge of vision, in the array beneath the till, the gleam of the thing he wanted, the thing he did not want to want'. He 'added it to his pile – this gleaming bag of salt and vinegar crisps'.

Here is a neat illustration of what Freud referred to as compromise formation, when conflicting forces within, part-selves, pull this way and that, each with desires, values and motivations foreign to the self that directs 'the other party in the inner parliament'.

Beard is dominated by his greed. The integrated person, occupying more of himself while acknowledging that there will always be, as on the old maps of the world, *terra incognita*, unknown territory, 'unthought knowns' (in psychoanalyst Christopher Bollas's phrase), is open to his rich – in parts dark – hinterland. Unlike Beard, he *inhabits* the broader self. This kind of depth of interior life can be sensed by others.

(I wonder if my fascination with Michael Beard gains traction for me from his having the same initials, the same first name, and several letters in common?)

Is there no 'I' in Team?

But what makes a group of human beings into a team?

Some years ago, I was invited by the Managing Director of a consulting group to work with their partners. At any time, the organisation had small teams working on a range of projects, usually led by a partner. Each section (oil and gas, say, or property, or the financial sector), and in many cases each partner, got on with their jobs separately from each other. Though the small teams usually functioned well enough, between teams there was little sharing of policy, little comparing of methodology. The managing director thought that the partners had become too isolated from each other, and that the natural rivalry between the individual consultants had become too prominent. He was asking me to help them become more team-oriented, more cooperative and collaborative in their working methods.

It seemed that many of the partners were almost as minimally linked to each other as a group of stallholders in a London market. At Spitalfields Market in east London, founded in 1638, as I recently learned from a trader there, pooling of methods is a matter of chance interactions between individuals, and the only functions of the traders' association are to discuss terms of rental, opening hours, fire hazards, toilet facilities and so on. For the most part, each stallholder is left to his own devices.

This lack of structure and shared projects contrasts with the need for cohesion in a sporting team – footballers, say, whose members cannot function as such without each other, with their different skills and roles, and who all appear (for all or much of the time) on the field together. This is why leadership is so crucial, helping make individualists into teams, and stodgy groups into teams that permit, encourage and enhance individual brilliance. (Leadership may also, of course, work against such developments.)

The main development in football during the last fifty years, started by Johan Cruyff's side, Ajax, in the late 1960s, has been a matter of putting more and more emphasis on plasticity of role. Cruyff was a key factor in this transformation. One of the most iconic players in the histories of the Dutch club (1964–73), of the Dutch national side, and of FC Barcelona (Barça) as a player (1973–8) and as manager (1988–96), Cruyff developed a style and philosophy known as 'total football'. The term first hit the headlines when applied to the Netherlands side he captained in the 1974 World Cup, where he led his team to the final (they lost 2–1 to Germany, but he himself was named Player of the Tournament). In 'total football', players have a basic role and position – defence, midfield, attack: right or left side, central – but their teamwork is predicated on the ability of each to play anywhere. In typical Barcelona teams of the past decades, one sees free-flowing passing, a capacity for quick thinking, the subliminal knowledge each player has of just where his team-mates will be at any moment – all this and more constituting their skilful teamwork – yet nothing is done by rote. The style was later adopted by the Spanish national team, becoming known as 'tiki-taka'. Barça have been called, by writer Simon Barnes, a 'team with a single mind'. It has the fluency and teamwork of a great jazz band.

In the consulting group I worked with, one problem for the partnership as a whole was perceived to be located in a man I'll call Nigel, who had many excellent qualities. He worked hard, had a fine problem-solving intellect, and formed productive working relationships with the senior executives who were his clients. He attracted a large volume of profitable work to the office, keeping many of the junior consultants busy. One colleague suggested the partnership needed four or five Nigels, not just one.

On the other hand he was described as a loner. What many senior colleagues found hard to stomach was the way he undermined them, particularly by pushing to extremes what was considered acceptable in manipulating so as to ensure that the most talented individuals were allocated to the teams he led. There was, people alleged, no give and take. The picture I formed was of a gifted child who chose and co-opted similarly gifted children to form special groups, to which other partners were expected to act as benign and indulgent parents. He appeared to perceive himself, and was perceived by some, as a wayward genius whose talent justified special treatment.

I felt sympathetic to both sides of the argument. But I also suggested to the partnership that he may have epitomised a systemic problem within the firm; that he was a scapegoat or lightning conductor for the *organisation's* conflict between overall team spirit and the requirement for individual excellence, between cooperation and selfishness. I suspected that people envied Nigel his personal success, and the benefits accruing to the firm because of him. I suspected that it was convenient for the partnership as a whole to 'park' their ruthlessness in him so as not to have to look at it in themselves. Was their fainthearted reluctance to stand up directly to him and to his sharp intellect a factor in the escalation of his perhaps egregious behaviour?

Nigel's personal qualities reminded me of ex-cricketer Geoffrey Boycott. But the England team behaved differently towards Boycott, accommodating and integrating him by robust and humorous confrontation while welcoming his skills and idiosyncrasies. Part of the consultancy firm's mission statement exhorted people to 'uphold the obligation to dissent'. Having papered over the cracks, they handed the problem to me. I tried to put it back to them.

'Who Will Get These Runs for Us?'

If individualists are too powerful, too divisive and selfish, the team suffers. And if they run riot, the notion of a team scarcely applies.

After the 2010 football World Cup in South Africa, France's manager, Raymond Domenech, published a book. Largely in diary form, it reads like an unedited set of rants veering from petulant criticisms of the players to an equally disparaging tone of *mea culpa*. During the tournament, the team had gone on strike after Domenech sent home the key forward, Nicolas Anelka, for 'insulting' him at half-time during their match against Mexico. Domenech described Anelka as 'an enigma who does nothing for others'. The manager seems to have lost all sympathy not only with this individual but with the team as a whole: 'I'm out of here, I couldn't give a damn about this bunch of imbeciles,' he rages. 'I couldn't bear to hear everyone giving their opinion on everything.' He also accuses Anelka, Thierry Henry and Franck Ribery, all gifted players, of being self-centred ('everything revolves around their belly buttons'). And Ribery's eyes reveal, according to him, contempt and jealousy when another player, Yoann Gourcuff, is told that 'the keys to the match' are down to him. Domenech also writes: 'I'm certainly to blame for something. I got it all wrong. I feel humiliated to have got it so wrong.' He seems to have had little idea how to control either his players or himself.

The French, one might say, were 'not a team', or 'not really a team'. A ragged bunch, rather, lacking leadership and team spirit.

At the other extreme, some teams become flat, conformist, dull. Far from running riot, individuality is suppressed.

In a match in 1972, the English professional cricket team Northants faced a paltry total of 76 scored by my team, Middlesex, in a forty-over match. The pitch was affected by rain, difficult for batting though not impossible. A par score, in those days and on that pitch, might have been around 140. As the Northants team were preparing to bat, there was, opening batsman Jim Stewart told me later, a gloomy silence in their dressing room. Stewart, who had only just joined Northants from another county, and had yet to work out, let alone succumb to, the team's deep-seated pessimism, remarked cheerfully, as he strapped on his pads: 'What's up, boys?' After a moment's silence, someone asked sombrely, 'Who's going to get these runs for us, then?'

The outcome? They were bowled out for 41 in thirty-six overs. The implicit prophecy was self-fulfilling. Their collective mindset was utterly negative. The team talked (or thought) themselves into defeat.

The group mentality of starlings starts young. They are communal birds, famous for 'murmurations', when thousands take to the skies simultaneously, usually just before dark, creating by their dense swarms fast-moving, sharp-edged shapes.

Becki Lawson, a veterinarian at the Zoological Society of London, has investigated twelve mass drownings of young

starlings observed in England and Wales. In all but two cases, ten or more juveniles had been discovered drowned together in 'water bodies in gardens, most commonly garden ponds, also swimming pools, a well, even a bucket'.

The birds, examined under the microscope for toxins or infectious diseases, were found to have been healthy, so their deaths could not have been caused by illness. It was probably, Lawson suggests, a result of gregariousness: 'If starlings fly to a pond to quench their thirst, they all jostle each other and get in each other's way. We think it's the flocking nature of starlings that predisposes them to these things.' The theory was strengthened by comparing starlings with blackbirds, which do not drown in this collective fashion.

Steep hierarchies and an atmosphere in which juniors should be seen but not heard are factors in the suppression of individuality. Surgeon and health commentator Atul Gawande tells a cautionary tale of rank being used in the medical profession to shut down insight and innovation. In 1929, a surgical intern in Eberswalde, Germany, called Werner Forssmann came across an article in an obscure medical journal that included animal studies. An illustration portrayed a horse with a tube threaded up its leg all the way into the heart. The researchers had then taken blood from the heart and were thus able to describe what was going on there. Gawande continues:

> Forssmann thought: 'We could do that to a horse, what if we did it to a human being?' So he went to his bosses, and made his suggestion. 'How about we take a tube and thread it into a human being's heart?' Their response was, 'You're crazy. You can't do that. We know whenever you touch the heart, whenever people have attempted it in surgery, the heart goes into fibrillation and the patient dies. You cannot do this.' Forssmann

replied 'Well, what about in an animal?' 'There's no point and you're just an intern anyway. Who says you should even deserve to get to ask these questions? Go back to work.'

Forsmann just had to know. So he stole into the X-ray room, took a urinary catheter, made a slit in his own arm, threaded it up the vein and into his own heart. He convinced a nurse to help him take a series of nine X-rays showing the tube inside his own heart. The outcome? He was fired.

And then, twenty-seven years later in 1956, he was awarded the Nobel Prize.

Forsmann was no doubt an exceptionally gifted researcher, but he was also unusual in standing out against the prevailing culture of his place and time. Most of us would have conformed.

An early victim of compliance culture is truthfulness: language is watered down. The anodyne word for a manufacturing defect is, businesswoman Margaret Heffernan suggests, 'discrepancy'; problems become 'issues'. There is a slippery slope towards the 'Newspeak' of George Orwell's *Nineteen Eighty-four*, where (for example) the word for 'labour camp' is 'joycamp', and 'deliberately alter the past' is rephrased as 'rectify'.

The most obvious example of this attitude on a large scale is North Korea. In a regime where citizens have from birth been terrorised and brainwashed into deference to the Great Leader, the requirement, buttressed by terror, for absolute conformity is all-embracing. A sort of security is acquired at the cost of wholesale loss of the self, of initiative and freedom.

A theory of the contrast between teams populated by selfish and disparate individuals and teams flattened by obedience and conformity was developed in 1975 by the then director of the Tavistock Clinic, psychiatrist Pierre Turquet, previously an Olympic fencer. Writing about large groups, he offers a systematic account of how teams work, or fail to work. He calls selfish members 'singletons', compliant members 'membership individuals'.

Nigel was a singleton: the indoctrinated conformists in Pyongyang are membership individuals. The former sacrifices the team in favour of his own desires, interests or glory; the latter sacrifice themselves and their liveliness to the team. In one group there is atomised individuality, in the other dull unanimity, at least on the surface. In one, any cohesive strategy is undermined; in the other, knowledge is felt to come down from on high and/or from the past. In the former it is each for himself; in the latter a high premium is put on loyalty as a prerequisite for security, and whistle-blowers are automatically seen as traitors. In one there is chaos, or unfettered rivalry (a young player in one professional cricket team described its mentality as: 'If you don't tread on them, they tread on you'); in the other rigid professional behaviour, with the skulls of the ancestors gazing grimly down on their successors from the roof-beams of the longhouses.

Often, singletons dominate membership individuals. As Edmund Burke wrote, 'It only takes good people to be silent for evil ones to flourish'. Most singletons are not evil: but they become rampant when others lack the courage to resist them.

Some of the most difficult and distressing situations for teams occur when a talented but tactless individual comes into conflict with a decent, team-oriented, perhaps over-tolerant authority structure. Cricket followers will recognise in this description the outlines of the intrigues and conflicts that resulted in the eviction of Kevin Pietersen from the England team in 2014.

Pietersen, born and brought up in South Africa, was the most imposing England batsman of his time. He played 104 Test matches, scoring twenty-three centuries at an average of 47.29. He had the capacity to change the course of matches. He had admirable team qualities, offering himself as a supportive mentor to promising young players. His hard work on his fitness and his own game were excellent models. In personal relations, however, he was liable to put his foot in it, and rub up those in authority the wrong way.

In 2009 Pietersen had been relieved of the captaincy after only three Tests in charge. Though he partly brought about his own sacking, he was hurt and bitter as a result of this demotion. No doubt he became as a result more difficult to manage and lead.

For most of the remainder of Pietersen's England career, the director of coaching was Andy Flower, the captain Andrew Strauss – the man who had replaced Pietersen as captain. My impression of the leadership of the two Andrews was that they were strongly committed both to the whole team and to the individuals. They tried hard to keep Pietersen on board. It is after all one of the main jobs of leaders to make the best of the talents available; and there were no other batsmen with talents to match his.

No single, indubitable narrative can be established for the ultimate breakdown between Pietersen and those in charge of England's cricket. Pietersen did some egregious and damaging things, most notoriously when he sent friends in the opposition, South Africa, texts that were uncomplimentary to players in the England team; though he denied that he offered hints about his team-mates' technical weaknesses. It has been rumoured that, in order to sow dissension in the England dressing room, the information about the existence of these texts was calculatedly released by the South Africans. Even if this was so, however, Pietersen is not exonerated from foolishness at best, disloyalty at worst. For six months afterwards, he was not considered for selection. He was eventually accepted back until, after the crushing defeat in Australia in 2013–14, he was told he would not, in the short term at least, be considered for selection for England. He then wrote an autobiography in which he 'revealed' the bad state of affairs in the England dressing room. Here is a mild example of what he wrote: 'A clique choked our team, and Andy Flower let that clique grow like a bad weed. Flower could never stop its growth, so he focused instead on managing upwards. He did this well.'

The singleton Pietersen saw his manager and captain as membership individuals, who suppressed his individuality while permitting the growth of destructive behaviour from the 'bad weeds'. He claimed that it was the dullness and dampening influence of Flower in particular that caused him, Pietersen, to feel left out and alienated in the England camp. (Flower and Strauss might argue that it was largely down to their man-management that England got 104 Tests and 8,181 Test runs from Pietersen.)

I have often been asked how I would have dealt with Pietersen, had he been in sides I captained. Of course I don't know. No two people are alike. One doesn't know without trying. And I wasn't close enough to the England team to gain a detailed picture of what went on. Pietersen seemed to me gauche rather than malicious. I got the impression that he would say things for effect, without much thinking. I am sure that my attempts to enlist Pietersen would, like Flower's and Strauss's, have been disrupted from time to time. For example, my keenness on team talks and reflection would have struck him as pathetic, and annoyed him. And he may well have got under my skin, with what could have become a drip-drip effect of negativity and a subtle undermining of authority. But I cannot answer for how I might have reacted to, and indeed contributed to, such a scenario. Much would have depended on the behaviour of the rest of the team.

In my playing days, I witnessed tension, even collisions, between the more abrasive and brash style of some white colonials, and our more sardonic, even cynical, British ways. The 'hypocritical British' may slyly undermine the brash colonial. It is often hard to put one's finger on such emotional enactments. They are rarely of a kind to be itemised in a public charge-sheet, and a decent reticence keeps lips sealed. But if such group mentalities get going, downhill spirals all too easily result, and are hard to shift into more productive patterns. It is not so much that there is an elephant in the room as a can of invisible worms. Pietersen no doubt felt scapegoated and misunderstood. Australian cricket teams might have been more blunt and upfront in such conflicts, and nipped them in the bud. It is impossible to know.

Turquet has another category of team member: the 'individual member', that is, a person who manages to keep his individuality, drive and uniqueness, while at the same time being alert to and contributing to the good of the team.

The *Mishnah*, the first written version of Jewish oral tradition, states: 'If I am not for myself, who will be for me? But if I am only for myself, what am I?' We must fight our own corner, develop ourselves, be selfish, or perhaps self-ish. But if we are only that, we are limited, stunted. We need also to be *unselfish*, to want the best for bigger groups than our little selves, as Derek Randall did with his 'Come on, Rags, come on England'. At times we have to constrain ourselves in the interests of the team; no one can do exactly as he wishes. We may have to bat in a different position for the good of the team, or bowl into the wind. By being in a team, we also, potentially at least, have the benefit of the team's support, especially when things are hard individually. Teams succeed when there is a happy balance between looking after the self and looking after the team.

The Second Great Snowball War

I once told my grandson, who was then eleven, that I was planning a talk about teamwork. Luka – a confident boy – said *he* would tell *me* something about teamwork, something that happened in 'the Great Snowball War, at school, the Second not the First.

'Three years ago there were these lumbering, shaving, huge people aged around sixteen, that big.' At this point he stood on his chair and raised his hand above his head. 'But *we* were organised. We waited for them to throw their snowballs, which they did all at the same time. We dodged them, and then they had to pick up snow for more snowballs and we could attack them. We had some people making snowballs, a second group making low walls for protection, and a third throwing. They backed off and stopped. And then we fought each other.'

Luka's last comment reminds me of the speed with which teams are liable to disintegrate and become sub-groups, or sub-teams, fighting each other. In 1979 the England cricket team were allowed a single evening's practice under lights in Sydney before the first of the day/night limited-overs matches against Australia and West Indies. Unlike most of our opponents, we had had no experience of playing under lights, or of the new arrangements limiting the number of fielders permitted outside an elliptical ring some 35 yards from the batsman. For this crucial practice, we divided our squad of sixteen into two, enlisting some local fielders. What astonished me was the speed with which rivalry between the two sets of eight, and altercations about 'rules' of engagement, occurred. Here was an England team, preparing to play internationals in a new format, squabbling about how soon a dismissed batsman could return in order to get practice crucial for us all!

Luka's snowball strategy typifies teamwork – the need for organisation and planning, for thinking on your feet, and for differentiation of roles – some making snowballs, some making a wall, some throwing. Luka and his classmates, aged eight, already knew what is called for in creating a team. They also gave, implicitly, guidelines for the role of leadership.

11

WHY SPORT?

Competition has been shown to be useful up to a certain point and no further, but co-operation, which is the thing we must strive for today, begins where competition leaves off.

Franklin D. Roosevelt

We talk about the little boy who fell in love with the game, and that's what we've tried to do as a group.

Brendon McCullum

The glorious thing about mountains is that they will endure no lies.

Heinrich Harrer

I have long been troubled by mutual scorn between sportsmen and intellectuals. Jonathan Smith devotes a chapter to one side of the argument in *The Learning Game*, referring to 'a certain kind of English-middle-class-one-upmanship-social-chat, a cheaply competitive way of putting down sport, particularly competitive sport'. And I have encountered sporting 'hearties' who are liable to deride 'loftier' (if that is the right word) forms of culture as soft, or effete. Both sides, I suspect, when they denigrate capacities that they lack or feel insecure about, are acting from, and protecting themselves against, envy.

For many years the argument went on inside my own head, too. In my second term at Cambridge, the university lacrosse match, which was to be played in Oxford that year, coincided with the Cambridge Greek play, Aristophanes's *Clouds*, directed by Dadie Rylands. I had auditioned for the play, and had been given the (significant) part of Leader of the Chorus. Soon after, I was selected for the match. I chose the latter. When at the first rehearsal I told Rylands, who as actor, director and academic had long been a grand figure in British theatre, let alone in Cambridge, that I was sorry but I would have to pull out, he announced the news to the cast with amused emphasis: 'This *dear* young boy is going off to play *netball* for the University.' But he kindly let me play the *deus ex machina*, the god who wraps things up at the end, in this case Hermes, standing on a pedestal wearing winged sandals to pronounce the last two lines, on the evenings I was in Cambridge.

Four years later, in 1965, I had switched sides, with a high-minded (and probably snobbish) idea that becoming a philosopher would be intrinsically more valuable or estimable than becoming a cricketer. I did postgraduate work for three years, followed by a similar period teaching philosophy at the University of Newcastle upon Tyne.

In 1971, I made a further change of direction. Now, I was inclined to give up university teaching to become captain of Middlesex. My ex-supervisor, Renford Bambrough, wrote me a letter of encouragement: 'This is one of those occasions when what one ought to do coincides precisely with what one wants to do.' (He also knew the quality of my philosophy.)

Now I would say that an academic or reflective life, in which one comes to understand things better, and to think with more clarity and a firmer basis of knowledge, is a good thing in itself. Disinterested thought (and occasionally, knowledge), along with the humility to acknowledge how much there is that we don't know, is not the only good, but it is *a* good. But so too is sporting skill and prowess. At its best a thing of beauty, it is appreciated and loved by players and spectators alike. It *can* lead to personal and moral growth. Albert Camus, the Nobel laureate, goes so far as to say, 'All that I know most surely about morality and the obligations of men, I owe to football.'

Both sets of abilities are, then, to be admired, though it is not a moral failing to lack either. We recognise and give credit for the dedication and hard work that enables Usain Bolt to run 100 metres in 9.58 seconds, but we also admire him for his innate talent and speed. Similarly we admire, for instance, the distinguished philosopher G. E. Moore's intellectual capacities, however far these are the result of genetic endowment.

When Moore died on 24 October 1958, his philosopher colleague C. D. Broad concluded Moore's obituary in the *Manchester Guardian* as follows:

> Apart from his immense analytic power Moore's most noticeable characteristic was his absolutely single-minded desire to discover truth and avoid error and confusion. Fundamentally he was a man of simple tastes and character, absolutely devoid of all affectation, pose, and flummery. He thoroughly enjoyed the simple human pleasures of eating and drinking, walking, gardening, talking to his friends, playing with his children, and so on. It is because ordinary, unpretending Englishmen are so often muddle-headed, and intellectuals so often cracked and conceited, that Moore, who combined the virtues of both and had the vices of neither, was so exceptional and lovable a personality.

For 'Englishmen' read 'sportsmen', and for 'unpretending' 'sometimes obnoxious', and the point is made.

The Appeal of Sport

But what, at depth, is the appeal of sport, this form of life that I have spent so much time involved in?

In his book *Homo Ludens*, Johan Huizinga argues that play, through being set aside from the practicalities of life, often both in time and space, is the central feature of culture. As we have seen, sport, psychoanalysis and theatre all have their sacred areas – playing field, consulting room, stage. These set-aside spaces are safe enough for serious play, and for emotions of all kinds to be expressed and explored, through which an individual may become more fully a person, a group turn into a real team.

Julia Stone, an Australian family psychotherapist, writes a poignant account of weekly therapy sessions with a disabled boy called Tom, who died three months after his third birthday. His body was tiny and withered. His understandably protective mother, Lisa, struggled to allow him to come truly alive; for him to use his body must have felt to her (and perhaps would have been for him) both dangerous and exposing. For his therapists, though, it was important that he 'be able to strut his stuff and to protest about some of the things he couldn't do . . . One of the therapy rooms was called the "pillow" room. It was a space with lots of cushions, mattresses and soft balls . . . a safe place for rough play.'

Tom's older brother Nick would go there with a second therapist; they would come back 'red-faced and clearly having had a lively time'. Tom's wish to have the opportunity to go himself was picked up, and after consideration of his mother's anxieties, he went. Stone continues:

Despite his pronounced limitations to independent mobility, he entered vigorously into doing what he could, showing us how he could kick and roll and throw, and so a dialogue began, describing Tom as the rolling boy, the kicking boy, the balancing boy. With each named accomplishment Tom's smile grew broader and brighter. Along with this new-found physical prowess, Tom also discovered play dough; he delighted in making and creating shapes with his mother and me, and vied with his older brother for the favourite shape-cutter . . . One afternoon, sitting at the table in the therapy room, engaged creatively with the play dough, Tom looked at me, and smiled. He said, 'It's a perfect world.' Lisa looked up, startled, and asked, 'What did you say, Tom?' He smiled at her and repeated, 'It's a perfect world.' It was a precious moment. Tom, a little boy, present in the moment of creative engagement, at one with his life, a perfect moment.

Tom's delight and sense of achievement underline the fact that one central element in personal development is physical development. Babies' movements start off being jerky and uncoordinated; there is satisfaction in the beginnings of coherence and control. Later, we take pleasure in going beyond what we have managed before. We need to resist the temptation always to compare our achievements with those of others, and instead would do better to measure ourselves by our own yardsticks. As my analyst once said to me, ambiguously, when I was being self-critical, 'we must all remember where we started from'; Tom's yardstick was not the same as his brother's, but his field of aspiration and pleasure was. A perfect moment.

For those to whom sport doesn't appeal, it seems futile or worse. They remember hours of misery at compulsory school games on cold (or indeed hot) sporting fields. Physically awkward, they were usually picked last. I can understand now what a torment all this must have been, especially if their more gifted peers treated them scornfully. And if they feel unloved, on this account and for other reasons, their lack of physical coordination is likely to create either a deeper self-dislike, or a self-protective superiority of mind over body.

Yet almost every small child, before self-doubt, and comparison with other children, gets a grip, takes pleasure in his or her bodily capacities and adroitness. Like Tom, most are keen to show their physical achievements: look at me, look how I dance, or jump, or climb. Gradually the child achieves a measure of physical coordination and mastery. Jumping, dancing, climbing, catching, splashing, kicking, using an implement as a bat or racquet – all these offer a sense of achievement, as well as sheer enjoyment. Sport grows out of the pleasure in such activities.

And playfulness, along with disciplined competitiveness and cooperation, is a powerful element in good form. We 'play' sport; playing is central to it, just as sport is a central form of play. Playfulness is, however, sometimes marginalised in the 'win at all costs' mentality of high-level sport. It may well be that the necessary late-twentieth-century backlash against a form of amateurism that pretended that winning doesn't matter led to an over-calculating and sometimes cynical reactive professionalism. Brendon McCullum, until recently captain of the New Zealand cricket team, actively championed the values of the amateur, with its etymological link with 'love':

> I loved playing cricket as a kid . . . Just because there's more
> at stake now, it doesn't mean you should lose the innocence
> of why you got into the game in the first place. For a long

time I (and I think the team) had lost that, but it's one thing that we've tried to recapture. It sounds corny, but we talk about the little boy who fell in love with the game, and that's what we've tried to do as a group.

I believe that McCullum's attitude enhanced his team's form more radically than increased doses of the 'scientific', technical approaches that had become *de rigueur* would have done.

Competition: Test Cricket

For very young children, then, dance and sport are barely distinguishable. Sport proper starts to emerge when, alongside the simpler delight in physicality, competition takes a more central role. Teams at times also thrive on rivalries *within* the team. Orchestras play *symphonies* (a word with an etymology that emphasises togetherness) but also, with soloists, *concerti* (whose root means 'fight' or 'compete' – a reference to the vying for prominence between soloist and orchestra).

Sport is a field where controlled aggression and the public demonstration of skills and character are permitted, even encouraged. For many who are inclined to be inhibited or self-conscious, sport offers an opportunity for self-expression and spontaneity. Within a framework of rules and acceptable behaviour, we can be wholehearted. Such people – including me – owe sport a lot; it helped me begin to find myself.

The individual's form in a team is based on both competition and cooperation, qualities that are intertwined. Playing alongside a more skilful team-mate may enhance our play. As a young man I played a few games at inside-right for a good hockey side, Richmond. On the right wing was a Dutch A international, Aard Moolenberg. Playing with him made me a better player, in ways that I could not have imagined beforehand. He was quick and skilful; he would give me the ball and in an instant be ready for the return pass 20 yards on; he would know when to gather and hold the ball, to recoup, to start again (and I could learn from this too); or he would subtly invite me to change places with him, to throw the opposition off their formal defensive arrangements. He invited a more fluid and less conventional range of performance – not quite 'total hockey' (as in 'total football'), but heading in that direction.

Competition in sport has cooperation built in, not only in the obvious way (teams will not be successful without it), but also in each side's need for opponents who will stretch them; the better they are, the more they do so, forcing us to develop our techniques and our persistence. Edmund Burke wrote: 'He who wrestles with us strengthens our nerves, and sharpens our skill. Our antagonist is our helper.' We are co-creators of excellence and integrity.

The fact of a shared project should bring together even political antagonists. Writer and (briefly) politician Michael Ignatieff has argued for an atmosphere in which politicians treat their rivals as opponents rather than as enemies. No one, no single party, has all the answers. The current opponent is potentially a future coalition partner, a possibility 'thrown away with a partisanship that, in taking no prisoners today, makes government tomorrow impossible'.

Ignatieff's further point is that both sides share in the overall project of democracy. They are on the same side in this. Respect for the process as a unifying force, however intense the antagonisms, is an equally salient fact in sport. Sporting opponents are conjoined by love and knowledge of the game. There are shared values between competitors, both teams and individuals.

Moreover, rival teams, like England and Australia, say, are united in being confronted by sometimes jeering crowds, and by at times sensationalist elements in the media. At the eye of the storm, top sportsmen on all sides are sooner or later the focus of the cricketing world's critical eye, embattled together. The twenty-two participants – the two teams of eleven – have a closer relationship with each other than fans, however partisan, have with them (or for that matter with other fans). They go through it together. Fierce rivalry on the field need not preclude admiration and friendship, nor does it rule out having a drink together after the match. Fair-mindedness and sportsmanship between competitors is not merely a matter of obedience to the laws or rules; it also involves consideration, respect and the recognition of limits – the ordinary civilities that oil the wheels of relationships and collegial activities.

Without such cooperation rivalry would run riot. Even within teams self-protectiveness would trump cooperation, or, if the team functioned as a collectivised individual lacking respect for rules, traditions and opponents, calculated cheating and mendacity would be prevalent, except when the risks of being caught and penalised were reckoned to be more disadvantageous. In the extreme, if competition becomes the unique value, why should teams not resort to violence and the infliction of bodily harm on rivals if that ensures success?

In sport, there are narrow lines between cheating, violence and boorishness at one end, through gamesmanship and attempts at mental disintegration, to unsettling the opposition, often by ordinary tactical shrewdness, at the other. In 1993, Steve Waugh, later one of Australia's most successful captains, batted most of the second day at Headingley with his captain, Allan Border. Next morning Border surprised Waugh by not declaring, despite the huge Australian score. Border told him his aim was to 'bring about England's "mental disintegration"'. The phrase made sense to Waugh. They'd have been expecting a declaration, and would be unsettled by Australia batting on. Border had added: 'When I declare, the openers will have to rush to get the pads on. Makes it just that bit tougher for them.' England duly lost the match by a wide margin.

'Making it just that bit tougher' is of course fair play, and unsettling opponents a part of everyday tactics. But mental disintegration? That may amount to virtual shell shock. If one's opponent really does disintegrate, not only losing his form but his ability to perform at all, it is shocking for everyone involved.

For Jonathan Trott, the England batsman who was forced by self-doubt and panic to return home after only one Test in the Ashes series in Australia in 2013, the encounters and exposures became simply unbearable. He had already started to feel a dread of having to go onto the field earlier the same year, in England. At breakfast before a big match, he would find himself hoping that a pylon had fallen on the ground and the game had been cancelled. His anxiety turned into panic. He felt sick and worried that the pain in his chest was a heart attack. Tears pushed their way forward from behind his eyes. His breathing became shallow and his head started to throb. His colleague Kevin Pietersen said of him that at such times, 'He disappeared within himself. His eyes were elsewhere, and you felt you could only keep his attention for a couple of seconds.'

When batting, anxiety exaggerated Trott's movements: 'I was bobbing up and down, and out towards off stump. Nothing smooth about it. It was sharp and jerky. My head movement made it impossible to pick up the length of the ball, and my body movements put me in no position to pick up the line.'

He found himself batting 'in a rush' and 'thinking like a fool'. 'It wasn't exactly that I couldn't see the ball any more,

so much as that I couldn't *watch* it any more.' Trott quotes
Martin Crowe, perhaps New Zealand's finest ever batsman,
who was once out on 299: 'Crowe said that he "swapped the
mind-set of *watch the ball* to Wow, *I'm going to be the first New
Zealander to score 300!* . . . I never even saw the ball that got
me out on 299!"'

Trott seemed to be suffering from a form of castration
anxiety, especially when the menacing fast bowler Mitchell
Johnson was after him. 'Struggling against the short ball erodes
your confidence in yourself as a man . . . Once the sharks smell
blood – you are in real trouble . . . The only way I knew out of
this slump was hard work, so I pushed myself on. And the more
I pushed, the deeper I sank.'

Much of Trott's disintegration came from internal sources.
His experience nevertheless invites the question: had the
euphemistically named 'banter' tipped over into gang warfare?
And more generally, where is the line to be drawn between
legitimate undermining, and behaviour that has degenerated
into a vicious boorishness, humiliation and gloating?

In 2013, when Trott suffered his disintegration, Australia
were seething after three successive defeats in the Ashes at the
hands of an England team that had not been above a certain
triumphalism. The Australians were nursing wounds and grievances. Moreover, the series came unusually thick and fast at
that time – there had been a recent series in England immediately before this tour; and yet another series between the sides
took place the following (English) winter, in 2015. This unusual scheduling may have led to an overfamiliarity between
the players, with too little time for resentments to fade. As winning teams resort to arrogance, so the loser who has not been
allowed to hide and recuperate after humiliating defeat is liable to become dangerous. A wounded cricket team that fights

its way back to a position of superiority over its recently triumphant rival is unlikely to celebrate faintly or politely if they smell success. Australia were no saints during this series.

In a more general sense, competition has, notoriously, its negative and cruel side, degenerating into arrogance or cheating. Doing well ourselves becomes entangled with relishing someone else's failure. A central feature of gang culture, and of gang conflict, is mutual humiliation. In relation to the opposition, your team collectively score emotionally off the other lot, putting them down. If they humiliate you, honour requires you to return the compliment. Indeed, being made to look weak may be felt as the ultimate shame; it may be unbearable, a matter of life and death. The only resource might be, with the help of your mates, to force the insult back down their throats.

In soccer, the professional foul – that is, a deliberate, calculated foul – is criticised, if at all, not because it goes against the spirit of the game, but on the grounds that the occasion did not 'warrant' it; a 'warranted' foul, according to this mentality, is one that prevents a likely goal without incurring the sending off of the perpetrator. Or, again, there is a notion that cheating should be avoided only if the risk of getting caught is too high. In such atmospheres and cultures, to admit mistakes is to open oneself up naïvely to public or group ridicule. Thus paranoid self-righteousness in individuals and groups is heightened, and viciousness escalates. A society that over-emphasises competition may act on the precept 'the devil take the hindmost'. Any sense of fairness is replaced by sheer bargaining power and market forces.

Yet most Test cricket, however hard-fought, is played with mutual respect and fairness. Ian Chappell was one of Australia's toughest captains, but his standards of behaviour were high. Against England at Melbourne in 1975, he was twice in the match incorrectly given out caught by Alan Knott, England's wicketkeeper: for 65 off the bowling of Chris Old and for 50 off Tony Greig. On each occasion, Chappell left the field without showing by the slightest gesture that he had been the victim of an umpiring error. He lived up to his own ethical code, and did as he would be done by. Once, when I indicated that the ball had bounced after I hit it, before being caught in the slips, Chappell remonstrated, 'Mike, you do the batting, we'll do the appealing, and let the umpire do the umpiring.' He was right.

In the epic Centenary Test, in Melbourne in 1977, the result was identical in margin as well as outcome to that of the original fixture, a hundred years before: a win for Australia by forty-five runs. On the last day of an absorbing match, Derek Randall, who was eventually out for 174, was well past a century, and we, England, were something like 250 for two. With Australia's champion bowler, Dennis Lillee (who in the end took eleven wickets in the match), tiring, there was a serious chance that we might reach what would have been a world record target of 463. Greg Chappell, the fielding captain, then bowled a ball that squeezed between Randall's bat and pad. Rod Marsh, Australia's wicketkeeper, dived forward to take the ball, and the batsman was quickly given out. Despite the high stakes riding on the moment, Marsh, having picked himself up, indicated to Chappell and the umpire that the ball hadn't carried, and Randall was called back. (Grinning, Rod adds in retrospect: 'Randall hadn't even hit it, but that was beside the point' – in other words, unlike the question of whether he had made a fair catch, that was in his view exclusively a matter for the umpire.)

All sport, I suggest, involves attempts to unsettle the opposition, an aim that may be achieved in a range of ways – by group solidarity and overt toughness, by the hostility of the bowling and batting, and indeed by tactical ploys. As a captain, there may be a number of rationales for putting a fielder in a certain position, the most obvious being to have him in place to take a catch or to prevent the batsman from scoring runs. But there are also mind games: part of a strategy to make the batsman wonder what on earth you are thinking of, so that he is shaken out of his steady mindset: 'If I put my best fielder at deep square leg you will expect a bouncer. Is this a bluff, a trap to make you think the ball will be short? Or is it a double bluff?' Or the message may be: 'We don't need a mid-off for you!' Or 'You don't like it at your throat, do you?' Or 'You can't play this bowler, we all know that, so I'm taking off the bloke who's just taken three wickets and I'm putting him on.'

In 1954–5, England captain Len Hutton would go through a charade of near-imbecility when the young Richie Benaud came in to bat for Australia. Benaud, Hutton believed, could not play England's extremely fast bowler, Frank Tyson. But Hutton did not simply put Tyson on to bowl when Benaud came in to bat. He would first allow the fielders to take their places for another bowler. Just as the over was about to begin, Hutton would hold up his hand, walk up to the pitch, and say, 'Hang on a minute, where's Frank?' all the while looking vaguely round the field as if he didn't know where Tyson was. At last 'spotting' him at third man, he would summon him in to bowl. Like a schoolboy at the hands of a sadistic headmaster, Benaud would thus be put through a nervous wait for his punishment. Fair play? Or against the spirit of the game? I would say the former.

Many great players have as part of their repertoire an intimidating ebullience. Viv Richards and Shane Warne for instance, a West Indian and an Australian from different eras, conveyed in their very walk the sense that the big cricket match, with a full

house, was their natural habitat. Both these charismatic and brilliant players had a certain strut. But the bravado was not placed in front like a mask, it was part and parcel of the skill itself. The international stage was where they belonged, and everyone, including their opponents, felt it with a degree of awe and apprehension. I have known bowlers who were nervous of Richards's very presence at the crease, and batsmen cowed by Warne's.

Warne's captain, Steve Waugh, wrote as follows about Warne's impact on South African batsman Daryll Cullinan:

> Warne owned the head-space of Cullinan, one of South Africa's better batsmen of the 1990s, and they both knew it. Every time Cullinan made his way to the crease when the ball was within Shane's sizeable grasp, we could see him shrinking both mentally and physically with each painstaking step, as if the inevitable guillotine was hovering above. It was always just a matter of time.

Richards for his part would not let an impertinent jibe against him go without a reaction. When Greg Thomas, the

Glamorgan fast bowler, having beaten Richards's bat a few times, announced audaciously, 'It's red, round and weighs about five ounces,' Richards hit the next delivery out of the ground into the River Taff. He quietly told the bowler, 'You know what it looks like, now go and find it.'

Playing for Your Country: 'But You Picked Me to Play'

Test cricket, especially between long-standing rivals like Australia and England, provides a quintessential context for both competitiveness and cooperation. All top-level sport has this feature, but given that Test matches last for five days, with two innings per side, there is time for all sorts of phases and reversals. Gratification often has to be delayed. Anglo-Australian Tests have been going on regularly, except during the world wars, roughly every two years for almost 140 years. Each series is a contest for 'the Ashes' – a strange little urn of a trophy based on a satirical obituary about the 'death of English cricket' published in an English newspaper in 1882. The tradition has lasted ever since, and will (I hope) continue well beyond our lifetimes.

But what is it like to play in a Test match? In one's first Test match? The experience is not always benign, but it is intense and often memorable. Is it unique?

For John Inverarity – who later became chairman of selectors for the Australian national team, as well as a friend – his induction into Test cricket, opening for Australia in England in 1968, was not uniquely significant. He writes that he had felt similar levels of excitement, pride and awe at notable moments in his earlier cricketing life. He cites his first innings for the school XI at the age of thirteen, and, four years later, his first appearance at the Test ground in Perth. He recalls the launch of his State career, for Western Australia, facing the bowling of the great Gary Sobers. For him, his first foray into Test cricket was not a world apart.

For my part, before my very first competitive game of cricket at the age of ten, I had a stomach upset; I was sick with anxiety. I agonised over whether I was fit to play, and withdrew. Three days before my second Test, against West Indies at Lord's in 1976, on a hot afternoon outside London, I had a stomach ache so bad that I was forced to lie down, curled up, under a hedge. In the ditch, a thought crossed my mind: how some newspapers would relish knowing where and how England's brave opening batsman was preparing to represent his country, especially if they had also known the location of the aforementioned hedge and ditch – inside the grounds of Shenley Mental Hospital (as it used to be called), where I was to attend a course. I didn't drop out of that match.

John Stephenson played cricket for Essex, for Hampshire, and – once – for England. The first day of his single Test, against Australia at the Oval in 1989, the last of a six-match series, was, he tells me, the most exhausting experience of his life. Much had gone wrong even before the game itself. England were at a low ebb, four-nil down. Morale was low. David Gower knew this would be his last Test as captain. The selectors had cast their net wide; Stephenson was the twenty-ninth cricketer to play for England that summer.

To arrive in good time for net practice that afternoon, Stephenson set off early for the Oval on the day before the Test. Getting hopelessly lost in bad traffic, he arrived late. The gate-keeper wouldn't let his battered yellow Vauxhall Cavalier into the ground. Once he made it to the dressing room, the embarrassed debutant apologised for his lateness to chairman of selectors Ted Dexter, who asked him what he was doing there, and directed him as a net bowler to the lower dressing room. 'But I'm John Stephenson,' he said. 'You've picked me to play.'

At the pre-match dinner, players and selectors were tucking into the red wine, which John assumed must be normal. Next morning he had no idea how to get to the Oval, and no one offered him a lift. Once he got there, he heard the public address system announce that England had won the toss and would bat. Stephenson, due to open the innings with Graham Gooch, started to strap on his pads. Shortly after, a correction was announced: Australia would bat. Stephenson took his pads off again.

England fielded for almost two days. It was after the first day that utter exhaustion set in. Stephenson still doesn't understand it. My guess is that the anxiety and tension of playing for England, combined with feeling unwelcomed in a demoralised environment, were significant factors.

On the evening of the second day, Terry Alderman, swinging the ball sharply, soon had Gooch lbw, at which the umpires took the players off for bad light. On the third morning, Saturday, the sun was shining, the ground full, the pitch flat. John struggled through his initial nervous dread, first in partnership with Michael Atherton, then Robin Smith, then Gower. At one point he said to his captain in mid-pitch: 'If I've batted this long it's OK, I can survive. They'll have to get me out now.' Just before lunch, Merv Hughes – he of the handlebar moustaches – Australia's fastest, and loudest, bowler in the match, went round the wicket and hit him on the wrist with a short-pitched ball. Bernie Thomas, England's physiotherapist, told Stephenson he should come off for treatment. John said, 'No, I'll keep going to lunch.'

There was one last over. He let several balls from Alderman go, swinging away towards the slips. For the fifth ball, Australia's captain Allan Border brought in Steve Waugh to third slip. Stephenson jabbed, edged and was caught by Waugh for 25.

I asked John about the Australians. He and Border had been team-mates at Essex, where Border had always played the game in a tough but positive way. But his attitude was different in the Test match, Stephenson thought; there seemed to be a policy of being 'aloof and aggressive'. He was shocked when Border swore at umpire Dickie Bird.

During that third morning, wicketkeeper Ian Healy, and David Boon, at short leg, within earshot of Stephenson, started to make clicking noises like horses' hooves, and snide remarks about horses. Stephenson was disconcerted. What were they on about? Why these sly and insidious noises and comments? Though puzzled, he came to the conclusion that he must have earned the right to be mocked; that it was a mark of respect, however inverted. Later he discovered from Boon that they had formed a picture of him with his upright stance as a horse-rider.

Apart from the almost affectionate grin apparent behind the bristling moustache of the sledging Hughes (another ex-colleague at Essex), Australia's overall attitude was that there should be no friendly interaction on or off the field. It was Border's way of differentiating Test cricket from county cricket.

'And England, were they the same?' I asked him.

'No,' he said. 'We were quiet. There was an air of inevitability, of expectation of defeat . . . Derek Pringle [another Essex man] said at lunch on the first day, when England had taken three wickets, "That's a really good result", as if we were surprised to get anyone out.' And he recalls Smith throwing grapes at the wall in celebration when tail-enders Nick Cook and Gladstone Small saved the follow-on.

Nasser Hussain, yet another Essex colleague, and later England's captain, was preferred for the upcoming tour of West Indies. Stephenson was not picked for England again.

Being Eaten for Breakfast or for Lunch

My own overriding impression of playing Test matches was that they were like an arduous expedition, through difficult terrain, with the enemy ever-present. The experience, somewhat as I imagine in war, veered between the frightening, the exhilarating and the tedious. But in contrast to the experience of Stephenson, who had little chance to acclimatise himself, my Test matches were expeditions in the company of friends. The arguments, quarrels, rivalries, dissensions – passions of all kinds – fell, as I now recall it, under this rubric of purposeful camaraderie.

I don't think it was because their bowlers were, as my father would have put it, trying to knock my block off that I wasn't keen on the Australian habit of drinking beers in each other's dressing room after a day's play. John Emburey, the England off-spinner, spoke of the advantages in seeing the likes of intimidating and extrovert fast bowlers Lillee and Hughes as ordinary human beings when half-dressed in the changing room. He reckoned the bubble element in their well-founded reputation as fast bowlers was pricked in this way, perhaps like seeing a great actor off-stage after the performance, reduced to human dimensions. In county cricket I enjoyed meeting up with fast bowlers and others in the pub. But during Tests, I was more uneasy, more tense, probably a sign that I rarely felt quite at home in Test cricket as a batsman.

(I love the story of Brian Statham, who after a long, match-winning spell of fast bowling during England's successful tour of 1954–5 poured his first pint of cold beer over his feet, saying, 'They've earned it more than I have.')

West Indies, the most powerful side in Test cricket from the late 1970s until the early 1990s, never sledged. They conveyed menace more subtly, letting the ball (or the bat) do the talking.

My first Test match was at Nottingham in 1976. Both teams were staying at the same hotel, and on the first morning I happened to arrive at breakfast at the same time as Andy Roberts, one of the greatest and shrewdest of fast bowlers. Roberts gave me a little look, not unfriendly, but appraising, enquiring, eyebrows quizzically raised; rather (I felt) like a predator eyeing future prey, not in anger but measuring it up for later consumption. (Ian Chappell told me not long ago of his tussles on the field with Roberts, both in Test matches and in World Series Cricket (the cricket matches staged in Australia by Channel Nine boss, Kerry Packer, in protest at being refused the rights to broadcast Test cricket by the Australian Cricket Board). He found Roberts's short ball harder to deal with than anyone else's. It was always straight, and, arriving around chest height, was never wasted. Chappell would fend the ball off, duck and take blows, waiting for a short ball just outside off stump that would give him room to swing his arms and pull or hook. Just once, during a World Series match, he got such a ball and pulled it away for four. Never again, Chappell said. Recently he had commented on this to Roberts. Roberts remembered it well. He wasn't going to give him such a ball again. And he never did.)

I Had it Covered for Everything Except Bad Bounce

It was not all deadly serious. I played two Test matches in 1976 with Brian Close, who was then forty-five. (This was the first year since his debut in 1949 that he had not written in his diary the details of the forthcoming summer's Test matches.) At Lord's, Close scored 60 and 46. In the second innings, he was caught and bowled by Vanburn Holder, who, bowling from the Pavilion End, with the slope favouring his tendency to move the ball away from the left-handed Close, was inviting him to plant his front leg and play round it to the leg side; if the ball moved off the seam, he might be caught in the slips or get a leading edge. The latter is exactly what happened.

Whenever Close was out, his team-mates would wait expectantly to hear his latest account of how unlucky he had been: how in fact the cricketing gods (or even ordinary mortals) had conspired against him. (He once said: 'that bloody little twelfth man, he gave me chewing gum of t' wrong bloody flavour.') This time it was: 'I had it covered for everything except bad bounce.'

Later in the match, when we were pressing for wickets in West Indies' second innings, left-hander Alvin Kallicharran, a brilliant puller and sweeper of the ball, had been kept quiet for some time by Derek Underwood. Close was known for his fearlessness; he had once famously declared: 'A cricket ball can't hurt you. It's only on you a second.' Now, fielding in direct line of fire at short square leg, he whispered to me at backward short leg: 'He'll have a lap [sweep] in a minute. I'll get in t'road, and you catch t'rebound.' And he meant it.

Test matches were extremely exhilarating. Winning close-fought games after five gruelling days was an occasion for celebration and relief, along with some trace of 'there but for the grace of God' on behalf of the opposition. Some defeats, however, were too shocking to be taken magnanimously. After Headingley 1981, when we won against all the odds, I went, tentatively, to the Australian dressing room, to shake hands and thank them in the usual way for the game. I was ready to invite them in for a glass of our champagne. The silence was absolute, the atmosphere heavy with the tension of dawning comprehension. It was like walking in on a major family trauma. I quietly withdrew.

In recent years I have become good friends with several of the old Australian rivals. Lillee, who I imagined regarded me on the field as a feeble Pom with a posh accent, told me recently that we should have shared more time together all those years ago. In fact, however modest my role, I was honoured to share the stage, even briefly, even as a rabbit to a fox, with one of the greatest bowlers of all time.

Keeping Us Honest

There is something honest about striving and competition. Mountaineer Heinrich Harrer writes, in *The White Spider*: 'The glorious thing about mountains is that they will endure no lies.' And batsman Maurice Leyland, who played for Yorkshire from 1920 to 1947, said: 'Fast bowling keeps you honest.' Visceral truthfulness is part of the process whereby we come to accept the urgency of our own subjectivity and the otherness of the other. We have to face without cowardice or self-deception the challenge of the intransigent mountain or the aggressive and skilful fast bowler. There is nowhere to hide.

In learning a foreign language, as Iris Murdoch writes, we have to face the fact that things are not as we would like them to be; irregular verbs have to be learned. Facing reality means having to give up some of our narcissism.

I was once a guest player for an English professional side on a short tour abroad. During the first half of the tour, we had tried our best but lost more games than we won. We had been facing talented players in local conditions. Though not part of any competitive league or series, the matches were played hard. In the next game, against one of the strongest sides, we were led by the regular captain, who had arrived late for the tour. He chose to emphasise the entertainment aspect of the next 'friendly' fixture, taking off his front-line bowlers, allowing the opposing batsmen to run riot and make an even bigger total than they would have without such (to my mind misguided) generosity. When we batted, our opponents bowled flat out and we limped to a crushing defeat. This gesture of 'giving' runs patronised the other team and robbed each party of the satisfaction of doing their best in striving to win. The gilt on our opponents' win was tarnished. And not really trying means not fully losing – though we *did* lose both face and respect.

Henry James puts the point neatly and ironically about the languid Gilbert Osmond, in *The Portrait of a Lady*. 'Osmond, in his way, was admirable; he had the advantage of an acquired habit. It was not that of succeeding, but it was something almost as good – that of not attempting.'

Such dilution of straightforwardness may also occur out of a wish to look good. One Test captain decided during the afternoon of the last day that his batsmen should play for a draw rather than take further risks in going for a win – a perfectly respectable decision. He was, however, anxious not to be criticised for being defensive. The match was the debut of a young batsman in the middle order, who had been unkindly barracked from the start by the crowd, having been selected ahead of their local hero. In the first innings, he had been given out (incorrectly) for a duck. When he went in to bat that last afternoon the captain gave him the following orders: 'Play for a draw, but make it look as if we're playing to win.' This was hypocritical and cowardly captaincy; the young batsman was in a difficult enough situation without having to act a false role. But the captain was more interested in how he himself looked than in standing by his own decision, supporting a young player and competing honestly. Instead, he hid behind him.

Boorishness and gloating, then, are not the only perversions of competitiveness. We may also inure ourselves to disappointment by denying the desire to win. It takes courage to risk all in competitiveness, to face the challenge and refuse to hide behind the self-deceptive indifference of 'I don't mind losing'.

It is not only in sport that we admire the unflinching performer. We value that quality in art of all kinds, and in everyday life. Think of (clichéd example notwithstanding) Rembrandt's self-portraits. Here is a man painting himself without illusions. What we observe in the late portraits is a lived-in face. We are presented with the face of someone who does not shrink from seeing and showing himself, acknowledging his flaws and the ravages of time.

This takes integrity and courage, as it did for Leyland. Both face up to whatever life (or the bowler) throws at them, to wherever life has brought them.

PART V: SURGEONS, DIRECTORS, AND CANOEISTS

12

SEEING THE WOOD AND THE TREES

You have to do the job in peace and in concentration.

Piraji Gajaj

I want to be taken to places in myself that I can't go to by myself.

Juliet Stevenson

I want to have love and confidence poured into me.

Simon Russell Beale

Great surgeons have bad memories.

Henry Marsh

———

1. Tree Acrobat

Watching tree cutters at work in western India, where I spend some time each year, has been for me one of those peculiar pleasures that are shot through with discomfort and anxiety. The man who climbed on the most recent occasion, Tina, works barefoot. He climbs trees up to eighty or a hundred feet tall without harness, helmet or safety net, usually without ladders. He carries only an axe (its handle perhaps twenty-four inches long) and ropes. Once up there, he attaches ropes to control the fall of the limbs, negotiates with other members of the team on the ground, and calculates how and where to lop. Then he will cut a branch to the point where it is on the verge of breaking. Before his colleagues on the ground pull on the ropes, Tina moves himself well away from the break point, sometimes embracing the trunk with arms and legs to keep himself safe as the tree shudders and shakes. The branch creaks, rocks, breaks and plunges down, held parallel to the trunk by the ropes.

From time to time Tina will wedge the axe into a joint, or stick it in the trunk, to give himself two free hands. The cutting has to be done while he clings to the tree with his free arm, or is balanced in a variety of awkward postures. He will have to reach over to cut underneath his body, holding on with the other hand. Or, holding the axe with both hands, he will cut the branch between his legs. The blade sometimes sticks in the wood and has to be jerked out. He has to turn round at these heights, on exposed branches. He spends several hours at a time up aloft, without much respite, bringing down a large, many-branched tree limb by limb.

Meanwhile, afraid of heights, I find my palms sweating, I feel slightly sick and apparently go pale. So identified am I with a fear-filled version of Tina that it is far more likely that I will fall to the ground I am standing on than that he will topple from his narrow perches. It is always admirable to watch someone proficient in his work; with Tina, this wide-ranging skill is combined with wonderful sangfroid. He is a graceful habitué of the tree-tops, as assured in his movements as an acrobat. Tina strikes me as a mightily impressive man: calm, patient, flexible, strong and totally deliberate in every movement. His overall bearing is serene.

I wonder about the notion of form for Tina. And I ask the organiser of the whole operation, a man called Piraji, forty-eight years old, who himself climbed and cut until ten years ago, if he will talk to me. He now runs the business, negotiating agreements with clients, getting his team together, hiring and arranging for a tractor to pick up the wood, selling the wood. He is also the trainer or supervisor of the cutters who climb. Nowadays he trusts Tina, aged thirty-two, to do most of the work independently; but he has to talk his number two climber, aged twenty-five, through his next moves while on the job. He has to keep his eye on him and look after him. And this man cannot go as high as Tina.

I first ask Piraji his full name. He tells me, 'Piraji Gajaj Marwadi Naroda Bethak opp. Bharat Petrol Pump, Mafatpur.' His identity is made up of his given name (Piraji), father's name (Gajaj), the community he comes from (Marwadi, in Rajasthan), and his present address and how it is to be found. Thus ensuring that he is not mistaken for any other Piraji.

I ask how he got into the work. Before his birth, his father was a camel herder in Rajasthan, who would climb and cut neem trees (a member of the mahogany family native to the Indian subcontinent) to get fodder for the camels. When Piraji's father was thirty the family moved south across the state border to Gujarat, where he started to cut wood as a job, especially in the military cantonment. As a small boy, Piraji carried his father's tiffin for him. He learned his trade by observing, and by using his own intelligence. Only when he himself was twenty did he start his training, and at twenty-five was given the opportunity to climb and cut. He had already become confident at heights up to fifty feet, he said. Of four brothers, Piraji alone became a tree-cutter.

He says that his men start this work only at twenty-five. Before that, they 'do not have the mind for the work'. They can usually continue up to about the age of forty-five. In his case, when he was thirty-eight he started to have pains and stiffness in his arms, hands and legs. His mind was, and is, sharp, but not his body.

I ask Piraji if he has children, and whether he is training any of them to follow him. He says he has six children – four boys and two girls – but he has not encouraged any of them to join him. They are, he says, city boys, expecting more money than those of his generation and country boys – 'times have changed'. (I doubt if the idea of female tree cutters would even today be any kind of option in India.) He has educated all six to tenth grade (to the age of fifteen or sixteen), and they are going into factory jobs and the like.

I ask Piraji about fear. He says categorically that he has no fear. Even today if he were to climb he would feel no fear, though after three or four days his body would suffer from the strain. There is simply knowledge of danger, and appropriate caution. He himself never had a fall. Of course many do. They are carrying something in an ungainly way, or they slip on a chiku tree, a fruit tree that can reach one hundred feet in height. Intoxication is another occasional cause of accidents.

I try to find out if there is any appeal or thrill in being on the edge in this way; it seems hard to formulate the question so that he understands me. I think he answers in the negative; he keeps emphasising that it was (simply) his job. I ask if there is a risk of becoming over-confident, intoxicated one might say, so as to be brash and incautious, and he agrees energetically to this, citing the example of Ravana, a king from the great Indian epic the *Ramayana*, whose certainty that nothing bad could happen to him led to his defeat; he thought he could get away with stealing Sita from the god Rama, but Hanuman, the monkey god, spotted her and Rama eventually rescued her. Piraji's point is that you mustn't ever lose that necessary caution and realism.

He speaks about fitness and training. The young men in his team, who all come from tree-cutting families, practise with the ropes (sometimes they descend from the trees by abseiling down on ropes they have attached higher up). At ground level they also practise with the axe, learning how to cut clean wedges, at different angles, with different stances; left-handed, right-handed, both-handed, forehanded and backhanded. They have to look after their health and bodily well-being. Each morning before climbing, a cutter will eat ghee (purified butter), milk and rotlis (chapatis) to ensure that his stomach is in good order, with no inflammation. (They are not by caste vegetarian, though Piraji now is.) They have to build up their strength. I mention that I have noticed that both he and Tina are over six feet tall, with long legs and arms, so they can scale exposed or dangerous passages with a few long, careful steps, or reach out to catch ropes thrown to them, or reach round the ends of branches to attach a rope. Yes, he says, they are strong in the shoulder, and in the legs. Their legs have to hold firm against the jerk of the axe as it gets unstuck from the wood, or while reaching over to cut at difficult angles. The cutters have to be able to sustain long periods in uncomfortable positions without losing their physical strength, poise and flexibility.

'Those who are heavy can't climb,' he says. 'You have to do this kind of training from twenty. Otherwise what happens is your axe slips and hits your foot; you must control it and know how to hit.'

But above all the mind has to be right; 'you have to do the job in peace and in concentration'. Piraji says he was never aware of being off form. If he was unwell, or had an injury (a pulled muscle or a cut foot, say), or if his mind was not in the right place, he would hope to be able to hand over to someone else, but if no one else sufficiently skilled was present, he would decline to climb, and the work would be called off for the day. So he knew when to say no; false pride did not interfere with safety and good sense.

I ask if he was ever distracted or put off by the ordinary irritations and frustrations of life, whether with clients, team members, or with anyone or anything that caused extra difficulties. He says no, he put all that completely out of his mind. He didn't let extraneous things affect him. He separated the two. There was only the tree, and being in the present.

Yes, he says, he is a calm person, and he has developed this natural trait by making sure he meets and sits with good men, with the tax collector, or people working at the Physics Research Laboratory, for instance; that is, with people of stature, seniority, education and goodness. This is how he learned to be stable and not influenced by evil, but by good. He trained himself from the beginning in this way. I ask him if this is true in other areas of his life. He says yes: he is able to put things out of his mind and concentrate on the now. I get the impression that he can accept life as it happens. He lights candles daily to three divinities, he says matter-of-factly; this is part of his routine, his background, but I don't get a sense that he is praying for help. It seems to be a minimal ritual. Nowadays, I suggest, he too must be an example of calmness to his team. He replies, modestly, 'They don't know who is a big and great person, so I have to make sure they understand.'

Piraji is, as I have mentioned, never off form. This reminds me of two quotes. One is by Picasso: '*Je ne cherche pas: je trouve*' – meaning 'I don't look for things, I find them'. The other is from Don Bradman, the greatest cricketer ever. Geoff Marsh, ex-player and ex-coach of Australia, says:

> We had him down for a seminar in 1997 . . . to come and meet the players. One of the questions I asked was, 'What sort of things did you do when you were out of form?' And he looked at me and said, 'I can't answer that'. I asked him why. He said, 'Well, when I played, I was never out of form.'

(Interestingly, Bradman had a high percentage of ducks in Test match cricket: seven in his eighty innings. Roughly once in every eleven or twelve innings he suffered this fate; to put this into perspective, his batting average in those eighty innings was 99.94. But as with Ken Barrington, scoring ducks did not mean that he was out of form.)

I ask Piraji when the greatest risks occur for a tree cutter. He says that rain makes trees slippery, so that descending is dangerous. And there are, he says, slippery trees. Then you have to be sure to have a rope to hand, tied securely above, to rely on if you slip. And no two jobs are the same. Yes, he plans how a tree is to be cut, in what order, and how each branch will come down. But he must also be ready to improvise and change.

I had watched the final cutting of a large, dead tree. After bringing all the branches down, the team were left with the trunk alone. It was perhaps thirty feet high. This could only be felled in one go, as there was nothing above to fix the top of the trunk to, so as to lower it (or half of it) slowly. It would have to fall directly to the ground. In its crowded site not far from a house, there was only one place for it to land, to avoid the building, a patio and other trees. The line of fall risked wrecking two beautiful, red-flowering, shrub-like bottle trees. Piraji said he would try to bring it down between the two shrubs. As the great trunk started to creak free, wavering in the seconds before falling, it became clear that it would fall to one side. Piraji urgently told the men manning the ropes to change their angle of pull, creating a different direction of fall. The tree crashed down precisely between the two shrubs, neither of which lost a branch or a flower. As with a cricket captain, the tree-felling captain has to be flexible. Not every move turns out initially as he hopes or plans. He has to make quick-thinking adjustments. In our conversation, Piraji recalls this particular tree, acknowledging that he did not get the angle right at first, but when the tree began to rock he could see what needed urgently to be done, and made the modification.

I'm told that one of Piraji's distinguishing features as a tree cutter is his willingness to take on tricky jobs like this one, cutting big trees near precious buildings, and facing the risks of substantial and costly damage. He is proud of his capacity to do such jobs where there is a lot at stake. He is like the brain surgeon who will tackle the most challenging tumours.

The Tina-figure up the tree is of course reliant on other team members, who man the ropes, give him advice, cut up the felled wood, and help load the large logs onto the trailer. If they let go, or pull in the wrong way, or have not fixed a staying rope securely, the log can hit the cutter, injuring him or knocking him off; or of course it can damage people or things on the ground. Piraji will not employ people who don't keep themselves fit, who are unreliable, who won't do as they are told, or who won't see a job through. They need mutual trust and loyalty.

He takes a proper pride in his care and professionalism, and in being an exemplar for the younger men. He says that only one climber in ten or fifteen could, on retiring from the actual climbing, do the job he now does. But there is also humility, in his awareness of his own need to learn from others. Partly this is a social humility. But it also has an Aristotelian ring to it; we need to habituate ourselves by being in contact with good people, so that good habits of mind become ingrained.

Finally I ask him, 'If you had access to harnesses, helmets and power-tools, would you use them?' Piraji replies 'Yes.' But then he adds, 'But we have faith in ourselves. We believe we can do it without.'

2. 'Creativity is just Practice that's Camouflaged'

In 2007, I spoke to leading figures in the theatre for a radio programme. Peter Hall, director for many years of the Royal Shakespeare Company, described a 'Road to Damascus' moment in 1957. At that time, it was *de rigueur* for directors to block out scenes in advance of rehearsals. He would have the moves and furniture in place, all carefully 'rehearsed' with his 'tin soldiers', and would announce this to the cast before they first went through a scene. Peggy Ashcroft – 'the first really great actor I directed' – was playing Imogen in *Cymbeline*. On the Friday of the first week of rehearsal, going routinely through the blocking for Act 5, he said, 'Dame Peggy, at this point you walk across the stage from left to right.' She said, 'Fine.' But a moment or two later she spoke out in a clear voice: 'Pete, I don't think I can do this.' He was temporarily flabbergasted; blocking was what you did! But he had the presence of mind to pause, sit down, and then talk about it. He came to see that he agreed with her. Not only was it 'a bad move', he would 'never again block in advance of rehearsal. We will start again on Monday!'

The director Katie Mitchell, another influential presence in British theatre, put hard work far ahead of other factors:

> Ninety-eight per cent of what the director does is hard work. There is a prevalent idea that directors spend their time sitting around at dinner parties, or going for a walk in the park, and get new insights. If only it were so, this romantic view. In fact this amounts to perhaps 2 per cent of what I do, when there is a moment of new insight into the material which will help articulate it in a stimulating way to the audience; but I never rely on it, and would never assume it's there. Each morning you get up and do more work on the text.

There are moments of inspiration; but they are both adventitious and provisional.

Sam Mendes, a highly creative presence in both film and theatre, argued that before embarking on a play it is vital to have a sense that you possess a key to it, whether from personal identification with one of the characters, or of a more overarching, conceptual kind; you need to believe you have something special that will illuminate the process of rehearsal, and no doubt the outcome. Leading British actor Juliet Stevenson agreed; she requires a director to have a 'compelling vision of the play'. Like Mitchell, she wanted the vision to be found in the 'heart of the text', not 'superimposed on top of it like an ill-fitting garment'.

Combined with this need for a vision, however, Mendes's ideal was to leave open as much as possible. He referred to 'by far the greatest book on theatre, Peter Brook's *The Empty*

Space'. Mendes favoured starting rehearsals with an empty stage and an empty-enough mind. There would be no blocking, of course; but also, ideally, no fixed design, nor any sets already made or in process of being made. As director, he said, you have to 'encourage the actors on a journey that will be independent of you; you want them to find the answers themselves. And in the course of working together, you must be ready to give up or modify some of your preconceptions.' (Echoes of bringing up children?)

The empty mind is, in short, a vital mental correlate to the Empty Space – like Greg Chappell and Wilfred Bion's recommendations for batsmen and psychoanalysts. Such an oscillation or tension between emptiness and conscious planning is part of the mind-set of much creative activity, and indeed of being fully on form. Sometimes we wake up with a solution to a troublesome problem; we may even realise in our sleep that something we thought we had solved has drawbacks that need attention. Experimenting with this idea at Harvard Medical School, psychologist Deirdre Barrett found that two-thirds of her student subjects had dreams that addressed their chosen problem, and one-third reached some form of solution within the dreams.

Is the director's work closer to science or to art? Katie Mitchell explained the Russian theatre director Konstantin Stanislavski's attempt to find as precise a method as possible for actors as his response to his personal susceptibility as an actor to debilitating stage fright. In his curiosity and his determination to find reliable tools to 'build' real people, he was, she suggested, being scientific. She valued similar methods regarding improvisations and the elaboration of back-history as vital means for achieving on the stage depth of character in its moment-to-moment detail. More than most directors, she said, she focuses on physical triggers to arrive at an emotionally convincing performance. She has respect for the text, but also wishes to go deep into it, or maybe beyond it, into its unconscious roots in the writer.

Another key element is the relevance of the visual. Ted Braun, former Professor of Drama at Bristol University, remembered an instance of directorial vision in the Berliner Ensemble's version of *Coriolanus*, which he saw at the Old Vic Theatre in London in 1965. Here the director brought an idea to life visually, as well as verbally:

> The part of Coriolanus was played by a 'little bull of a man' called Ekkehard Schall. At one of the turning points in the play, Coriolanus, proudly refusing any longer to eat what he experiences as humble pie, announces explosively, 'Thus I turn my back. There is a world elsewhere'. In this production, as Schall strode off, he shed his bright, blood-red cloak. The mesmerised on-stage crowd looked on, aghast at this vivid symbol of abandoned authority.

The audience shared the shock of this spectacular *coup de théâtre*.

In the film *Throne of Blood*, his version of *Macbeth*, the Japanese director Akira Kurosawa turns Cobweb Forest (Birnam Wood) into a kind of character in the story, a site of madness where human characters get lost, going round and round desperately in a swirling fog of disorientation. It is the locus of the siren-witch voices intensifying Macbeth's regicidal, patricidal fantasies. Only the equivalent of Macduff, Noriyasu, a character who knows the wood – that is to say, who knows the paths and pulls of madly desperate ambition – can in the end defeat him by bringing Birnam Wood to Dunsinane.

The capacity to imagine in visual terms such dramatic symbolic moments is one central feature of a mind that is fully alive. Pictorial fantasies strike me as an earlier form of thinking than 'rational' cognitive thought. If we are to be creative and remain on form, we need to keep in touch with these down-to-earth and striking images, alongside verbal narratives and argumentation. Certainly this principle applies in my work as a psychoanalyst.

Juliet Stevenson, speaking about what she seeks from directors, stressed her need to be stretched if she is to reach top form. Another leading British actor, Simon Russell Beale, prioritised rather the confidence that arises from the director's regard for him. Once he knows the director not only loves him but also fully believes he can play the part, then he can take tough, critical remarks – especially from a director he knows well, like Mendes – and learn from him.

This fits with my experience in sport and in psychoanalysis. When there is a good relationship between captain and player, analyst and patient, tough words can be spoken by the captain/analyst and, over time, made use of by the team member/ patient. If the person in the position of the 'director' has not found or been able to build a relationship of trust, then what he says and does is liable to be regarded with indifference or scepticism. The stretching that Stevenson spoke of is more possible within a relationship that has grown into, or in some cases starts with, mutual respect, but, as she implied, the reverse is also true: trust sometimes grows from the director's tough-minded willingness to speak truth to power, and to stretch the actor. Much depends on the tone of, and the unarticulated attitude behind, the comments, interpretations or criticisms.

Both Stevenson and Mitchell dig into the characters' psychological hinterlands. Stevenson described her 'thrilling collaboration' with Mitchell on Samuel Beckett's plays. She admired this director's 'love and respect for the writing' and her 'healthy disregard for all the old imperatives, including Beckett's own idea that his texts should be read as song, without any struggle to understand the underlying psychological meaning'.

For Mitchell, the part-self (the Mouth in *Not I*, for example, which becomes a 'character' by being all that is visible to the audience of the actor's face), had 'just the same flesh-and-blood reality as a character in a nineteenth century play like *The Seagull*; I want to know her back-history. I want to know where she got the shopping bag from, and what happened to her in her life that led to the strange buzzing in her ears.'

Stevenson added that there are two types of actors: those who go into acting to flee from who they are, and those who want to discover and reveal who they are. This rings bells for me, too; we all are ambivalent about really knowing ourselves, but some are more open and unflinching about it than others. There is a parallel question about sportsmen and women – how far is a player keen to stretch himself, to face up to his fears and his shortcomings? Or will he settle for something well short of his potential? I remember a crushing remark made about a fellow county cricketer, that when he retired he knew no more about either cricket or himself than when he had started as a young professional fifteen years before.

One point on which Stevenson and Mitchell differed was the issue of whether inhabiting a role means, necessarily, having a strong emotional identification with the character. Stevenson has to feel the character's emotions 'or [else] it feels agonising. I work hard to generate them.' On the other hand she knows well enough that the regulated structure of the profession, which means you have to feel destructive envy, say, at 7.30 every evening, and 2.30 for the matinee on Thursdays, makes it hard; but she attempts to 'tune up or down' her emotional range in order to get inside her character. Mitchell demurred; she regards the emphasis on feeling as not sufficiently repeatable or reliable; the aim is to get the *audience*, not the actor, to feel something, and how that is done doesn't matter. She believes it is better to think in terms of being *credible* as an actor rather than being truthful. She added: 'there is a danger that if you feel sad when you act sad you will end up depressed.'

Like Mitchell, Braun too saw it as a flaw in Stanislavski's theories that, despite his attempts to focus on the body and on repeatable gestures, he assumed that if the actor truly, and 'freshly', experiences an emotion, then so will the audience. The debate goes all the way back to the French encyclopaedist Denis Diderot, who wrote of the 'actor's paradox', advocating the priority of physical representation over emotional experience. For me it remains unclear how much the actor's form relies on his inner state of unconscious identification with the role, and how much it relies on his credibly representing such a state, whatever is going on inside.

Mendes was more easy-going about this issue, less prescriptive. He suggested that great actors manage to convey something by a mixture of being 'real and being fake'. It doesn't matter which. The proof of the pudding is in the doing, and in the eating by the audience of the meal offered, however it was cooked.

In a separate conversation with Juliet Stevenson, I asked her about the link between conscious hard work and the apparently more unconscious, more automatic state of living the part. Echoing Mitchell, she spoke first of the discipline involved. There is the whole training to become an actor in the first place. And in any particular production, there is the work of rehearsal, the trying out of different interpretations or meanings. There is the hard work of learning how to interact with the other actors, who are themselves striving to inhabit their parts. But in performance, Stevenson hopes to feel the emotions of the character and enter into the part. On stage, then, is she, I want to know, *trying* to do something? Does she any longer have to *work* at it? She responded with the idea that there is a benign split in the actor's self. She is familiar with this experience of being in a zone, of not having to watch herself, not having to *try*. She *is* the part and the part plays her. But always alongside 'being' the character, she said, there is a professional side of the actor watching herself and the whole scene, alert to everything, and especially ready to step in with solutions in case of errors or accidents – a broken glass, say, or a missed cue – and able to calculate with often incredible sureness and swiftness how to save a scene, while and by remaining as far as possible in character.

I find this notion of a benign split helpful. In the words of Marion Milner, 'The internal gesture required is to stand aside.'

In the end, we need to allow room for an element of mystery in how the director elicits something extra from the text and the actors. Like Diderot, Peter Hall spoke when interviewed for the BBC programme of paradoxes in the art of directing. He recalled asking Sybil Thorndike what it was like for her as the first St Joan to be directed by the play's creator, George Bernard Shaw. After hearing about Shaw's rigid approach – 'Come at three, know the scene, we will go through it, I will give you notes; we will go through it again and I will give you more notes. I don't want wasteful discussion' – Hall commented, 'How absolutely awful!' To his surprise, Thorndike replied, 'Yes, but we adored him.' Hall went on to say that he had seen brilliant directors speak rubbish and get wonderful work from the cast, and less good directors talk brilliantly and get nothing. In speaking we all convey more than mere words, and in listening we hear more (or less) too.

3. More Tar, More Poison

This conundrum of how leaders communicate seems to be even more striking with orchestral conductors. Orchestral players speak about conductors creating their own personal kind of sound with different orchestras. This arises not only as a result of the conductor's musicianship, – his understanding of the music and of the marks on the page that constitute the score – but also from his personality, conveyed largely through the body.

Violinist Kathleen Sturdy, who as a young woman in the 1950s played in the Philharmonia Orchestra, recalled the great Otto Klemperer conducting from a wheelchair in advanced old age. She said that he was so impeded in his movements that it was hard to know how the orchestra knew when to start, yet there was something magical in the interaction. 'It came

from somewhere inside him. He was a great man. Do you have to be a great man, or woman, to be a great conductor?' She answered her own question with a tentative 'yes'. So perhaps part of what a conductor or director conveys is a sense that he or she has gone through and faced up to the predicaments of life that artists explore and express.

One clear aim is to make space for successive significant musical events. Australian conductor Charles Mackerras, describing rehearsals of the first movement of Brahms's First Symphony, speaks of slowing and broadening the tempo at one point 'so that the melody can be heard in all its beauty; I make sure the accompanying instruments don't get in the way of the clarinet and oboe answering each other.' Later he says, 'Now [it's] big chords, so I have to conduct proudly and confidently.'

This reminds me of a gardener ensuring that whatever is most striking at any given season is planted in a setting where it can be fully appreciated. Mackerras's comments also evoke the physicality emphasised by Stanislavski and Mitchell: much emotion is transmitted by means of body, gesture and emphasis.

Most musicians seem to agree that interpretation is vital and sometimes unique. Harrison Birtwistle, the composer, is more sceptical. What he wants from conductors and players alike is 'for them to realise my intentions'.

> It's not so much the content and getting it across to people that exercises me; the hardest part of my work is to make this clear through the notation, through the squiggles on the page . . . There are performers who want to bring out the form and structure of the music, whatever the parameters are. And there are those who use music as a vehicle for their own egos. The world is full of such nonsense. There is a danger of pushing the barriers and distorting the object.

More recently, he has spoken about his two chamber operas, *The Corridor* and *The Cure*, and of his pleasure in being in on the rehearsals for the double bill performed at Aldeburgh in 2015. As a result of this collaboration with the performers and conductor, he made some adjustments to the score. But, he remarks, these were in the service of making what he had in mind crystal clear.

As Birtwistle is suspicious of conductors who might use his music to show off, I imagine he would not have admired Sam Mendes's frank and disarming admission of his own early attempts to make a mark by showmanship (without, hopefully, cheapening or distorting the work): 'Revivals of Shakespeare are often self-serving, self-publicising, more about yourself than about some simple basic truth. I'm concerned with what will amaze others and draw attention to myself.' Novelty is also important, Mendes added: 'You can't set *Much Ado about Nothing* in the Raj, for example, since John Barton has already done that.'

Birtwistle is clearly right that the main task is to realise the text. However, there is surely no single realisation. The squiggles cannot be absolutely definitive. The task of interpretation is complex. Whichever orchestra he conducted, Klemperer made a distinctively Klemperer sound. Moreover there is, I suggest, the possibility of *unconscious* intention in author or composer, who may not fully understand all the interrelations or alternative possibilities inherent in his own composition. Once it has gone public, his piece becomes, I would think, public property. Whereas Birtwistle seems to believe that there could be a single definitive performance of his music.

There are, clearly, differences between conducting and theatre directing. There is usually less discussion, rehearsal, and give-and-take between performers and these musical 'auteurs'. There is less democracy of input towards a final form. The differences must in part be to do with various practicalities. You can't engage in detailed, free-ranging discussions with the hundred or more players in many modern orchestras. And conductors frequently fly in for a few concerts in as many days, and fly out again.

One intrinsic distinction is that the language of music is so different from the language of a play, whose meaning is to be found, largely or at least primarily, in the words of the text. Conductors rely less on words, though occasionally the right words do win over the players. Even more occasionally, conductors engage orchestras by the depth of their understanding of a composer, as, I understand, Mackerras himself did with the music of Czech composer Leos Janacek.

Carlos Kleiber, the Austrian conductor born in 1930, is regarded by many as the doyen of conductors. One recording shows him conducting rehearsals with the Stuttgart Symphony Orchestra of the Overture to Johann Strauss's *Die Fledermaus*. There is evidence of much hard work, by orchestra and conductor alike, during these rehearsals. For his part Kleiber uses words fluently, vividly, evocatively. His method seems to be to chivvy the instrumentalists into the spirit of the music, into playfulness. I am reminded of the Bushmen dancing the animals they hunt. One passage of music is heard by Kleiber as, and to be played as

Virginal, sensual, dishonest; depicting (if you like) someone charming their way in, touching 'first the hair, then the skin . . . It's not an honest touch, unlike a robust handshake; don't play it as if you're overweight! . . . A rush of hormones here! . . . Here he dances lightly . . . This next bit must be played commandingly; a gorgeous woman with long legs floats by, the more affecting because of her slight look of contempt . . . It's too studied here, too academic . . . You're

tickling her too hard, it must be very light or it doesn't work
... This bit isn't very clear; it's more malicious than crazy,
as if you took off with the cash box!

All these words are said quickly, lightly, expressively and intensely. Kleiber makes movements with his whole body, indicating the gait, the dance, the rhythm and meaning of each passage, all interspersed with his humming of themes and his tripping indications, with fast verbal trills, or crisp beats of hand or baton, of the rhythm and the mood.

From time to time Kleiber asks the orchestra to bear with him, to be patient with his interruptions. It will come right. He doesn't know how to conduct this part, and 'Perhaps that is the point – it's crackling with tension – we want it to come together but it won't. It's very dirty' (the German word is *schweinisch*). He asks one section of the players to 'be nutty for a bit. Let the others play.' He wants one phrase played with 'nicotine, more tar, more poison', another sharply – as if a musical phrase is 'equivalent to saying "Be quiet"'; and then he proposes an image of 'a violinist who wants to kill a conductor – do these violinists', he wonders aloud, 'want to kill me for all this interference?' Kleiber voices his own reaction to the music, sees it in the reaction of the players to his conducting and his rehearsal methods, using all this to get the sound he wants. At one point he says he is after a sound that is 'hard but light'.

So: hard work and inspiration; preparation and letting go; excellence as a human being and technical knowledge; authenticity and wanting to make a mark. And, most notably with Kleiber, a use of words and bodily gesture to coax the orchestra to give him in rehearsal, and the audience at the concert later that day, the energy, drama and emotion that he finds in the score. Kleiber says at one point: 'The technique *is* the expression.'

4. Fierce Concentration, Shaky Hands

In his job as a tree cutter, Piraji Gajaj carried his life in his hands. Doctors like cancer specialist Siddhartha Mukherjee carry the lives of their patients in their hands. They risk being overwhelmed by the uncertainties and complexities of their responsibility. When Mukherjee started his advanced training in cancer, a colleague took him aside. 'It's called an immersive training programme. But by "immersive" they really mean "drowning".' Mukherjee began his Pulitzer Prize-winning book *The Emperor of All Maladies* in order to keep himself afloat.

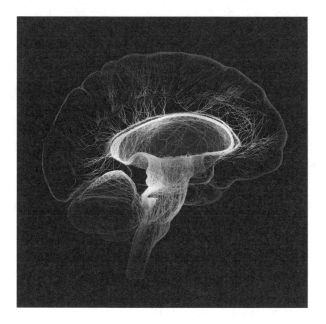

Unlike Piraji, Henry Marsh, a British neurosurgeon, acknowledges anxiety, fear and guilt. He admits to wishing he could avoid facing those who have suffered as a result of his mistakes. There are constantly difficult choices to be made: to operate or not, to get out the last traces of a tumour or to be satisfied with a job that is imperfect, and so on. He recognises the role of luck, good and bad, but this does not remove the inevitability of remorse and misery when things go wrong. He also recognises the negative impact on his state of mind, and potentially on the quality of his work, of what he experiences as irritating NHS management initiatives, and the absurdities of some health and safety requirements.

Marsh is strikingly honest, not least about the ever-present temptation to surgical heroism. The catastrophic outcome of one operation, which he undertook as a relatively inexperienced consultant, taught him never again to be tempted to take on a job that a more senior surgeon had declined.

'In those years', he writes, 'I was in awe of the big names of international neurosurgery, whom you could hear giving keynote lectures at conferences where they showed cases like the man in front of me, and the amazing results they achieved, quite beyond anything I had yet done.' The case arrived as a result of a flattering phone call from Professor M, a senior neurosurgeon for whom 'self-doubt never seemed to be a problem', offering him the job as a sort of 'papal dispensation'. The first few hours of the operation went perfectly. By midnight, after fifteen hours, it looked as though most of the tumour was out and the cranial nerves were not damaged. 'I started to feel', Marsh suggests, with more than a tinge of sarcasm towards his own pretensions, 'that I was joining the ranks of the really big neurosurgeons, whose keynote lecture scans never, of course, showed residual tumours.'

Hubris drove him on, and disaster struck. He 'tore a small branch off the basal artery . . . the blood loss was trivial, but the damage to the brainstem was terrible. As a result the patient never woke up, and that was why, seven years later, I saw him curled into a sad ball, on a bed in the nursing home.'

Mukherjee reports that in his field, too, there have always been dangers of over-confidence, notably in the use of radical mastectomy in the 1970s. Cancer surgeons thought, mistakenly, that each radicalisation of the procedure was progress. 'Bristling with conceit, and hypnotised by the power of medicine, oncologists pushed their patients – and their discipline – to the brink of disaster.'

The neurosurgeon will inevitably often have good reason to be uncertain. For instance, it may be impossible to predict whether a tumour will peel off the brain easily, or will stick and tear. More generally, the worst torments suffered by doctors arise when they are uncertain about whether they can, or should, help.

Marsh is unflinching in telling us about his own flaws and disasters. Among the lessons he learned from the awful outcome of the damage to the brainstem of the patient referred by Professor M was that he needed to become more cautious in his methods, operating in stages, if necessary over some weeks, and with a colleague. As a result, he would rarely let an operation take more than seven or eight hours (that earlier one went on for eighteen). He developed a healthy scepticism towards keynote lecturers.

But there is no getting away from the agonising dilemmas of the job. Surgeons are human beings, subject to 'cognitive biases'. They are also liable to be torn between the fear of cowardice if they refrain from intervening, and of grandiosity if they make the attempt. In fact, despite the case just referred to, Marsh became bolder with experience. It is 'only with endless practice that you learn you can get away with things that at first seemed far too frightening'. On reflection, he says:

> You only get good at doing the really difficult cases if you
> get a lot of practice, but that means making lots of mistakes
> at first and leaving a trail of injured patients behind you.
> I suspect you've got to be a bit of a psychopath to carry on, or

at least have a pretty thick skin. If you're a nice doctor you'll probably give up, let Nature take its course and stick to the simpler cases.

Marsh hopes that he is a good surgeon, but thinks he is not a great surgeon. But then perhaps those thus acclaimed *are* psychopaths.

Another dilemma is the constant need to balance optimism against reality, or, as Mukherjee puts it about cancer: 'the queasy pivoting between defeatism and hope'. A doctor needs to offer patients something to look forward to or to soften terrible news. Under pressure from patients and their families to 'do something', he may find it easier to go against his better judgment, and operate, than to be honest and let nature take its course. Marsh writes of the family of one young woman, Helen, who would look at him with such an intensity of hope and desperation that their 'eyes felt like nail guns fixing him to the wall'.

Doctors are anxious to help, but wary in their sympathy. Mukherjee again: 'Walking across the hospital in the morning to draw yet another bone-marrow biopsy, with the wintry light cross-hatching the rooms, I felt a certain dread descend on me, a heaviness that bordered on sympathy but never quite achieved it.'

Patients become objects of fear and anxiety as well as sympathy, Marsh says. And the less responsibility you have the easier it is to feel compassion. The result: anxiety tends to grow as you climb the professional ladder. Sympathy is a burden.

Detachment and compassion present conflicting claims on the surgeon. To be able to enter the mysterious and private space of someone's body, with sharp knives, risking disaster, doctors probably need to depersonalise their patients to some extent. One form this takes in neurosurgery is the still-current practice of shaving the heads of patients before operating. Marsh suspects that the real – albeit usually unconscious – reason is that it is no longer a *person's* head you are entering, but a patch of bone covered by skin.

When Marsh himself was about to undergo an operation for a detached retina, he was struck by the incongruity between his predicament as a patient ('in a gown and paper knickers') and his regal professional standing as the consultant surgeon. After describing the agonies he and his wife experienced when their own baby son was diagnosed with a brain tumour, he comments on how personal anguish provides a useful lesson for doctors: 'Doctors, I tell my trainees with a laugh, can't suffer enough.' Yet at the same time, 'It would be impossible to do the work if you felt the patient's fear and suffering yourself.'

The reader (and potential patient) is shocked to be told what we ought to be able to imagine for ourselves, but would be reluctant to, that our neurosurgeon occasionally finds his hands shaking as he operates, sometimes from anxiety (for example after a recent failure or bad outcome), or, on one occasion at least, from anger at the absurdity of some hospital management directive. Do such intrusions on the surgeon's serenity interfere with his calm professional skill? Usually not, Marsh says; when operating, he is taken up with 'the thrill of the chase' and then the 'morbid fear disappears', and he works in a state of 'fierce and happy concentration'.

Marsh describes vividly the amazing and beautiful world of the physical brain. 'The view down the microscope into the patient's brain is indeed a little magical – clearer, sharper and more brilliant than the world outside, the world of . . . paperwork and protocols.' He 'loves the microscope that takes him close up into this world, which, after so many years of operating with it, has become an extension of my own body . . . It feels as though I am actually climbing down the microscope into the patient's head, and the tips of my microscopic instruments feel like the tips of my own fingers.'

His job takes him hard up against the incomprehensible wonders of metaphysical questions. Soon after describing his mother's death, he ponders the 'binding problem' – the philosophical question 'how can brute matter give rise to consciousness?'

Marsh's description of his journeys into the brain is conveyed with many images of his role. These pictures animate and inform his sense of his own work. He is a 'medieval knight going to slay a mythical dragon', the patient is being 'stalked by death'. He is engaged in 'single combat with an enemy within'. He is a 'bomb disposal expert' (except that 'in his case a mistake will kill only the patient'). He is 'in a war zone'. He may feel after a successful operation that he is 'a conquering general post-battle'. He is the 'captain of a ship'. (I am reminded of Freud's description of himself as a 'conquistador'.) At the same time he is modest: 'Doctors like to talk of the "art and science" of medicine. I have always found this rather pretentious, and prefer to see what I do as a practical craft. Clipping aneurisms is a skill, and one that takes years to learn.'

One image links him with Piraji Gajaj. Marsh is talking about occasions where patients might sue. 'When I receive one of these letters, or one from a solicitor announcing the intention of a patient of mine to sue, I am forced to see the great distance beneath the rope on which I am balancing and the ground below.'

Tightropes, power and the ever-present possibility of a catastrophic misjudgment. It is disconcerting to know how flawed and limited our doctors are, but good to realise that there are some who can face and learn from such limitations.

13

A TINY MISTAKE IN
THE BLINK OF AN EYE

The important thing is to approach the next event as if nothing has gone on before.

David Florence

———

David Florence has twice been world champion at canoe singles (C1), once world champion at canoe doubles (C2), and three times silver medallist in the Olympics – at Beijing (in C1), and in London and Rio (both in C2, with his partner, Richard Hounslow). We've arranged to meet in a large café in his home town in Essex; arriving, I take up a position near the door. I have little idea what he looks like, having seen only one picture of him, intensely elated in the water, and he has no idea what I look like. I notice this tall man, wearing a University of Canterbury, New Zealand, tracksuit top, pushing a pushchair with a small girl in it, and wonder. It is indeed Florence, who minutes later phones me from inside the café.

From that first T-shirted glimpse, I retain the image of those New Zealand cricketers I have known – lean, strong, fit; modest but assured. And I recall the fact that many early-nineteenth-century settlers in New Zealand were indeed

Scottish, like Florence; tough and determined, as well as quiet and unassuming.

I had been shown an article in the *Guardian* newspaper about his experiences in Rio. On Tuesday 9 August 2016, the day after his thirty-fourth birthday, he had finished last in the C1 final, when he was the favourite to win. A mere two days later he and Hounslow won silver in C2. What caused the poor result on Tuesday, followed by the excellent one on Thursday? Were these fantastic shifts in form, or a matter of luck? Why did this top athlete veer about in such an apparently crazy way?

I ask him first about canoeing and how he came to it. His father, who was a Scottish canoe champion, kept a canoe by the side of their house in Edinburgh, not far from the Water of Leith. One day David and his younger brother, Fraser, who also became a top British canoeist until he suffered a common canoeing injury – a dislocated shoulder – tried it out, and were quickly hooked. David was fourteen.

At eighteen he chose Nottingham University, where he read mathematical physics, because it was the site of the National Watersports Centre, with a slalom course, on an offshoot of the River Trent. By the end of the third year, his results on the water were good enough for him to win a grant that enabled him to be a full-time athlete: not quite a professional in the sense of having a contract, he tells me, but enough to keep going and compete at the highest level. He was pleased not to have to bother any more with exams and lectures, and to be able to attend all the camps.

He had no qualms or uncertainties about this course of action. He loved canoeing and still does. Several times in our talk he mentions enjoyment. 'I love training, too,' he says. 'Not every moment, of course, but I love what it builds towards, and always enjoy the sense that I am improving myself. Even on a winter's day, practising on my own, not for anyone else to see, I feel good that I'm an athlete, good that I'm good at it.'

I ask him about luck. 'It comes in quite a bit,' he tells me. 'There is no direct racing against competitors, side by side. As in skiing, races are against the clock, with two-second penalty points if you touch a gate. The breeze may get up during the competition, behind you or against you. The water changes. And in the Olympics, all hinges on one run, which you have been four years training for.'

Florence tells me that the margins are so fine that it is rare for anyone to be a medal-winner in several competitions in a year. It is possible to be ranked number one in the world if you come, say, first, second, tenth, fifteenth and thirty-seventh in the major tournaments. In one European Championship, a 'guy who had come fortieth – last – in the heats won a medal in the final'. Only rarely does someone 'sit on top' for a whole season.

In the Olympics there is a preliminary round, judged on the best of two runs each. In the C1 event at Rio, Florence didn't bother with his second run, as he had the fastest time on his 'perfect' first run. He thought it a small advantage not to tire himself. 'Of course, they might have all done marvellous times, so that I wouldn't have qualified, but it was extremely unlikely.'

The night before the semi-finals, the gates are repositioned in a configuration not known to the competitors before the day's competition. (Virtually the only requirement the event organisers need to comply with is that there must be between eighteen and twenty-five gates, six of them upstream on the edge of the eddy.) In the semi-final, Florence made a mistake off the start, 'eddying out' (which I gather means losing momentum) and having to flip back. But he got into the final easily enough, for which the fastest ten qualify, coming seventh without forcing the pace.

In the final, the order in which competitors set off is the

reverse of their positions in the semi-final, so he started fourth, a position he was happy with. Sometimes it is hard to keep level-headed when you know people going off before you have done exceptionally good times. In fact, a journalist noted that in Rio no canoeist who had come first in the semi-finals won a medal of any sort. (Florence thinks this is probably a random event, but he isn't sure. However, in the London final in 2012 he and Hounslow had gone last, and won silver.)

The results of the earlier rounds have no bearing on the final. The slates are wiped clean. At the final stage, all depends on the single run. So what happened?

David tells me he was in good shape and good spirits. His training had gone well. The British team had spent two weeks in Rio in each of the four months preceding the Games, and had got to know the whole river and its channels well. He had competed in only two other international races that year, for one of which he had had no time to practise following the birth of Josie, now quietly present in her pushchair beside him. He had won no medals, but this had, he felt, no bearing on his success or otherwise at Rio. In the four years since the last Olympics, Florence had won three World Championship golds. His morale was high. And after the two rounds, his performance had been 'ninety-nine per cent spot-on'.

River conditions were perfect for the final. In the first third of the course everything went well for him. Then, on a more inconsistent piece of water, he 'cut the line too tight, was left struggling to get through the next gate, and had to paddle back'. This left him needing to make up time. Then, disaster: 'Punting' (that is, pushing off the bank with his paddle to move upstream), 'the paddle slipped on the bank. I ended up in the wrong part of the eddy, which made manoeuvring slow. I was a fraction off, one mistake on a single move.'

And that was it. It was not easy for someone ignorant of canoeing to understand all the technicalities, but even I could see how small the margin was.

So how did he cope with it? How did he turn things round, with Hounslow, a mere two days later, when the first round of the doubles took place? According to the *Guardian*, he himself had said that he 'got over his defeat by brooding'.

'It wasn't quite like that,' he tells me. He was of course 'hugely disappointed'. He was also 'quite surprised; I expected to win, or at least to be in contention. But these ups and downs are part of the sport; part of what makes it exciting, but (again) hugely disappointing when you have done so much right, and one run in four years . . . From an external view I had failed.'

I read to him another part of the newspaper article, quoting his doubles partner as saying that he, Hounslow, 'did his best to get Florence up . . . But with David you don't need to do too much. He is a professional. Sometimes you've got to let him go off and stew in his emotions. I guess controlled anger is almost a good thing.'

Again, Florence demurs. 'For me, so-called constructive anger doesn't work. I'm not saying it won't work for everyone. It's not right for me. There is a risk in going in aiming to do something you're not capable of. I *was* very quiet for a while. I can be insular. But the important thing is to approach the next event *as if nothing has gone on before*. I think that for C2 I was calm, measured, focused and ready, no different from how I'd want to be if I'd won the C1.'

'Quite an achievement,' I say, 'to manage this internally. And this seems to confirm that doing well is not just a matter of technique?'

'Definitely there is a psychological element,' he replies, 'not just in competition but in training too, in not wasting training time in frustrating ways. It was', he repeats, 'a tiny mistake that happened in a blink of an eye, with an awful result.'

'By being insular, quiet, you managed to get back to a fresh, open, optimistic attitude, then?' I suggest.

'It was a time to think. I was quiet, but not unpleasant. Next day I was on the bank to support my mates on their big day. You wouldn't see all the team do that.'

'Did you do it through gritted teeth?' I ask.

'No, I felt a responsibility. I didn't want to throw my disappointment in their faces.'

'You must be the senior member of the team, so do they look up to you?'

'Don't know about the most senior, but the most decorated. It's hard to know if they look to me. In sport people also do their own thing.'

What he was looking for in C2 was a 'solid performance'. He wasn't drawn to attempt anything too glamorous, he was not going to go over the top. 'That's what we try for most, we try not to do anything wild. It's so hard to be consistent. We try to deliver what we're capable of, Richard and I, and be in control.'

He refers to the privilege of taking part in the Olympics: even some world champions have never made it to the Games. 'It is an amazing place to be. It is great fun, the aim is to focus only on the moment, from start to finish. In C1 I had a fantastic start, ruined by one small mistake. In C2 we were in a medal position the whole way through.'

We speak more generally about form and attitude.

There are times when it feels as though nothing can go wrong. I have had that experience and then had things go wrong. But sometimes they've gone fantastically well, too. It's not all random, of course. On average some regularly perform and win lots of medals, while others never win a medal in their entire career. On the whole, if you're in a good frame of mind your chances of delivering are higher, though it's not a 100 per cent correlation. Poor thinking, lack of confidence' – it seems hard for him to remember such a state, though he thinks it must have been so for him at times – 'then one is much more likely to do badly.

I ask if his 'hinterland' helps his form and performance; besides the mathematical physics, there is the remarkable fact that before Beijing he taught himself Mandarin, before Rio Portuguese, both times from audio and from books, so as to be competent to discuss the races with local journalists. I mention too the fact that he plays the bagpipes. Does all this help him?

I still get interested in maths problems from time to time, though not as much as when there was another mathematician in the team. Nor are these problems as difficult as those I was working on for my degree. As for the languages, that's a hobby, and I like it. Yes, it makes my focus broader. I enjoy it. There is a lot of downtime in our sport. In Rio we were on buses, stuck in traffic. The other guys would look out of the window, or listen to their music. I got on with my Portuguese grammar. I reckon I come out of it with something. And it takes my mind away. I'm as committed as anyone, I love it, the canoeing, but if slalom ceased to exist tomorrow, I'd have a fantastic life anyhow. I'd have to find another job, though,' he grins. 'Whereas for a younger chap, for whom it is all there is, that may be all right when things are going well. But when they go badly, there's nothing.

David Florence clearly does things his own way. He was the first slalom canoeist for decades to compete in both single and double forms of competition. The latter is a very different skill, he tells me. 'When Hounslow and I started together, eight years ago, we were really poor. It turned out that a French guy, Fabian Lefevre, was doing the same, doing both forms. It means of course that you train for half the time at singles that your opponents do, and also half the time at doubles.'

Florence and Lefevre have transformed the sport in this way. Now several canoeists do both.

He is totally autonomous in his training. He almost never goes to the gym. He believes in training by canoeing. He tries not to waste time, though the team may want the gates set up in ways that are not so helpful to him at certain times. He has a coach, Mark Delaney, who is there for 80 per cent of his training. But as with Graham Gooch and the England batsmen, what he offers is not so much technical advice, and certainly not 'authoritarian' coaching, as sometimes happens with the younger players, although Delaney does sometimes spot things from the bank, or suggest a route through a gate that the German guy, say, has found works better.

I ask Florence if he feels the best equipment gives a cutting edge. He doesn't think so. All the players use the same firms, often the same boats and paddles. The England team had new paddles made for the Olympics. He says a Slovakian canoeist (one of the gold-winning pair in C2) agreed about the same boat they each have, that it isn't much different from others. I say: 'So there is camaraderie among the top canoeists?'

'With some,' he says. 'Others are more insular, but a lot are surprisingly open. Bizarrely, the secretiveness can be greater within one's own team, especially for the Olympics, where only one boat per country is allowed in each class, whereas in the World Championship, up to three are allowed. The Olympics are such a big deal in the sport.'

We are nearing the end. I ask him about planning and spontaneity. Which is more important? He says they plan a lot. 'You get to know the water in advance of the competition. But if you ask me where exactly I put my hands for a particular move, how I do it in order to put the bows around as I go through a particular gate, I wouldn't be able to tell you. If I thought about it too much I probably wouldn't be able to do it.' As to general approaches, he says simply: 'If the water is massively difficult I concentrate on trying to position the boat the right way. The flatter the course, the more I must attack.'

Aiming at Consistency

In slalom canoeing, in white water, one mistake within an otherwise perfect run can have disastrous results. This fact of life makes consistency Florence's primary aim. In this respect he is like the batsman, for whom a single error or good ball may end his innings, and unlike the bowler, who has many opportunities – six an over – to regain the initiative and end up on top. Canoeing also resembles both neurosurgery and tree surgery. Like Piraji, Florence strives to keep himself on an even keel; not only in his primary concern to avoid mistakes, but also in his efforts to avoid emotions such as anger or fear that could disturb his inner calm, and lead him to try to do more than he is capable of. His aim in competition is to put in a solid performance as often as possible, to do what he can do and trust that it will, often enough, be good enough. Only on flatter water will he really attack the gates to gain the crucial small advantage. The more choppy or difficult the conditions, the more his task, as he sees it, is to put and keep the boat in the right place. He does not go in for 'glory shots'. He knows he has no second chance after a mistake like the one in the C1 final at Rio, when his paddle slipped on the bank.

Tiny mistakes can have awful outcomes.

PART VI: AND NOW FOR SOMETHING COMPLETELY DIFFERENT

14

FREUDIAN SLIP

I couldn't come without the 'orse, m'Lord.

Fred Winter

In 1961, my first summer at Cambridge, I kept wicket for the university. Fielding at first slip, next to me, was Edward Craig, a Lancastrian studying Moral Sciences, the formal name for philosophy. Much later he became Professor of Philosophy at Cambridge. We had plenty of days in the field when nothing much came our way, not least against the Australian tourists, each of whose first four batsmen scored centuries in the same innings. Halfway through that afternoon, Richard Jefferson, our best bowler, bowled a ball that passed the outside edge of some-one's bat. Enthusiastically, I said to the captain, David Kirby, 'That was a beauty, it moved off the seam.' Kirby replied, in his Eeyore voice: 'You've got to move one if you bowl all bloody day.'

To help pass those long days in the field, Edward would pose philosophical questions to me, sometimes between deliveries. 'Can we ever not know the contents of our own minds?' 'Are aesthetic judgments all subjective?' 'Is there such a thing as freedom?' And so on. I'm not sure we were sophisticated enough to apply such questions to our own activities: was it really a subjective question whether that ball of Jefferson's was a beauty? Or: did we have a *free* choice whether to play forward or back?

But I found these long conversations stimulating and mind-opening. In my second year, I went to lectures by Renford Bambrough, later my supervisor at St John's College, on Greek philosophy, a topic in Part One of the Classical Tripos. He made what seemed incomprehensible at least thinkable – I was even naive enough at this stage to be puzzled by the idea of beauty lying in the eye of the beholder. Here was another pull towards Moral Sciences, to which I changed in my third year. And, though academic British and American philosophy in the 1960s did not focus on Freud, his account of the nature of mind, and his elaboration of self-deception as not only conceptually possible but actual and ubiquitous, questioning Descartes' starting point for the possibility of knowledge, quickly became an area of fascination for me. I soon gave up wicketkeeping, and spent a lot of time fielding at slip.

In 1963, not long after these momentous events, the first professional limited-overs competition, the Gillette Cup, became part of the regular fixture list. One day Richard Hutton, the son of Leonard, and another member of the university side, pronounced balefully: 'Limited-overs cricket is not cricket.' He was comparing this form of the game unfavourably with traditional time-limited versions. In the latter, there is a logical space for what is in fact a regular result, called a 'draw', when the side batting last has not reached their target, but nor have they been bowled out. In limited-overs games, there is no room for such an outcome. Richard was trying to persuade me that this real difference is a crucial one, sufficient to differentiate cricket from what is not cricket. He was in fact making a philosophical point about the concept of cricket. Like many philosophers, he made it as a paradox, for limited-overs cricket is no distant relative to time-limited cricket – if we follow Ludwig Wittgenstein's notion of 'family resemblances' they are siblings rather than second cousins twice removed.

In the course of writing this book, conceptual, philosophical questions have arisen about the notion of form that I am writing about, and about other versions of 'form'. In this chapter I will reflect on some of these: on form versus content, for instance, and on formal as opposed to material explanations of events, particularly of actions.

On Form: A Psychological Concept?

But first another set of questions. How much is being on form a concept that signifies an inner state, verifiable by how we feel in the theatre of the mind? Or is it a concept that refers to the shared, objective world?

Many years ago, I wrote an essay for a postgraduate seminar at the University of California at Irvine led by Daniel Dennett, now a prominent philosopher of science, entitled 'Is "know" a psychological predicate?' The main point was that, for a claim to *knowledge* to be verified or falsified, something other than the subject's inner state must be the case. 'Know' is a term of solidity of achievement, as well as a term for someone's mental state. When my beliefs are in question, by contrast, I have special authority (though not ultimate authority; we may say of a politician that 'he believes in free trade, but look at his actions – whenever we have a trade imbalance, he wants to slap import duties on!'). When I make a claim to knowledge, my authority is much more easily and categorically overthrown – for example, by the demonstration that what I claimed to know is false. I no doubt believe many things that are not true, but I can't (as a matter of logic) *know* things that are untrue. There is false belief but not false knowledge. Moreover, to know something we also need to have grounds or evidence for it: belief in something that is true does not necessarily amount to knowledge.

So one question that arises in trying to write about form (in the sense I've been doing) is: is being on form more like knowing, or more like believing? Is being on form an achievement term, which we agree to attribute only if the person's state of mind is corroborated by his actions in the world? Is it thus an 'objective' concept? Or is it, like 'belief', subjective?

We know what we would say if someone pronounces himself to be in excellent form, but to outside observers he keeps failing, or looks disjointed and out of shape; or if he disclaims form, saying he doesn't feel right, or something is missing, and yet he looks to us assured in his performance over a period of time. Would we not think ourselves justified in overruling him as mistaken, without ignoring what he has to say? Whatever his internal state, we might say, he is in the first instance *off* form, in the second *on* form. His self-image is unreliable. His view of his form is distorted, in his own favour or self-disparagingly. Whether or not he is on form is mainly a matter of how he is in the world.

'In the zone' seems to me to be somewhat different. I think of it as being closer to a psychological concept, more about a state of mind, more like 'inspired' or 'ecstatic' or 'detached' or 'calm'. Pelé could say that in the final of the 1958 football World Cup he felt euphoric, in the zone. He felt he could 'run all day without tiring', he could 'dribble through any of their team or all of them'. He said he could 'almost pass through them physically' – a comment that, though materially impossible, seems to epitomise being in the zone: it's more about a person's feelings than his performance, more a matter of the *sense of* being on top of the world than of evidentially, to the impartial outside eye, being there.

This distinction needs qualification. First, the concepts of mind and body are more mixed, more mongrel, less pure, than we tend at first to think – including 'on form' and 'in the zone' themselves. We have moved away from the Cartesian world of mind and body as different substances, worlds apart, mysteriously connected by a gland in the brain. Terms for emotions, for instance, refer to bodily as well as mental phenomena. We make a psychological assertion when we say of someone that he is jealous, or angry, but the truth or falsity of the assertion is also a matter of how that person behaves; others are in a position to confirm or deny it. We may well be mistaken about our own states of mind. We are self-deceived, we have illusions about ourselves, we de-form our inner worlds. Psychoanalysts are particularly concerned with self-deception, with unconscious motives and states of mind, especially those we don't want to know.

But even if I am resistant to knowing, or unable to know in my own case, I am an authority on my own states of mind *in a way that no one else is,* as John Wisdom, my philosophy professor at Cambridge, put it.

Form and Content/Matter

Approaching a book titled *On Form,* as this book is, one's first expectation might be that its topic would be form as related to content, or perhaps form as related to matter. What makes a good novel, work of art or piece of music, say: is it form or content, form or matter? How are the two related? Are there rules of composition? But I have not been primarily concerned with such questions. Mine are to do with what it is for someone to be on form in whatever activity he is engaged in. Is a batsman or a team on form on the field of play? Is a writer 'back to his best form' in his latest novel?

There is though, I suggest, an overlap between these two uses of the term. Form replaces chaos; light, darkness. The second verse of the Bible reads: 'And the earth was *without form*, and void; and darkness was upon the face of the deep. And the Spirit of God moved upon the face of the waters' (italics added). In the New Testament, St John's Gospel proclaims: 'In the beginning was the word, and the word was with God, and the word was God.' The Greek for 'word' is *logos* (λόγος), which also means rationality; having a structure and a purpose. Thus darkness is transformed into light, agglomerated particles into structured entities; chaos into meaningfulness, random physiological movements into purposeful actions and thinking. 'God' – the god in us, the quintessence of humanity – is capable of transmuting the thing into the animal, the animal into the human, the instinctual human creature into the self-aware person. Entropy evolves into order. New kinds of order evolve. Form (as opposed to matter, content) means coherence, order – and so it does in being on form.

Aristotle

Aristotle was possibly the first to theorise the distinction between matter (*hyle*; ὕλη) and form (*eidos*; εἶδος or *morphe*; μορφή). He rejected the abstract Platonic notion of Forms, arguing that every sensory material object is to be construed in terms of both matter and form, neither of which can exist without the other. For Aristotle, matter was the (relatively) undifferentiated primal element: that from which particular things develop. Such a development – from this base matter or material, from content – consists in differentiation, the acquiring of the particular forms of which the knowable universe consists.

According to Aristotle, the matter of a thing consists of those elements of it that may be said to constitute it; and the form is the arrangement or organisation of these elements, as the result of which they have become the thing that they then are. Thus, bricks and mortar are the matter that, given one form, becomes a house, or, given another, a wall. As matter they have the potential to become many different kinds of things. Here 'matter' is a relative term: a brick, while potentially the constituent matter of a house, is already formed into a brick; i.e. it too is a composite of form and matter, clay being the basic matter out of which the brick is formed, just as the brick is the material for the house or the wall. The word for unmade-up cloth is 'material'.

One may be more struck either by a lack of form, or by a lack of substance, and these possibilities make sense of the fact that we use each term both pejoratively and to praise.

Form Good, Matter Bad or Disruptive

Following one line of thought, 'form' suggests creative and benign organisation. The word 'shape' may help us get hold of this notion of form – we speak of 'being in good shape', or 'shaping up well'; of 'being ship-shape'. When things are form-less, twisted out of shape, when matter lacks organisation, there is disorder, even chaos. A team, a social grouping, or the team within the individual, falls apart into anarchic disharmony. This use of the concept amplifies the loss of form that results from fragmentation and conflict, as in, for instance, the antagonism and chaos of civil war. Things fall apart.

Sometimes there is a need for a radical transformation, or re-formation, as when an entire field – physics, or philosophy, or psychology, say – is revolutionised; or a whole personality, even a whole culture, having been disrupted beyond anyone's capacity to anticipate the kinds of change that will emerge, reconfigures itself.

For concrete to fulfil its role in load-bearing, builders create plywood forms. They pre-stress the concrete, that is, they put it under pressure by means of a slight curvature in the wooden form, to allow it to ease into a more rectilinear shape under the stress of its load. In similar ways, we humans sometimes train ourselves – subjecting army recruits, for instance, to hardship. Surviving stresses may toughen us, with the result that later we are able to bear the loads that come our way.

Imposed, Oppressive Form – Insubstantiality

A contrasting version of loss of form is that it is a result of *imposed, repressive, distorting,* as opposed to *inherent,* form. Or 'form' becomes the be-all and end-all.

Each individual human being has potential, which may or may not be shaped into satisfactory form. Potential form may be inhibited or distorted, just as a tree grows crookedly because of its environment. Like the tree, the person will of course also have some genetic tendency to grow in one of a limited number of ways. An oak may be bent out of shape, but it is not bent into an ash.

In these types of loss of form the basic matter, the potential, the seed in the self or in the members of a team or society, is not given a chance to develop, but is stereotyped or suppressed by adverse, often external forces. Largely unarticulated personal and cultural demands and assumptions set the parameters for our lives, often restrictively. Man (or child) is reduced; he becomes closer to being a mere robot or machine. He fits in with a controlling plan laid out for him. Donald Winnicott refers to a 'false self' personality, someone who, unable to develop his own spontaneous self, lives a false life of compliance. A cage may be gilded but it is still a cage. Agendas that are inappropriately imposed create resistance to a full or spontaneous engagement with life.

These suppressing agendas are also internalised, resulting often in passivity and lifelessness. The harshness of our super-egos may be predominantly the result of a harsh upbringing, or they may be more a result of a projection of harshness onto authority figures, which are then internalised as such. Either way, a severe superego is likely to exaggerate errors into major failures of character, thus preventing us from living up to our potential. 'There you go again, you are *always* like this.' Skilfully and subtly, we talk ourselves down. In ways that are destructive to our egos, we condemn ourselves not only with 'You always do this' (when we don't), but also with 'And that means you are worthless not only as a performer/player but as a person.' We set up before ourselves ideals of perfection, which mean that any-thing less is of no value. We undermine ourselves.

It is not always easy to put one's finger on the difference between two types of superego: a firm constructive guide, on one side, and a tyrannical master, whether internal or external, on the other. Exactly the same words may be used by two ana-lysts, say, or parents, or superegos, in similar contexts, to convey very different messages to the patient, child or self. One voice does so with an undertone of disdain and moralistic blame, exaggerating the individual's ordinary errors; the other is more simply blunt, willing to call a spade a spade, kindly confronting things that need to be faced. One person speaks from a supe-rior position, as if such tendencies were beneath him, another from a context of acknowledgement of his own destructiveness, aware at some level that 'there but for the grace of God go I' – or 'there, hoping for the grace of God, go I'. We might be tempted to say that the same matter (words) may be *formed* differently by different subliminal intentions, feelings or messages, that in these contrasting cases the material (content) is the same but the form (expression) is different. In fact I think shifts of form are also shifts of content. Form is not a kind of curlicue added to what is already there.

Within human lives there is a spectrum from being a plaything of external and internal forces, a thing in the world, to being a person – a subject and agent – in a fuller sense.

One element of being a unique person, capable of being on form in a solid way, is the ability to see things for what they are. Psychoanalysts attempt to clear their minds of fixed expectations and filters, in order to be open to the new or the different in the patient. They are aware of how readily a moralistic attitude prevents us from seeing how things really are. They may be too narrowly fixated on theorics, which act like blinkers rather than helpful frames for thought.

Form can also degenerate into *mere* formality, so that people become shallow or refined in their way of being. They go through the motions. They are, we say, *insubstantial*, that is, superficial. Mere manners have become to them more important than getting things done, or than having anything frank or robust to say. We prejudge, are prejudiced – dismissing strangers too quickly because they wear the 'wrong' clothes or speak with the 'wrong' accent. From a Soviet point of view, much modern art was corrupted by the crime of 'formalism', the lack of a substantial substrate of passionate support for the class struggle, as Julian Barnes writes, the sin of 'writing for the perverted taste of the bourgeoisie, pandering to a narrow circle of gourmets'.

Leading steeplechase rider Fred Winter was once criticised by an aristocratic owner when his horse, the favourite, finished last. 'Where were you?' demanded his lordship tetchily. 'I couldn't come without the 'orse, m'Lord,' the jockey replied. Horse is matter, rider form. We find form as a result of a helpful balance and collaboration between horse and rider. There is a need for substance, matter, as well as for a guiding principle.

Aristotle's notion of form combines with his teleological – that is, directed forward towards an end or aim – viewpoint to give the conclusion that a human being's behaviour has direction, goal or function. A central feature of Aristotle's account of form and matter is the kind of explanation that is offered in each sphere. He points out that explanation can be given in terms of material causation (along the lines later proposed by David Hume) – when preceding events without which the later event would not have happened are cited as causes. Thus the movement of one billiard ball accounts for that of another; my friend's death was caused by the mycobacterium tuberculosis.

But the question 'Why?' may be asking not for a Humean material explanation but for a formal one. It may call for an answer in terms of the meaning of the event. Philosopher and psychoanalyst Jonathan Lear reminds us how activities also make sense, are explained and unified, when seen under the rubric of their *telos* (τέλος) or aim. A man breeds cows, feeds them with special food to condition their skins, slaughters them, pays particular attention to curing their skins, and then punches holes in the treated skin. What is the meaning of these apparently random actions? Lear shows how they make sense when one knows that he is a shoemaker, plying his trade. Similarly, many different activities, thoughts, images and ways of interacting make sense, are unified, once one understands the conscious or unconscious assumptions, mindsets or aims that link, animate and give them sense.

In this *telos*, this teleological or aim-oriented explanation, we see the link with goodness and desirability (from some point of view) that underlies form in its many meanings – in a sportsman or violinist, as structure in a poem or a play, and as central to Plato's Forms.

Plato

In trying to answer the question 'what do all things of a certain kind, like the [hackneyed] table, or indeed goodness, have in common?' Plato arrived at his answer in terms of Forms, intuited as supra-sensible realities, which, he argued, provide the essence of meaning. They are what make things what they are, of one kind rather than another. The Form of the Good, like the Form of the table, is that without which people are not good, things are not tables, whereas with them they are.

Plato realised moreover that what is essential for something to be of a certain kind is also what makes it good of that kind. If a thing alleged to be or described as being of a certain kind K deviates too far from its excellence as a K, it at some point ceases to be a K (as Richard Hutton proposed about limited-overs cricket). Plato's Forms were the yardstick for things being of a certain kind; a table can hardly stand on two legs alone, so a two-legged table is hardly a table. Something raked at forty-five degrees can scarcely be a table, though it may be a broken table. Similarly, being on form is being excellent in whatever area or category of life one is functioning.

Plato proposed, then, that the Form of a thing has to do with its excellence qua table, or human being, or whatever. The notion of 'good form' (as of the violinist, say) arose from the idea that there is a shape or model for the performance of a skill, whether a general Form (as for Plato) or a personal one. I think the link between form in art and an on-form artist lies in the fact that exemplifying either requires an idea of goodness, of excellence, in approaching its *telos* or aim.

Restrictive Forms of Life

For many of the activities to which we readily apply the notion of form, there are as we have seen bounded physical spaces

– frames, stages, consulting rooms, areas specifically designated for games or play. In these special spaces, in relation to the specific activity of each, different rules apply from those current in everyday social life, and illusion is willingly entered into, whether for escape or for self-discovery. On the stage of psychoanalysis, the analyst will become, and be responded to as, the representative of an internal figure, so that old and underlying scenarios are enacted 'in the playground of the analysis', as Freud suggested. They are then worked on, and over time may become less compulsory. In sport the freedom to throw ourselves into competitive activity, with all the striving at our disposal, puts us in touch with spontaneity and wholeheartedness. For the child, a room with two sofas becomes a beach. These activities – theatre, sport, psychoanalysis, play – have in common a more or less temporary suspension of focus on everyday utilitarian ends; many entail also a suspension of disbelief.

Psychoanalytic and other fields of thought reveal too how unconscious scenarios – complexes, one might almost say – about how things are (or how they 'must be') pervade our thinking, feeling, desiring and acting in many different ways. We expend a lot of energy in arranging our lives according to such scenarios. There are 'games' we all play.

Jean-Paul Sartre, as we have seen, put 'bad faith' at the centre of his philosophy, giving examples of people who, playing such roles without self-awareness, deny or constrain their own freedom. We are all more or less conditioned, of course. Our families, our cultures surround us as the water surrounds, sustains and conditions the life of fish. Two young fish meet an old fish swimming the other way. The old fish asks, 'Morning boys, how's the water?' Politely, the young fish reply, 'Fine, thank you.' Once out of earshot, one says to the other, 'What the hell does he mean, "water"?'

Many of our patterns of thinking are 'hidden in plain sight'. The assumptions of our culture are too familiar to us to be easily noticed, let alone questioned. And even if we do interrogate and disagree with some of these assumptions, we are conditioned by them. As Jawaharlal Nehru said to Bertrand Russell, who was enthusiastically proclaiming their affinity in both being atheists, 'No. You are a *Christian* atheist, I am a *Hindu* atheist.' Where we come from casts its shadow over what we can be, even in our rebellions.

One question is: how enabling or how constraining are these constructions for an individual or a whole population? Can they be questioned? How immutably are they laid down for each of us by society, family, or other elements of our environment? One person may retain a degree of freedom to think, feel and act with independence both at work and away from it, while happily donning the uniform, metaphorical as well as literal, of his job; another *becomes* the uniform, for him there is no alternative to submitting to its presumed or actual standards, to following rules.

The fact that someone – a novelist perhaps, or a philosopher or a psychoanalyst – may be able to point out the possibility that there is unconscious or collective pressure on individuals, whether from internal figures in the self, or from collective processes such as from the presuppositions of the broader culture, exemplifies the possibility of standing out against these pressures. And psychoanalytic treatment aims to free us from having to live out (or react against) such fantasies blindly. Becoming less driven to adopt default defensive 'solutions', we give ourselves the chance of more realistic, more thoughtful ways of being.

There have always been courageous people who have stood out against such pressures, even to the point of death. A

photograph taken under the Third Reich in 1936, at the launch-ing of the naval training vessel *Horst Wessel*, shows a densely packed crowd of mostly seated men, perhaps two hundred of them, all with right arms rigid in Hitler salutes. All, that is, except for one man near the back. Broad-faced, burly, already (or is this a figment of my imagination?) physically shunned by his neighbours in the same row, his upper arms relaxed by his side, his forearms partly obscured, perhaps linked at the hands or wrists, he looks dispassionate. But imagine how his heart must have been thumping in his chest. The man is believed to have been August Landmesser, a shipyard worker from Hamburg, who loved a Jewish woman, Irma Eckler and had already had a baby girl with her.

There is in life, almost always, a degree of freedom, however costly. Landmesser managed to claim some freedom. He told truth to power. But the pressures constituted a powerful and dangerous rip-tide to swim against.

Like Freud, the philosopher Baruch Spinoza links freedom with knowledge and understanding. According to him, the free man thinks and acts according to his own nature, rather than reactively, passively. Acquiring freedom, he is less a victim of social and personal forces than before. He understands the causes of his own states – not fully, not in Spinoza's terms *sub specie aeternitatis* (under the aspect of eternity), since we are imperfect creatures, but from a position closer to that than when ruled by passions. He has found another place to stand, from which to view his own compulsions or patterns. He has distanced himself from the tendency to fit in with others' expectations, and to construct experience in ways he has no control over.

Wittgenstein's Forms of Life

Ludwig Wittgenstein's 'form of life', explored in his *Philosophical Investigations*, is to be understood as referring to a wide or narrow domain of beliefs and practices governed by rules and norms. As a thought-experiment, he imagines what he calls 'language games', primitive versions of language. Whereas Sartre focuses on the pathological aspects of the games we play, Wittgenstein is more interested in the *inevitability* of forms of life as shared bases of people's lives and practices.

Wittgenstein's 'games' are based on ways of relating and interacting that, because of how primitive they are, reveal how language works. Language games may, like the forms of life that give them their meaning and context, be defined narrowly or broadly. We may thus think of the form of life which belongs to being human, so that a vast range of activities constitute being human, of which any particular group of human beings will partake in some, but none will partake in all. 'Form of life' may also be used narrowly – to pick out games, say, or more narrowly again, card games or ball games. There will be 'family resemblances' between the different activities, to use another important phrase of Wittgenstein's.

I suggest that forms of life provide the context not only for language games, but also for the possibility of form. We show form in whatever game we are playing. Inside a form of life, a shared set of activities governed by detailed or vague rules and values – the good or bad form of, say, a cricketer or a violinist – makes sense and is possible. Someone is in good form *qua* cricketer, or *qua* violinist – in the relevant 'form of life' that characterises playing this game or this instrument.

When on form we are most truly ourselves in some particular sphere of life. But when we are inclined to use the phrase 'in the zone' we think in terms of something 'coming out of nowhere'; this is DeLillo's 'secret aspiration', his 'rapture'. One might even think of 'ecstasy'. Then we might ask: is this a state in which he *finds* his true self? Or in which paradoxically he *loses* his self? Is he fully present? Or not there at all? It seems hard to find the right words. The etymology of the term 'ecstasy' is 'standing outside ourselves', and we can see the point of this. We are inclined to say: we find ourselves by losing ourselves. Perhaps what we mean is: we find ourselves by losing or lessening our self-consciousness, or our need always to be in conscious control. We are able (at times) to hand the reins over to the trained and observant true self, recognising that we may be best served if we stand aside. The focus is utterly on the task, as in a child absorbed in an activity. But we do not get rid of the observing ego, which holds the reins loosely. There is a benign split. In best-case scenarios, the ego is not out of the situation altogether, but is, like the jockey, an integrated, trusting and trusted partner to the horse part of the self.

PART VII: THE CENTRE CANNOT HOLD

15

HORSE OR SNAFFLE?

*Perdition catch my soul, but I do love thee! And when I love
thee not, chaos is come again.*

William Shakespeare

I would prefer not to.

Herman Melville

Which is worse, the fire or the death?

Michael Eigen

————

Horses are by nature 'flight' animals, instinctively geared to run
from threats. When a horse takes off, its rider may try to stop
it by violent use of the reins. This is not advisable. It causes
extreme pain to the horse, which makes it run yet faster to get
away from the pain. A more efficient and humane method is to
turn the horse in a large circle, gradually decreasing the diam-
eter. This unbalances the horse and forces it to slow down.
Riding master Nuno Oliveira writes: 'To practise equestrian
art is to establish a conversation with the horse, a dialogue of
courtesy and finesse . . . The secret in riding is to do only a few
things but to do them right . . . The horse is then a partner,
rather than a slave who is enforced to obey a rigid master.'

The horse may bolt, or it may have the life squeezed out of it. Here is South African Roy Campbell, regarded by T. S. Eliot as among the best of the inter-war poets, writing about some (then) current South African novelists:

> You praise the firm restraint with which they write.
>
> I'm with you there of course.
>
> They use the snaffle and the curb all right;
>
> But where's the bloody horse?

The expert rider has access to all the horse's power without loss of control. A partnership. Otherwise there are the risks of being thrown from the saddle, or of not moving at all. Emotions and desires present similar problems in our personal lives.

Rampant emotions sometimes defeat our efforts to regulate them. Shakespeare's Othello is fragile. As the general in charge of Venetian forces, he brings his young wife, Desdemona, to army headquarters in Cyprus, where his task is to repel a threatened Turkish invasion. There she becomes friendly with his lieutenant, Michael Cassio, whom he not long ago promoted ahead of his 'ancient', or standard-bearer, Iago. Seething with resentment, Iago (who calls Cassio a 'great arithmetician . . . that never set a squadron in the field, nor the division of a battle knows more than a spinster') has cunningly contrived to get Cassio demoted. When Desdemona intercedes with her husband on his behalf, Iago elicits and stirs up Othello's suspicion that she is having an affair with Cassio.

For as long as Othello is confident that he loves Desdemona (and, we might add, that she loves him), his military exploits and responsibilities keep at bay some primitive terror. When he believes her to be unfaithful, what has held him together as a man and a capable military leader collapses.

Here is loss of form so far beyond the ordinary as to be (almost) not a matter of form at all. Othello is overwhelmed by suspicion that quickly becomes delusional conviction. His security and sanity are shattered. Like a man perched on a bolting horse, he is powerless to change course, or to rein the horse in.

At times of transition, too, our metaphorical, emotional horses are liable to unseat us. Psychoanalyst Anna Freud writes of the problems posed by physiological maturation in adolescence:

> Aggressive impulses are intensified to the point of complete unruliness, hunger becomes voracity . . . Oral and anal interests, long submerged, come to the surface again. Habits of cleanliness, laboriously acquired . . . give place to pleasure in dirt and disorder, and instead of modesty and sympathy we find exhibitionist tendencies, brutality and cruelty to animals.

A patient of mine dreamed of rooms slipping, houses splitting, floors tipping away; I came to think of this as an expression of his fear of some old, perhaps infantile, experience of feeling insecurely held, when the shoulder on which he was carried, his personal horse, had not been steady enough. Donald Winnicott alludes to the infant's terror of falling endlessly; Wilfred Bion to 'nameless dread'.

By contrast, loss of form and functioning may arise from the other side, from the annihilation of emotion and desire, from overuse of the curb. Profound reactions to disappointment or trauma, or self-curative efforts to control or suppress states of anxiety or terror, may result in a shutdown of life and liveliness, so that instead of being overwhelmed we are deadened. Getting someone in such a state to do something may feel like flogging a dead horse.

Lying Down in the Snow

Our passivity may amount to a death-wish. Novelist V. S. Naipaul writes about writing, 'The idea of laying aside the ambition was restful and tempting – the way sleep was said to be tempting to Napoleon's soldiers on the retreat from Moscow.'

A compelling literary example of the suppression of life, and its replacement by death or near-death, is to be found in *Bartleby the Scrivener,* a short novel by Herman Melville. The story is simple. The narrator, a New York lawyer, takes on an additional copyist, Bartleby. The latter, described at the out-set as 'pallid, thin, quiet and mechanical', gradually ceases to do anything. His response to any request or requirement to work is 'I would prefer not to.' He hardly eats. Facing the 'dead wall' a mere three feet from the window beside his desk, he stands motionless. He occupies a small, screened-off area of his employer's office. Eventually it becomes clear that Bartleby sleeps there. He has moved in; he has become an incubus.

The employer finds himself reduced to impotence by Bartleby's passive aggression. He feels anger as well as pity. Increasingly, he finds the strange man who occupies not only his office but also his mind impervious to both kindness and reproach. He tries to get rid of him.

As the story develops, Bartleby is more and more explicitly associated with death. He stands, as I say, at the 'dead wall'. He is likened to the 'last surviving pillar of an ancient temple' – scarcely animate, scarcely human. Eventually he is removed to New York's place of detention, called (appropriately) the Tombs. The story's final revelation is that in his previous job he had been a subordinate clerk in the 'Dead Letter Office', dealing with envelopes containing, in the narrator's suggestive words, 'bank notes sent in swiftest charity for someone whom it would not relieve; pardon for those who died despairing; hope for those who died unhoping, good tidings for those who died stifled by unrelieved calamities'.

Bartleby has become anorexic to the point of death, both literally (he hardly eats) and metaphorically (like the posthumous recipients of charitable dead letters, he is unable to receive hope or sustenance from those who reach out to him in his needy state). But he is also powerful, arousing strong feelings in the initially well-disposed but naive narrator. Bartleby rids himself of life, of its desires, guilt, agitation, anxiety; he has no compunction about loading the other with all such turmoil and responsibility. Bartleby provides an unforgettable image of a deathly negativity and refusal of succour: 'I would prefer not to.'

The story ends: 'Ah Bartleby, ah humanity.' We all, Melville suggests, have a Bartleby in us, a tendency to say no to life. Indeed, Bartleby's occupation of his employer's office, behind the screen, suggests a secondary reading: that Bartleby is also an aspect of the narrator himself.

Fire or Death, Wild or Tame, Romantic or Classical?

Othello and Bartleby represent opposite tendencies writ large. On one side, our structure collapses. Losing our shape (our form), we become unrecognisable to our saner selves; uncontrolled emotions 'run away' with us like bolting horses. Or, by contrast, we are all snaffle and curb, losing touch with the lifespirit within.

The New York psychoanalyst Michael Eigen discusses a patient's dream, in which a fire in the basement threatens the top floors. He interprets this as her awareness of a painful dilemma: to suppress erotic and angry feelings to the point of death, or to release her passions and risk hot destruction. This fire below

was associated with sex and rage . . . Lynn was caught in a war between her controlling mental ego (top) and pulsating body ego (below). She paid for her controlling attitude with bouts of confusion and, finally, deadness. A too-controlling attitude might kill the fire. The question raised in the dream was: which was worse, the fire or the death?

One may not know which poses the greater threat, horse or snaffle.

Something of this conflict is to be seen in our choices between the glittering and the dull, between the wild and the tame. We are inclined to elevate unfettered emotionality, to romanticise the unusual, the unquestionably creative or distinctive, above a solid orientation in work and life that may in reality suit us better. The saying 'those who can't write, teach' (compare: 'those who can't act become theatre critics'), finds glamour in the arts, while downplaying the apparently more mundane values and satisfactions to be found in less brilliant activities. Yet there are quiet, unglamorous, even at times heroic satisfactions in a career like teaching.

Jonathan Smith, a teacher all his working life, describes a dinner party given by a successful lawyer:

> I told the [women] guests on either side of me at the table that I was a teacher – no doubt accompanying the confession with the appropriately apologetic body language. One was beautiful and sexy (even a teacher could spot it) but she . . . turned her back on me and her eyes on [the man to her right] . . .

Later in the meal, his friend across the table refers to the current TV adaptation of Smith's novel: 'You must be pleased. This week's *Radio Times* front cover!' At which point

The woman on my right, the woman who I had spotted was sexy, was now stirring. She quickly disengaged herself from the Boring Bloke on her right. She looked at me. 'You mean *you* wrote that?' . . . I wasn't just a teacher. Now I could hold my head up in any company.

Within professions too there are contrasts between the dashing and the orthodox. It has been remarked of England's two wonderful pre- and post-war star batsmen that while Denis Compton was a romantic, in personality as well as in style of batting, Len Hutton was classical. Compton was gloriously free, impulsive; for Hutton, as poet and cricket writer Alan Ross put it, 'grace and levity seemed almost excluded as indecencies'. Compton was uninhibited, improvisatory; Hutton balanced, correct, disciplined. One man was exuberant, even lavish; the other ascetic. One batted flamboyantly (though with a basically sound technique); the other regarded anything florid as indulgence – Hutton once said, drily, to Ross, in response to the latter's comment about his repudiation of flourish: 'I am a Yorkshireman bred and born, you know. I have bought a drink but not too often.'

Hutton was thrifty in his whole way of being. When at one period short of runs, he found it strange to contemplate that 'although', as he confided to Ross, 'a hundred or two will put me right', he even dreamt of 'a few runs made for fun'. Ross comments: 'It is precisely in this subservience of the personal to the impersonal, the sacrificing of the imp of human impulse to the demands of the situation, that classicism consists.' For Hutton, batting for fun was an anomaly, an extravagance.

That Hutton and Compton were both great batsmen indicates that there is no single form of form. Each person has to find that area between extreme classicism and extreme romanticism that suits him best. There is, we might say,

'Compton-form' and 'Hutton-form', Romantic form alongside that of the Enlightenment Rationalist.

Straight off the Boat

Between leaving school and going to university, I got a holiday job working for a construction company. The site was the grand Lancaster House in central London. After its renovation, to which I made my contribution as a 'carpenter's mate', it served as the venue in 1979 for the agreement bringing independence to Zimbabwe, and for many other Commonwealth meetings.

There were two types of carpenter on the site. One was embodied in three or four old (as they seemed to me then), unionised, white British men, unhurried in their work. The second consisted of a similar number of young, ebullient, black Jamaicans. Though in the early 1960s racism was more open and raw than it is now, in Lancaster House there was no outright antagonism, but there was a sort of stand-off. The white men, doing the delicate job of repairing ill-fitting, damaged window frames and replacing the lead weights in the elegant sash windows, would tell me: 'These fellows get straight off the boat, pick up a saw and a hammer in a chain-store, put them in a paper bag, and call themselves carpenters! They can't do anything complicated. They're bandits. What will happen to our profession?'

They moaned, slowly and steadily, rather as they worked. Their work was, so far as I could judge, solid. Their day revolved around tea breaks, which they knew how to extend. Along with their well-stocked toolboxes, they carried as emotional luggage the long trade union history of fights for rights and status. They were suspicious of anyone different in background or style. I imagine they had a point: that the Jamaicans had limited skills.

In overt personality and working style, these young

immigrants were the opposite of their British counterparts. One day I was assigned to help them put up a false ceiling in one of the less grand rooms. They did everything at speed, relishing their work. Their banter and storytelling, in to me mostly incomprehensible patois, was non-stop. The ceiling was up in a flash. They did not voice any complaints in my hearing about their indigenous colleagues, but one could imagine what the gist of such comments, if they were to have made them, might have been.

These observations, familiar in racially sensitive environments, illustrate cultural differences. Both parties might have been right, not only in their criticisms, expressed and supposed, of the other group, but also in what they could justly have claimed for themselves. There was a stark dichotomy between the two modes of working, each with its virtues. Though it would have been absurd and unproductive for either group to mimic the other's style, they could have learned from each other.

It is important to find our own style of working. In the old Yorkshire saying, 'It takes all sorts'. What's more, as teams and as individuals, we need to give house-room to a range of qualities. My being on form looks different from yours, and my own form changes as it must with varying challenges and moods. There are different forms of form, and of loss of form. Working with patients, I may in one session keep quiet, allowing the patient space, sensing that he is opening up and should not be interrupted or confronted; in another I may speak more, holding on to my line of interpretation, seeing it exemplified in one manoeuvre after another by the patient.

Harsh Inner and Outer Voices

Form implodes as a result of harsh inner voices that rubbish the self, as we saw with Jonathan Trott:

I'm in the nets and I'm caught behind. I'm thinking: what are my team-mates going to think of me? What are the opponents going to think of me? The spectators? When in fact the bowler is probably thinking he delivered a good ball, and half my team-mates didn't even see it.

When this sort of spiral gets going, any happy or companionable relationship with the self is eroded. Kipling's 'two imposters', triumph and disaster, become tyrants, making life a misery and good form an impossibility. Horse and rider are no longer harmonious partners.

Such severity towards the self lies behind much lack of resilience. We write ourselves off in certain fields, as many children do with maths, say, and older adults with computers. If something doesn't work at once, we panic. We demand instant help. We give up too soon.

I once heard the CEO of a Japanese electronics firm say on the radio, 'I like problems; problems give chance of solutions.' And he said it with such relish, and with an almost naive enthusiasm, that I fully believed in his willingness to face disappointment in the confident expectation of ultimately finding a way.

Similarly, scientists steadfastly face up to negative experimental results, seeing them as small steps forward in the never-ending development of their field. The scientific attitude proposes that all progress is provisional; that each individual and each generation are guardians of the ongoing tradition, standing on the shoulders of those who went before, themselves providing shoulders for the next generation.

Judgmentalness is not only an internal force. Without always realising its impact, I can be hypercritical, a harsh outer voice, towards others. Ten years before his tragic death at the age of just thirty-four in 1989, Wilf Slack had been a shy newcomer to the Middlesex team. After some games in which Slack and I opened the innings together, other members of the team commented pointedly that he had done better when I had been absent. After some pressing on my part, Slack managed to tell me that he felt inhibited when batting with me, that he experienced me as a disapproving eye.

I had to face two facts. One was that I was indeed, without being clearly aware of it, unhelpfully conveying disapproval when my junior partner played a loose shot. Second, I had to take seriously the fact that even if I wasn't doing so, or wasn't doing it as harshly as he experienced it, this *was* how he experienced me. My disapproval undermined his confidence. For him, it felt, I suspect, like that of a parental figure constantly conveying to a child that he or she is no good. In the extreme, some children sense that they have been unwanted from the beginning. In our case, we were both able to move beyond quick, subliminally driven reactions, making constructive adjustments in our attitudes. This openness led to a much-improved partnership, and allowed Slack to play with more freedom.

Closely related to the severity of the superego is the idea that we have to be perfect. Trott was convinced he was a failure for not living up to his exceptionally high average – 90 at one point – against Australia. The best had become the enemy of the good. His fantastic inner demands were more traumatic than anything the Australian team and its bowlers could hurl at him.

We may believe that an object of desire might, even should, be attained in its completeness, all at once, and unendingly, in a perfect union. A musicians' agent tells me that for many artists the offer of a job is the high point – the artist is wanted, and important – and everything, all the small or large snags and dissatisfactions, is downhill from then on.

Sartre writes about a young man who is waiting for someone he loves and has not seen for a long time. His 'emotional joy' at the impending arrival is mixed with impatience:

> Although the object is 'imminent', it is not yet there, it is not yet *his* . . . And even when it is present, even when the friend so long desired appears upon the station platform, he is still an object that delivers itself to one only little by little; the delight that we feel in seeing him again soon becomes blunted; we shall never get so far as to have him there, in front of us, as our own absolute possession and to grasp him all at once as a whole . . . He will yield himself to us only through numberless details.

The young man has the idea, then, that the whole relationship, in all its excited fullness, could, or should, be consummated there and then, with nothing lacking, and that it should remain permanently in that state. He wants the other as his 'whole absolute possession'. 'Joy', Sartre says, 'is magical behaviour which tries, by incantation, to realise the possession of the desired object as an instantaneous totality.' This wishful fantasy is what advertisers appeal to when offering to 'take the waiting out of wanting'. A person disposed to experience this kind of emotion will be dismayed by the ordinary ups and downs of relationships, the minor disappointments and misunderstandings, a partner's moodiness or passing preoccupation with someone else, the jokes that fall flat. This young man would not appreciate the point of the vows of the marriage ceremony, to 'have and to hold, in sickness and in health, for better for worse, for richer for poorer'. He is unlikely to accept that activities and skills, like relationships, have their phases, and that there are bound to be *longueurs*. Easily dislodged from equilibrium, he will be constantly disgruntled.

Fitting in

The superego is not always harsh. It may be indulgent, or even go missing. We may be thrown off our values by deep-seated needs to fit in. Belonging and not letting others down may become more of a priority than taking responsibility for our actions and showing ordinary concern for others. We then betray our standards in 'just following orders', or in simply complying with the social or work norms of the group. We hand over our consciences to others. We become spinelessly compliant, destructively obedient.

Margaret Heffernan, businesswoman and writer, gives several examples, starting with Stanley Milgram's famous experiments at Yale in the 1960s, in which subjects who were not in any obvious way coerced were nevertheless willing to turn on, and up, switches that, they believed, produced electric shocks of ever-increasing severity in people who had done nothing more sinister than misremember word pairings.

A similar moral blindness affects people in real-life scenarios. In 2004, along with the other component branches of British Petroleum, the Texas City group was instructed to make a 25 per cent cut in 'fixed cash costs across all the refineries'. Its executives went ahead with these mounting cuts despite clear knowledge that the infrastructure was in a poor state, and that safety was being put at extreme risk. 'We cut 10 per cent, cut 10 per cent, cut 10 per cent . . . without regard for risk,' said one. The 'effect of the cost-cutting directive was to block out other considerations' – in particular the likelihood that people would die. Managers on site 'turned a blind eye to the problems and obeyed', even though they were later grief-stricken at the accidents and deaths that resulted a year later, when fifteen workers were killed (and 180 injured) in an explosion.

Group pressure, especially in hierarchical organisations

where questioning those in authority is regarded as disloyalty, is likely to lead to an ethos in which everyone is fearful
of stepping out of line. Then form is compromised not only by
excessive caution, but also by the sacrificing of ordinary moral
values, which in other circumstances would have ruled out the
resultant courses of action.

We also find it impossible, at times, to think outside our
boxes. The psychologist Mihaly Csikszentmihalyi tells a chilling story of a parachute training exercise during the Korean
War, in which a man is fatally distracted from reality by being
stuck in old routines. He loses his head – and his life.

> One day, as the group was preparing for a drop it was dis-
> covered that there were not enough regular parachutes to go
> around, and one of the right-handed men was forced to take
> a left-handed parachute. 'It is the same as the others,' the ser-
> geant assured him, 'but the rip cord hangs on the left side of
> the harness.' The team went up to eight thousand feet and
> over the target area one after the other they jumped out.
> Everything went well, except for one man: his parachute
> never opened and he fell straight to his death on the desert
> below. There was nothing wrong with the equipment. The
> man had become fixed on the idea that to open the chute he
> had to find the release in its accustomed place. His fear was
> so intense it blinded him to the fact that safety was literally
> at his fingertips.

The dead soldier was the one who had the left-handed parachute: the right side of his uniform and even the flesh of his
chest had been gouged out in his desperate attempt to pull the
non-existent right-side cord.

16

FEAR OF FAILURE

Phantasy (imagination) . . . has the power to create what it represents.

Neville Symington

Try to hear their comments as straightforward questions, not as criticisms, let alone as humiliations, whether they are or not.

Renford Bambrough

'I will have no man in my boat,' said Starbuck, 'who is not afraid of a whale'.

Herman Melville

———

Form may be impaired by fear, especially fear of failure. As with other factors in loss of form, the degree of disablement varies. Fear of failure ranges from healthy awareness of risk all the way to retreat or collapse.

Though age brings, in my experience, a reduction in anxiety about failure, or about how others see us, such fear never goes away altogether. As Kathryn Hunter, the 'astonishing shape-shifting' actress who was one of the leading figures in the theatre company Complicite, said, we have to learn to *live with* Mr Doubt and Mr Fear. We can, she suggested, come to find a degree of acceptance in being with such uncomfortable companions. One question is: do Mr Doubt and Mr Fear master us, or can we respectfully tolerate and even master them?

The most experienced psychoanalysts suffer anxiety; indeed it is essential to the task. Betty Joseph, a redoubtable and highly regarded analyst who worked in the field for half a century, was well aware of how difficult it is to start up with patients after the summer break, when we are out of practice and perhaps ambivalent about resuming, and patients harbour resentment and other complicated feelings about our having left them for the holidays. She used to advise younger colleagues: 'Don't give up the profession in September!'

'You Won't Want to Talk to Me!'

Fear may also be self-fulfilling. The psychoanalyst Neville Symington writes: 'Phantasy [imagination] . . . has the power to create what it represents.' We create the outcome that we most fear. We convince ourselves that we will have nothing whatever to say when interviewed, and we become tongue-tied. We create the very thing that we most strive to avoid. We are like the actress who, seeking to make a good impression on an influential producer, invites him to dinner; she drums into her twelve-year-old son that he must on no account mention the producer's prominent nose. When after the tense meal the boy goes to bed, having stared at the nose but said nothing, she breathes a sigh of relief. Turning to her guest, she says, 'Will you have some coffee with your nose?'

A woman I know was convinced that people would not want to spend time with her. One day, she and I were having an enjoyable conversation at a conference before lunch. As we moved towards the buffet, she suddenly came out with, 'Of course you won't want to talk to me any longer, will you?' Here is another example of the thought creating the feared situation that made her voice it. Before her self-belittling remark I had had no such thought. After it, I was inclined to sit with someone else. Others, perhaps as a result of having been mocked for 'being slow' as children, are so worried about not understanding an ordinary conversational opening that they anxiously pepper their interlocutor with questions about what he means, almost before the latter has made his point. The worry about not getting it, about being thought 'stupid', leads to a sort of stupidity.

'I Gave Him t'slow Death'

In high-level sport, failure is swiftly visible and public. Spectators and media pounce on it. The night before my first Test as captain of England, against Australia at Lord's in 1977, I had two dreams. In the first I was trotting anxiously after Tony Greig (my immediate predecessor as captain, and a member of the team) while he was running towards my room, perhaps to collect his things from it. The second dream took place in a small theatre where actors on stage asked the audience to mime their own characters. While others seemed uninhibited, I wondered what mime to perform. Finally I decided to be a shell with me peeping out. In the second dream I am, I think, behaving just like the small, frightened rodent in Kafka's story 'The Burrow' (which I comment on later) – I may be peeping out, but the timidity is undeniable. Nor does 'trotting after' suggest confidence, let alone a willingness to assert myself.

In cricket, batting is a particularly precarious business, and nervousness is never entirely eradicated. For the batsman, a single error may lead to his 'dismissal'. He 'gets out', a phrase that indicates his departure from the arena, and suggests that he has been extinguished, like a flame. He leaves the field like a killed-off character in a drama. (One leading umpire, Dickie

Bird, used to say, of some of his decisions that meant the batsman was out, 'I had to give him t'slow death.') Adrian Stokes,
who wrote about art and psychoanalysis, likened the batsman
to the (ageing) father defending his wicket; he fears being
'castled' – a slang term for being bowled – that is, having his
home and wife assaulted and overthrown by the raiding sons,
the bowlers and fielders. Thus batting has built into it extra
layers of insecurity. Many batsmen are continuously apprehensive, expecting disaster every ball, half-aware of an open-ended
catalogue of potentially fatal scenarios. Moreover, while every
innings (except for those of the opening batsmen) begins at
a moment of triumph for the bowling side, buoyed by their
recent success, the batsman himself is 'cold', new to the crease.

Fear of failure typically results either in timidity or its
opposite. When I batted, especially at the highest level,
I often operated in a stiff-upper-lip mode, physically and
mentally uptight. But similar fearfulness often lies behind a
different type of 'solution' – a reckless need to throw off the
chains. Some feel compelled to break the tension quickly

and definitively, at one fell swoop. Ambitious but imprudent attack may be as much an expression of fear of failure as over-caution, and may have the same result – a quick death. When a batsman comes in to face top-class spin bowlers, for instance, in conditions that suit them, he is surrounded by an excited, effervescent set of close fielders, ready to pounce on the slightest error. There is a lot of chatter and appealing. Each ball is a drama. In such a context, it takes nerve to trust one's defensive technique, to be relaxed enough to play those first anxious balls and overs with soft hands – an important element in defensive technique – and to refrain from trying to hit one's way out of the tension. Most batsmen have to 'play themselves in' with care, and get the pace of the pitch, before blossoming into a more attacking mode of play.

What's more, fear of failure is often entangled with fear of ridicule and humiliation. A low score may be the result of any number of factors, among which poor performance may have played only a small part, or none at all. Yet internally we may be over-sensitive to any hint of humiliation, and thus prone to experience the dismissal as epitomising our overall weakness in ability or personality.

In 1967, when I was about to give a philosophy paper to an audience of professional philosophers for the first time, my former supervisor, Renford Bambrough, advised me to reframe their responses: 'Try to hear their comments as straightforward questions, not as criticisms, let alone as humiliations, whether they are or not.' Anxiety may be transmitted to us by means of the contempt of others. But are we bound to take it on? Or can we frame the scenario in such a way as to refuse to have our well-being shattered? A story is told of the Buddha's response to an intemperate attack on him when he was giving a lecture:

A Brahmin got up and began insulting him. He raved for a while, and when he had finished the Buddha said, 'If somebody laid out a banquet in front of me, to whom would it belong?' 'Obviously it would belong to the person who put it there,' replied the Brahmin. 'And if the person offered it to me,' said the Buddha, 'and I declined to accept it, whose would it be?' 'Well, obviously it would remain the property of the person who put it there,' replied the Brahmin.

'Just so,' declared the Buddha, 'just so'.

The Yips

Aiming to be the best is an important element in maintaining and elevating one's skill. But this aspiration needs to be combined with the realistic acceptance of facts about the world and about ourselves. Jared Tendler, author of *The Mental Game of Poker*, speaks of the dangers for the poker player of over-confidence and wishful thinking, or of its opposite. In particular, he says, you can't always be at the top of your form. When things go your way, don't swagger or imagine you are the king: for the flip side of such illusions is despair, or a feeling of being cursed when luck turns against you. In either state, further errors in thinking creep in, such as superstitions, or an obsession with taking revenge – a mentality that poker players call 'tilt'. The only way to play poker is to bear in mind that there are no guarantees of success. This search for consistency and a straightforward attitude through good and bad spells reminds me of both Piraji, the tree-cutter, and David Florence, the canoeist. As we have seen, batsman Jonathan Trott suffered from something akin to 'tilt', his confidence and technique crumbling.

Not that such traumas are restricted to batsmen. Bowlers, even the best, may lose all control of their skill, becoming unable to propel the ball onto the cut pitch. Early in his career when his coach at Surrey tried to get him to change his action to be more 'side-on', fast bowler Bob Willis went through just such a phase. In the nets, the ball kept hitting the side netting.

For some reason the type of bowler most prone to the 'yips' is the slow left-armer, mirror image to the right-arm off-spinner but generally a different psychological animal. Two such bowlers come to mind. One was my Middlesex and England colleague, Philippe Edmonds, the second, India's Ravi Shastri. Both were top-class spin bowlers, yet both were, for a few weeks or months, reduced to the ineptitude of serving up double bouncers or high full-tosses. From being class acts, they performed like beginners. If these disruptions had not been so painful and mystifying, they might have been a bad joke. In the event, both cricketers were able, by taking things slowly, step by step, and thanks to their resoluteness – Edmonds's rehabilitation included bowling ninety overs in a Middlesex second team game – and the procedural memory of their substantial skills, to find their way back to their old form and ability. Others, with less skill, experience and support, give up the struggle, whether in sport or in life.

Such bewildering loss of an established skill is liable to happen in any field, as in stage fright or writer's block. These are disasters that go beyond mere loss of form, removing the individual from the field in which he was an expert.

Writer's Block

John, a successful novelist, had suffered from a shutdown in his ability to write. He found himself blocked from communicating at all levels. A private person, he didn't want to talk, to show himself, whether in speech or in writing. He could express himself only through this withdrawal. He went into psychoanalysis. In a few months he was writing again.

John puts his recovery down largely to the analytic process, though there were other factors, including a friend's encouragement to start writing again on a theme close to his heart; the friend also read the first drafts of what in the end became a new novel. In his analysis, it was not that he suddenly discovered what was causing the block. There was no specific insight. Rather, he said, it was as if through analysis he found himself picking up and playing with the bat he had put down. He was aware of being once again capable in its use. The key seems to have been the regular process of speaking in a context where someone really listened to him. It was also important that there was an invitation, even a *demand*, to speak; he was paying to do so in this 'boot camp of the soul', as he put it. (I had not previously thought of psychoanalysis as a boot camp of the soul!) John rediscovered a way of being that he had years before found possible, even though it had been then, and was now, often agonisingly difficult.

To call this a 'rediscovery' is not quite correct. For since he has been in analysis, John's writing has, he says, been undergoing a transformation. For instance he has become aware that there is more in him than he knew, a disconcerting as well as an empowering realisation. And in this recent rebirth, he has been writing more about feelings, and more from the child's point of view.

Now, a few years later, he is again a bit blocked, sometimes scared, but not to the previous extent. 'But it is always with me. I am beginning to recognise the shape of it. I am temperamentally torn between an urge to be silent and an urge to express.'

Fears that Interrupt the 'Tranquil Vacuum'

Fear of failure or exposure may impede us in job interviews. It is often easier to perform well either when you believe you have no chance of getting the job, or when you are not sure you want it – when, as we say, using terms that fit my horse metaphor, 'nothing rides on it'. When I left university, it was partly because I was uncertain whether it was what I wanted, that I was able to enjoy (and do well in) the two-and-a-half-day interview process for entry to the Civil Service.

When by contrast we are especially keen to succeed, when the outcome matters a lot and we have high expectations of success, then the stakes are raised, and pressure and anxiety are liable to mount. Our focus narrows, and our capacity to think creatively shrinks. We cease to enjoy the moment, or to be open to the unexpected. Alongside doing the necessary homework for an interview, we need to say to ourselves at times, 'it's only a game, not a matter of life and death'. Moreover, more often than not, opportunities will recur.

For similar reasons, children's birthdays are often traumatic: the child's best friend is playing with someone else, the icing on the cake is not the right colour. Expectations run riot, and so does disappointment. 'Good enough' is no longer good enough.

Realistic Fear

Yet despite all this, realistic fear is both natural and useful. In *Moby-Dick*, Herman Melville writes of Starbuck, the mate of the whaling ship *Pequod*, and his healthy fear:

> Much more did his far-away domestic memories of his young Cape wife and child tend to bend him still more from the original ruggedness of his nature, and open him still further to those latent influences which, in some honest-hearted men, restrain the gush of dare-devil daring, so often evinced by others in the more perilous vicissitudes of the fishery. 'I will have no man in my boat,' said Starbuck, 'who is not afraid of a whale.' By this he seemed to mean that an

utterly fearless man is a far more dangerous comrade than a coward . . . Starbuck was no crusader after perils; in him courage was . . . a thing simply useful to him, and always at hand upon all mortally practical occasions. Wherefore he had no fancy for lowering for whales after sun-down; nor for persisting in fighting a fish that too much persisted in fighting him. For, thought Starbuck, I am here in this critical ocean to kill whales for my living, and not to be killed by them for theirs; and that hundreds of men had been so killed Starbuck well knew. What doom was his own father's? Where, in the bottomless deeps, could he find the torn limbs of his brother?

Operating in the service of survival, fear may save us from Melville's 'gush of dare-devil daring', and failure may be the starting point for development and change. A measure of anxiety forces us to concentrate fully on the task in hand. Appropriate fear, with its incitement to caution, is part of what distinguishes bravery from bravado, and helps us avoid going over the top. In the words of Samuel Johnson: 'When a man knows he is to be hanged in a fortnight, it concentrates his mind wonderfully.'

17

FEAR OF SUCCESS

Herschelle, you've just dropped the World Cup.

Steve Waugh

Mirror, mirror, in my hand, who is the fairest in the land?

Brothers Grimm

Fear of failure is basic, and often plain to see; what is less obvious is fear of success, self-sabotage, when we veer away from the sharp jaws of victory.

In the 1999 British Open Championship, French golfer Jean van de Velde had a three-stroke lead at the last hole. To win the tournament, he knew he had only to finish with a safety-first five or six on the par-four hole. His tee shot, however, was daring, pushing the limits; he was lucky to land up just short of the Barry Burn, on a small peninsula near the seventeenth tee. Van de Velde continued going for glory. His next shot, also ambitious, ricocheted off a stadium railing, and then off the wall guarding the burn, into thick rough. From the rough, he landed, if that is the right word, in the burn. He famously took off his shoes and socks to see if he could hit the ball from the water, but decided against. Having dropped the ball, stroke number five fell into a sand bunker beside the green. He then holed with only two more strokes, taking seven for the hole and by the skin of his teeth qualifying for a play-off. This 'tragi-comedy' was described as being the result of his swashbuckling 'd'Artagnan approach'. He lost the play-off.

Over the past decade and a half, South Africa's top cricketers, no doubt much to their chagrin, have been labelled 'chokers', especially in the World Cup, a competition in which they have lost several matches that they were expected to win, often from good positions. This reputation was first gained when they lost twice to Australia in 1999. In a key match in the competition, South Africa scored 271 for seven in their fifty overs, a substantial score in those days. Australia, who would have been eliminated had they lost, won by five wickets with two balls to spare. Steve Waugh scored a match-winning 120 not out off 110 balls. Halfway through his innings he was dropped by South Africa's best fielder, Herschelle Gibbs (himself a century-scorer earlier in the day), who let the ball slip out of his hands while in the act of throwing it up in celebration. Waugh is alleged to have said, 'Herschelle, you've just dropped the World Cup.'

The two teams played each other again four days later, in one of the semi-finals. South Africa faced a target of 214. At the start of the last over, they needed nine to win with one wicket in hand. Remarkably (and far from chokingly), all-rounder Lance Klusener hit the first two balls of the over for fours. The third ball almost resulted in the other batsman, Allan Donald, being run out. Off the fourth, Klusener embarked on a panic run. Donald did not, and was this time run out by the length of the pitch. The match was tied, and, as a result of their lower run rate, South Africa were out. Three days later Australia won the final, against Pakistan, by a comfortable margin.

It is too easy to attribute psychological qualities or states as causative in such sequences, when clearly there are other factors, including bad luck. But having a reputation for being chokers inexorably leads to tension, even to an inability to breathe freely, to literal choking, so the repetition may in the end be a matter of increased fear of failure as much as a fear of and prohibition on enjoyment and success. Certainly the psychological attitudes of teams and individuals make them prone to fail when objectively well placed. Losing, like winning, becomes a habit.

Getting close to victory may arouse either anxious circumspection, a crawl towards victory, or, as with d'Artagnan-van de Velde, a wish to finish with panache. Either way, we stop playing with the relaxed concentration that has got us so far. At the same time, our opponents may improve their game – some individuals and teams show full commitment only when their backs are to the wall – so that, with 'nothing to lose', *their* anxiety and constriction decrease, and they think 'what the hell, I might as well go flat out for winners.' So the 'choker' is more likely to fail against an opponent who gets most aggressive and engaged when on the verge of defeat.

There are many reasons for self-sabotage. Some people mistrust their achievements or improvements, believing such things never last. For them hope is too vulnerable a hostage to fortune. Having plucked up the courage to ask a girl to dance, the young man retreats from taking it further. Better not to attempt what would satisfy, rather than risk disappointment. Success may alternatively arouse a sneaking suspicion of fraudulence. Or it may lead to heightened expectation, or indeed envy, from others or from within. A sensitive person is inhibited by shame as a result of his tendency to gloat. Some are attracted by the role of victim, eliciting sympathy for their 'bad luck', finding, as the Joker or the Fool, alternative routes to a version of acclaim. Some want to go out with a bang, courting rather than seeking failure. Others are dead set on forestalling or spoiling any gratification in those who have helped them, preferring that grim pleasure to the ordinary satisfaction of doing well.

Failure to live up to one's talents may also have to do with guilt, and the seeking out of punishment. One patient of mine, Frances, was unable to consummate any of her undoubted interests and skills. Unconsciously, we discovered, Frances believed she was a criminal, who deserved to be punished for sexual 'crimes' against her mother. These crimes were, it seemed, two-fold. First she had had a close and flirtatious relationship with her father, displacing her mother in his affections. Second, she had been initiated into sex as a teenager by an older, married man, who was also the husband of her mother's best friend. Thus she became (in her own eyes) a criminal by proxy, the husband standing in for her father. Years later, when she and her husband were mutually aroused, she would suddenly be tormented by sudden loss of desire, a sort of frigidity provoked, it seemed, by the same old wronged, envious and punitive Oedipal mother inside her head. Another symptom seems to have been her asthma, which became most acute whenever they were trying to have sex. Frances seemed to be forbidden to enjoy life to the full, especially but not only sexually. Perhaps this kind of experience underlies the term 'choking' as applied to sportspeople.

For some, the success of a project which has been carried through with ruthless energy and ambition leads to break-down. In his essay 'Those Wrecked by Success', Freud refers to two fictional characters, Shakespeare's Lady Macbeth and Rebecca West, a character in Henrik Ibsen's *Rosmersholm*, as examples of people who become riddled with guilt and neurosis once their ambition is achieved. Lady Macbeth has boldly, indeed decisively, championed the plan to murder the king and seize the throne. But this previously steely, even manly, woman is unmanned, and goes mad, once the crown has been won. With Rebecca West the situation is even more explicit. Rebecca has been living with the Rosmers as Beata's friend and helper. A year before the play opens, Beata drowned herself in the mill waters. It becomes clear that Rebecca drove Beata to despair, even encouraging her to commit suicide. She and Rosmer were in love. But when Rosmer asks her to marry him, hoping to escape *his* guilt by erasing the memory of his wife, she rejects him outright. Rebecca's collapse results from her linking all this, including her love for Rosmer, to her childhood incest with her adopted father. Filled with guilt arising from the distant as well as the recent past, she proves her devotion to Rosmer by agreeing to commit suicide herself. Still in love with her, he joins her. They jump together into the mill-race, dying in the same way as his wife did. This Oedipal story involves symmetrical self-punishment, an eye for an eye.

The Envy of Others

The envy of others often hinders or precludes us from reaching or enjoying our potential. In the Indian epic the *Mahabharata*, Ekalavya, a young forest tribal, surprises the archery teacher Drona by asking him to be his guru. Drona refuses; he teaches only youths from high-caste families. Ekalavya is not deflected by this rejection. Out of the mud gathered from a forest pool he makes a life-size statue of Drona, whom he still regards as his master. He begins to practise 'with faith, devotion, and pure discipline'.

Times passes. One sparkling afternoon in winter, Arjuna, Drona's star pupil, is hunting in the forest along with his brothers. They come across Ekalavya, who astounds them with the skill and speed of his shooting. 'Who are you? And where could you have learned to shoot like that?' they ask. The youth tells them his name and says he owes his skill to Drona, his master.

Pale with jealousy, Arjuna rebukes Drona. 'How can you be teaching, secretly, that lowborn boy, an archer so accomplished he makes me look like a mere beginner?'

Drona decides to do something about this and sets out to visit Ekalavya. The young lad falls at his feet. Drona says: 'Ekalavya, if I am your teacher, you should now give me my fee.' The fee is his right thumb. With total acceptance, the boy 'sliced off his right thumb, and placed it, dripping, at Drona's feet'. Then, sitting alone,

> He listened to the creatures of the night/as they went about their earnest purposes/constrained, and free. In the dawn light, he rose/and bathed, then stood in front of Drona's statue./In respect, he touched its feet. Then, straightening,/ he took his bow, began again to practise.
>
> From now on, he would never shoot/with such breath-taking speed./And Drona's words would not be falsified: Arjuna/would be the greatest archer in the world.

The story is significant in more ways than one, not least about the capacity of love and devotion, after a no doubt dark night of the soul, to overcome extreme hardship. But what I want to emphasise is the power of another's envy to damage a person's ability to perform to his potential. It may be safer to cut off our thumb and allow someone else to be the favoured and the best. We may fear success and its consequences as much as failure.

There are poles of envy, an emotion that ranges from admiration and aspiration for what is good in another to a destructiveness that spoils and hates them and their excellence. In a county cricket match in the 1950s, Dickie Dodds, the Essex opening batsman, was out without scoring on a pitch that was perfect for batting. Two hours later, at lunch, Essex had reached 150 without further loss. Dodds, who had watched the proceedings with some chagrin, said to his captain, Doug Insole, one of the not-out batsmen, 'Skipper, I hope you haven't been troubled by any bad vibes this morning?' Insole replied, 'Can't say I have, Dickie, I've been too busy enjoying myself – why do you ask?' 'Because I've been so full of bitterness I've not been wishing you well.' A degree of envy is ordinarily human, and acknowledgement of it disarming.

Arjuna is different. He cannot bear not to be the best. Seeing Ekalavya handicapped at his behest, he feels no guilt; on the contrary, he 'glowed with confidence restored'. We all, I suspect, know the impulse to be top dog at any price, and to envy and resent others who threaten to overtake us; equally, we have all been recipients of destructive envy.

Snow White is almost killed by the envy of her stepmother. Her mother has died in childbirth. The new queen (possibly also to be thought of as the bad side of the actual mother) is gratified by her magic mirror, which for years has told her that she is the fairest in the land. One day, however, the mirror informs her that her stepdaughter Snow White is a thousand times fairer than she. The queen instructs a hunter to kill her young rival. He does not carry out the order. Later, as the envy and pride 'grow in her heart like ill weeds, taller every day', the wicked queen makes other efforts to get rid of her stepdaughter. Eventually she poisons her with an apple, a sign perhaps of the girl's burgeoning sexuality. The daughter faints, and is presumed dead, until a prince, seeing her in her glass coffin, falls in love with her. As he carries her away, the bumping of the coffin in the carriage causes the apple to be dislodged from her throat, and she wakes up. The queen, invited to the wedding, is again consumed with jealousy and envy. Compulsively, she puts on red-hot shoes and dances till she drops dead – her frenzied, narcissistic, sexually based inability to accept her own ageing and the beauty of her daughter eventually destroys her mind and herself.

If a mother's envy of her daughter is poisonous, it may make coming alive too dangerous. Snow White has hidden in the forest to avoid being killed, and the coffin represents her as dead to life. Only the love and desire of a man can jolt her from her coffin-state and awaken her into emotional (and sexual) life. Teenage girls may similarly go into a sort of sleep or retreat from life if they feel that their mother is threatened by their growing up.

I have taken examples from mythology – Indian and German – rather than everyday life, since without the narrative and symbolic insight of myth it is hard to be sure of the reasons for loss of skill in public figures. Another site for conviction is psychoanalysis, where we focus as closely as we can on patients' inner, often hidden, motives.

It is not unusual for us to encounter patients who attribute envy to others. Unable to tolerate their own lack or need, these people, seeing themselves as the superior ones, assume that it is others who envy them. They may even subtly manoeuvre others into envious positions. One patient would come back to sessions on a Monday with stories about herself having been treated as royalty over the weekend, while the analyst was both seen as her retainer or lackey, and made to feel dependent on the patient for her grace and favour. I was to be the one left out and envious, not she .

There are also, by contrast, people who idealise others and diminish themselves. For them the possibility that the other might feel envious of them is hard to imagine. When they are scorned or ignored, they feel embarrassed and small rather than angry. Martin, a patient I heard about in supervision, was a young professional opera singer, like his older brother, Clive. Both were doing well in their field. Clive had stayed in the north of England, singing in a well-regarded opera company near their original home, and was beginning to get small solo parts, while Martin was in the chorus of one of the big opera houses in London. Clive was the more extrovert of the two; he had always been the 'clever' one.

On his visits to his home town, Martin felt envious of this idealised brother. They had always had a good relationship, but now, he felt, he was at times ignored by Clive. What gradually emerged in the analysis was that this disregard occurred mainly in work contexts, backstage after concerts, for example. Martin felt hurt and puzzled, understandably, but also embarrassed and infantilised, taking on the projection of being the incompetent little brother.

After some time, the analyst raised the possibility that from Clive's point of view, Martin was the one at the heart of things in London, with access to the best teachers and singers. At some level, Clive may have felt that his solo parts were less significant than Martin's presence in the more prestigious chorus. Once this possibility – that it was Clive who was envious of Martin, more than the other way round – was raised and considered, Martin became more confident. He began to see the put-downs as his brother's problem rather than his own. He recognised that Clive's envy of him was unconscious, that the latter, always the older brother, the leader, the one who 'knew', could not conceive that he himself might also have areas of insecurity, even inferiority, towards his younger brother.

Martin was not only invigorated by this reframing, he was also saddened. He would have to give up the somewhat fawning closeness to his brother – there was a distance between them that his insight created and contributed to. But there was, too, a solid advantage: he could now hold his head high and go for his own success. He felt less oppressed and reduced by his brother's painful rebuffs; instead of confirming his own insignificance, they were a back-handed tribute to his worth.

Other Sources of Fear of Success

Another motive for embracing failure rather than achieving success is the idea that, if we attain a higher standard, we will be faced with escalating expectations to live up to. So we build in errors and failings in order to keep expectations low.

The young Middlesex fast bowler Simon Hughes had a habit of bowling one bad ball each over. Once, against Essex at Lord's, his first four balls in one over were all excellent, and he took a wicket with the fourth. I simultaneously encouraged and remonstrated with him: 'If you can bowl four good balls an over, why not all six?' His response was a hangdog but also self-satisfied expression. 'I'm afraid I can't bowl six good balls an over,' he almost boasted. I felt he preferred to risk provoking irritation at his variability and at his air of self-satisfaction, rather than have to live up to the expectation of a higher standard, and this prevented him from raising his game an extra notch.

Unless big fish become canny, they are easier to catch. Another motive for avoiding success is to reduce possibilities of exposure; we fear the resultant prominence and scrutiny, which may reveal hitherto concealed sources of shame, embarrassment or guilt. Become prime minister and everyone learns you were once a member of a disreputable undergraduate club, with its arrogance, unpleasant initiation rites, and the trashing of restaurants. The foolishness or depravity of youth, whether at the age when such errors are to be expected or later, will be exultantly exposed. Safer for some to keep their heads below the parapet.

Another source of the seeking out of failure and the exaggeration of distress is the temptation to foster and nurse grievances. Fall into this way of being, and you 'arrange' not to win in order to prove to the world that you are hard done by. You use defeats to extract sympathy, to be the victim and to justify revenge, unconsciously choosing and directing such scenarios so as to occupy the moral high ground.

In some couples, both parties are caught up in this kind of inverted, even perverted, competition. A man and his wife are discussing where to go on holiday. The husband wants to go camping in the Lake District, the wife favours a tour of Italian cities. After a brief presentation of their preferences, both start arguing with peculiar force for the other's proposal. When the last date for booking the Italian holiday arrives, the husband capitulates triumphantly. Now the wife argues even more strongly for the camping option. Having booked the Italian holiday, the husband 'milks' his 'disappointment' with sanctimonious satisfaction, exulting in his defeat, even taking masochistic pleasure in it, as well as using it sadistically to punish his wife. Both want to lose the argument, in order to feel justified in saying 'we always have to do what you want'. Being 'defeated' in smaller battles is part of the campaign to win a longer war.

Negative Therapeutic Reactions

Psychoanalysts have a term for some forms of self-sabotage: negative therapeutic reaction. Something therapeutic, developmental, happens, such as enhanced self-esteem, and the patient reacts against it, saying no to progress. There are many sources of such reactions. Here are some examples of what, schematically, these patients might in effect be thinking.

One: I don't deserve it. How can I ever tell if my success is earned? I am like a beautiful girl who hides or disguises her beauty because she can never tell whether she is loved and admired merely for that, rather than for something more to do with the person she really is. She hides her light under a bushel, and avoids relationships.

Two: I'm bad and must be punished, I don't deserve it – not because of some existential lack, but because I've been unforgivably bad. I can't allow myself to do well, or enjoy any success, until I have properly repented for my crime. But like Claudius, the King in *Hamlet*, who says: 'I am still possess'd of those effects for which I did the murder – my Crown, mine own ambition and my Queen', I cannot take the drastic step of giving up my pride, and eating humble pie.

Three: if I come to realise how ill and destructive I've been, I have not only to repent but also to really experience how much I've been responsible for this wreckage of a life. I would never be able to catch up with my peers. It's unbearable to know this. Better to revert to my drugs and my omnipotence rather than stay with a more constructive, but also painful, form of life.

Four: I can't enjoy or achieve since success makes me feel fraudulent. Whenever I have got somewhere, I've tricked someone. I've hired papers to cheat my way to a university degree. I've asked a woman to marry me not out of passion or conviction, but in order to elicit an expression of love from her. How can I now trust any expression of love from another, or believe in my own?

Five: I can't bear to be beholden to you, or to my wife, or anyone else, it makes me feel small and insignificant. Better Lucifer-like to reign in hell than serve in heaven.

Six: I envy you for helping me, and for seeming to be a better person than I am, and I would rather stop you enjoying your contribution to my success; I'd even prefer to spoil your satisfaction than to have any satisfaction myself.

Our underground agendas are, then, diverse. We may be creative at losing, successful in avoiding success. Like Gilbert Osmond, in Henry James's *The Portrait of a Lady,* we excel at not attempting. We put a lot of work into self-presentation, creating masks of success or power. We are in form at being out of form.

18

ONCE-BORN, TWICE-BORN

There he was – complete honesty born of complete experience had entered the room and unobtrusively taken a chair.

Graham Greene

One can live only so long as one is intoxicated, drunk with life, but when one grows sober one cannot fail to see that it is all a stupid cheat.

Leo Tolstoy

———

Leo Tolstoy, quoted by William James, describes a man on an expedition with his brother, spending the night in a barn. Getting onto his knees, he mumbles his customary evening prayer. His brother says, quietly, 'Do you still keep up that thing?' Suddenly, the scales fall from the young man's eyes, and he realises that 'that thing' – his Christian belief – is a mere formality. James construes the shift as occurring

> because the words spoken by his brother were like the light push of a finger against a leaning wall, already about to tumble by its own weight. His brother's words showed him that the place wherein he supposed religion dwelt in him had

long been empty, and that the sentences he uttered, the crosses and bows which he made during his prayer, were *actions with no inner sense.*

The road to Damascus may be the setting for conversion in either direction, away from or towards religious belief. This man experiences an apparently abrupt loss of faith, where what is revealed to him is the inauthenticity of what have become token gestures towards religious belief. He recognises something of who he is, and who or what he isn't. Though his belief system is turned upside down, we are also told that he has almost reached the point of disbelief himself: 'the place where he had supposed religious belief dwelt in him had long been empty'. His belief has degenerated; it no longer has any underpinning. The push of a finger topples it.

James differentiates between the 'once-born' and the 'twice-born'. We know too little about the life of the man in question to be sure, but it seems that he has slipped without crisis into this new orientation. If so, we can see him as once-born, not having to go through the labour of a second birth. It was a very different experience from Tolstoy's own loss of belief and his subsequent regeneration of it, differently configured, which I shall come to later. For Tolstoy, the shift in his tectonic plates was seismic.

The Once-Born

The once-born appreciate life without deep crises. Their world is broadly benign and harmonious. They have slender if any metaphysical tendencies; they don't struggle with a sense of sin, or with existential questions about reality; nor are they likely to be self-righteous. They lack the acute sensitivity and over-thinking that makes the worst of a bad job and leads to perennial angst. Rather, James says, they don't think of themselves at all. They are inclined to see the good in life and in other people.

Such people have emotional resources which, as in the New Testament parable of the talents, they use profitably, so that their well-being and self-confidence are enhanced. A benign cycle is set in motion. A conjunction of optimism and practicality serves the once-born well. They are naturally accepting. They tend to be straightforward and spontaneous; they wear their gifts lightly. They have much of the grace, joy and exuberance characteristic of happy children. Their growing-up seems part of a natural process, not the result of cataclysmic changes of heart. They tend to find the world and the people in it on the whole kindly, offering gifts in abundance. And they make it an easier place for others, who in response are inclined to like them.

Even for the once-born, form varies, of course. But they do not suffer from extreme zigzags, nor do they agonise over poor form. They assume they will get over it; they have simple remedies for its restoration. Recovery is unlikely to involve a revaluation of a whole style or way of life. Good form seems to them like the celebration of what is natural, not a precarious ideal.

William's brother Henry presents us with a similar distinction in his wonderful novel, *The Europeans*. The aptly named artist, Felix Young, has a felicity of equanimity and conversation. He accompanies his sister, the more weightily named (and burdened) Baroness Eugenia Munster, to New England to visit their cousins. Her project is to make her fortune by finding a wealthy American husband. She has an eye on their cousin Clifford; and also on Robert Acton, a neighbour of the cousins, who wants to marry her. In the end she declines to follow through with either prospect. Felix, by contrast, travels with an open mind and leaves with a bride, a fellow-spirit, his cousin Gertrude. Once-born, he is not wracked by doubts and worries.

Novelist Graham Greene sketches a similar personality, that of art critic Herbert Read:

> He was the most gentle man I have ever known, but it was a gentleness which had been tested in the worst experiences of his generation. The young officer . . . gained the Military Cross and a DSO in action on the Western Front . . . Nothing had changed in him. It was the same man twenty years later who could come into a room full of people and you wouldn't notice his coming – you noticed only that the whole atmosphere of a discussion had quietly altered, that even the relations of one guest to another had changed. No one any longer would be talking for effect, and when you looked round for an explanation, there he was – complete honesty born of complete experience had entered the room and unobtrusively taken a chair.

The once-born possess the valuable qualities of directness and simplicity. They do not need to show off. The other side of this simplicity *may* be – although clearly not for Read – shallowness, a lack of seriousness and intensity. They may be complacent – there is 'nothing wrong with me!'

The Twice-Born

The twice-born are more complicated. They may be irritable, exasperated, suspicious, wracked with self-loathing or self-consciousness. They are liable to depression, anguish, a sense of fraudulence. William James quotes an asylum patient as saying, 'It is as if I could not see any reality, as if I were in a theatre; as if people were actors and everything were scenery . . . I weep false tears, I have unreal hands, the things I see are not real things.'

The twice-born nevertheless manage, out of crisis, to reinvent themselves. Then their world is transformed – 'as utterly', James writes, 'as the sunrise transforms Mt Blanc from a corpselike grey to a rosy enchantment'. James quotes Tolstoy, writing in *A Confession* about the sudden onset of a lengthy depression that dragged him down into near-suicidal despair, but which later led him into a second birth, a new form of life and a new set of values. About his despair, Tolstoy says:

> I felt that something had broken within me on which my life had always rested; that I had nothing left to hold onto, and that morally my life had stopped. An invincible force impelled me to get rid of my existence in one way or another. It cannot be said exactly that I wished to kill myself, for the force which drew me away from life was fuller, more powerful, more general than any mere desire. It was a force like my old aspiration to live, only it impelled me in the opposite direction. It was an aspiration of my whole being to get out of life . . . One can live only so long as one is intoxicated, drunk with life, but when one grows sober one cannot fail to see that it is all a stupid cheat.

This description of a force 'more powerful than any mere desire' strikes me as an apt account of what psychoanalysts refer to as the death drive, which is usually unconscious. It took a man of Tolstoy's depth of self-awareness to articulate it so accurately.

All this was happening, Tolstoy remarks, when his external life was one of apparently boundless benignity. He was blessed with a good wife, a glowing reputation, an ability both to labour with the peasants and to work intellectually for eight hours at a stretch without fatigue. But for him, as for Hamlet, what was this life but the 'quintessence of dust'? 'Why should I live? Why should I do *anything*?'

Yet he eventually, two years on, came to a resolution:

> The very thing which was leading me to despair – the meaningless absurdity of life – is the only incontestable knowledge accessible to man . . . [Moreover,] something else was working in me too, and kept me from the deed [suicide] – a consciousness of life, as I may call it, which was like a force that obliged my mind to fix itself in another direction and draw me out of my situation of despair.

He called this force a 'thirst for God'. And he came to the view that what was without meaning was the way he had been living his life, and the values on which it, like other lives led in society, was based.

Tolstoy's recovery, and discovery of peace, was not, James suggests, a matter of a 'simple addition of pluses and elimination of minuses from life'. For Tolstoy, renunciation and despair were the first step in the direction of truth. He needed to give up what had felt natural in order to move on from it, to reach the spiritual. For someone like Tolstoy, only via sickness could real health be apprehended and approached.

Another thinker who seems to me to sit squarely in the category of twice-born is Ludwig Wittgenstein, the philosopher who turned his field upside down not once but twice, transforming the subject with his *Tractatus* (1921) and again much later overthrowing his own system, leaving as his posthumous work *The Philosophical Investigations* (1953). Wittgenstein suffered from mental anguish and a lacerating disappointment with himself (and, often, with others). Around 1913, as his biographer Ray Monk tells us, he wrote to Bertrand Russell: 'Deep inside me there's a perpetual seething, like the bottom of a geyser, and I keep hoping that things will come to an eruption once and for all, so that I can turn into a different person.' Monk writes further of a 'life that is marked by a series of . . . transformations, undertaken at moments of crisis and pursued with a conviction that the source of the crisis was himself. It is as though his life was an on-going battle with his own nature.'

Monk then offers, through Wittgenstein's own words, an apposite statement of the contrast between once- and twice-born:

When someone remarked to him that the childlike innocence of G .E. Moore (the prominent Cambridge philosopher some years older than himself) was to his credit, Wittgenstein demurred. 'I can't understand that . . . unless

it's also to a child's credit. For you aren't talking of the innocence a man has fought for, but of an innocence which
comes from a natural absence of temptation.'

Wittgenstein had no such natural absence of temptation, no
such absence of fighting for an innocent, fresh view. In James's
terms, Moore was once-born, Wittgenstein twice-born.

Zidane the Both-Born

The wonderfully talented Algerian-French footballer Zinedine
Zidane seems to have combined both sets of qualities. In the
film *Zidane: A 21st-Century Portrait*, the camera focuses for
almost all its ninety minutes on Zidane himself, mostly in
close-up, following him in a match between Real Madrid and
Villareal in 2005. In the film I was struck by the animal-like
quality of Zidane's presence on the field. In the midst of hectic
activity, he has periods of utter stillness. Suddenly alive with
anticipation, as when a browsing deer pricks its ears at a sound
or sniffs the air for a dangerous smell, or like a lion that sees
a chance of catching prey, he is all alertness. As if in preparation for imminent flight or fight, he paws the ground with the
toe of his boot. Whenever he senses a chance or possibility,
his spring into movement is incisive, his acceleration electric.
He is urgent in his anticipation of a return pass, but also not
noticeably disappointed if, as frequently happens, the pass does
not materialise.

All this strikes me as typical of the once-born. But then there
is Zidane's tragic flaw, suggestive more of the twice-born – his
tendency, apparently out of the blue, to lose self-control and
get into a fight. Football lovers will remember the 2006 World
Cup final between Italy and France in Berlin. For 110 minutes,
Zidane behaved with admirable restraint through relentless

provocation by defender Marco Materazzi, until, in extra time, Zidane reacted by head-butting Materazzi and was sent off. This was the fourteenth time in his career that he had been shown a red card. I was struck by the fact that, in the match against Villarreal, the occasion of the film, which took place a year before the final, here too Zidane was sent off minutes before the end for getting involved in a brawl. Some devil of self-destructiveness, some need to get himself punished, whatever it was, a tendency that may also have been a cry for help, struck me a characteristic of a twice-born.

Jonathan Smith quotes psychotherapist Anthony Storr: 'Genius is most significantly found in *unresolved* people.' Smith agrees: 'Many of the most interesting pupils I have taught are angular; they're not easy or chummy . . . They may well not get on that well with their peers, and may well not be particularly keen to get on with you.' Smith doesn't blame them for that; as he says, he often doesn't get on with himself. I too see Storr's point. Those who have a sense that they are unresolved have more reason and drive to find ways of expressing themselves anew than those who are satisfied with how they are.

Form and Rebirth

In the give and take of everyday life, the once-born get along with ordinary support and sound advice, and smoothly improve their skills. For others, a more radical approach is needed, whether they attempt to find it through their own unaided thinking, as Tolstoy did, or through a more formal attempt at change of heart, through religion, or psychoanalysis, or meditation.

In sport too, an individual or team may attempt a radical reorientation. They reinvent themselves. Cricketer Bob Barber, who early in his career as captain of Lancashire had been a dogged batsman, metamorphosed into a dashing opener when he moved to Warwickshire. No longer trammelled by the burdens of captaincy, which for him demanded an inhibiting seriousness, he became a successful England player in this new incarnation, through which he also revealed a satirical attitude towards the absurdities and the solemnity to which those in authority are prone. He was reborn a different kind of creature.

A second cricketer to reinvent himself was Bob Willis. For him it was not so much a new self as a rediscovery of an old one. On one hand, he needed to go back to the old way, from which he had been diverted. In this he was like the once-born. But he also needed to make what felt like a radical change. He is, or was, a fierce personality, who oscillated between gloom and elation. He had strong convictions – this tends to be a feature of the twice-born. And his crisis was more dramatic and intense than Barber's. He was more twice- than once-born.

For Willis, as for Barber, the change involved a move to Warwickshire, in his case from Surrey, where the coach had attempted to turn him into a more orthodox bowler. The classical approach comprises a curved run-up, leading into an action where the left shoulder points at the batman, facilitating 'outswing' – that is, a bend from right to left in the ball's flight before it bounces. I have already given a picture of the Goose pounding in to bowl, as if about to take off. From that classical point of view, his approach was irregular, not only in its frenetic style but also in being very straight; he ran in from behind the umpire. This resulted in an action that was open-chested. Willis was more likely to swing the ball 'in', that is, from left to right.

That early-career coaching led to a breakdown in his basic ability. Both pace and control deserted him. Only when, under a different coaching regime, he returned to his old approach did he regain his natural style, which formed the basis of his move to become the spearhead of England's bowling attack over many years.

Finding One's Calling: Amit Ambalal

To discover a self that has been suppressed, some people have to make a radical change in their whole lifestyle or career. Indian painter Amit Ambalal was the sixth child, and only son, born into a dynasty of mill-owners. Painter, writer and curator Timothy Hyman writes:

> From birth, his fate was sealed . . . As heir to an industrial empire, the future Director of Sarangpur Mills in Ahmedabad, India, the boy was subject to a regimen that was both cosseting and strict. 'I was a kind of a sad child,' he recalls. Often when other children had holidays, he would be taken to the mill to attend the meetings of senior employees. At home the boy was in thrall to his grandfather, a charismatic Sadhu (a sort of holy man), whom Amit recalls 'seated on his tiger-skin, giving darshan (audience), with devotees washing his feet'.

Following desultory studies in commerce and law, and in spite of 'contrary currents', Ambalal 'submitted to the path marked out for him'. At the age of twenty-seven he became managing director of the company. His fate seemed sealed. But:

> 'Privately I was trying to find another way. I didn't want to die as part of a machine.' He would doodle at meetings. ('You might say my art is still an extension of that doodling.') Clearly he felt 'straight-jacketed into the smiling, impermeable mould of the tycoon . . . so contrary to [my] . . . impulses. I wanted to be transparent.'

When he was thirty-six, in 1979, Ambalal took the huge step of selling the mills, a first move in divesting himself of his imposed identity. (Shortly afterwards, when the mills in India started to fail, having to compete with the emergence of booming synthetics industries in the Far East, people congratulated him on his wise decision to sell. He says, drily, 'The Fool knows what's best'.)

Hyman refers to a 'transformation of his mode of being-in-the-world; Ambalal saw the task as "to be yourself, and to construct the language". Naturally, "It took some while. Changing your whole frame of mind inherited from six generations is almost like changing one's genes."' His early sculptures, sketches and doodles reveal busts of 'fatuously smiling men, often garlanded'. This satire, which included anger and a sense of his own former compliance, was a record and expression of his working towards a new identity, his 'gene-changing'. Hyman describes the work also as a 'reparation for what [Ambalal] calls a "chained childhood"'. His upbringing had been that of a prince. He had to fight his way out of the gilded cage.

Struggles don't suddenly stop. One ongoing challenge for Ambalal is to avoid falling into a further imprisonment, the bars this time fashioned within himself. Ambalal speaks of preparing for an exhibition of his own work, for which 85 per cent of what is to be shown is finished and ready. He has a few months to complete the show. Now, under pressure of time, and with the lure of a grand display in prospect, he finds his work constrained, academic. It is as if he is copying himself with a blueprint in mind. He has to resist the temptation to 'be the artist', to be a 'painter of good paintings'. Conceiving himself in these ways indicates a reversion to the means-to-end thinking of his business days; he is unable to work freely. He risks becoming a parody of himself.

While leafing through his sketches of an elderly man consumed by lust, he says that one is too close to a cartoon, and that the next is edging towards being too much 'a painter's drawing'. He had been looking for the area that felt just right to him, between the two extremes. He speaks of the pull towards being a 'proper artist', rather than trusting himself to paint like the six-year-old girl who painted the tiger. She was not at all making a copy; rather she had imagined her way into the posture of the tiger, which she drew with a sure hand.

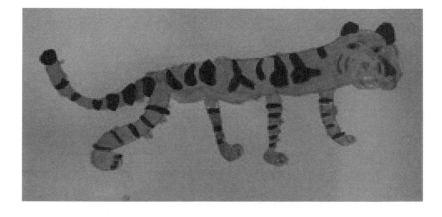

As Georges Braque said, late in life, of Picasso: 'he used to be a great painter: now he is merely a genius.'

I imagine that, had he lacked the courage to make a clean break, Ambalal might have grown into a bitter, dissatisfied man. He might have become split, continuing to doodle as an amateur, chairing not only his own board (seated at times on his grandfather's tiger-skin or its twenty-first-century equivalent), but also a board-member of various charitable artistic ventures, trapped in a false self, with a fixed but fading smile on his face. However successful he might have become as the heir to his family's business empire, it is difficult to believe that his heart would have been in it, that he could have produced more than a reactive, inauthentic sort of form in his work and life.

These revaluations and new starts may be crucial to integration, making external life consistent with our passions, beliefs and capabilities. Decisions of this kind perhaps appear in retrospect to have been natural, even inevitable, At the time they may have felt anything but.

Know Thyself and Born Again

The maxim 'know thyself' was a main tenet of the temple to Apollo at Delphi, and was one of three aphorisms inscribed in its forecourt. One interpretation of this phrase (in its Delphic context) was that it was particularly applicable to 'those whose boasts exceed what they are'. Wilfred Bion said that he 'would like to say to [the patient] "You are really expressing" and then I say whatever I think my interpretation is. The object of that is to introduce the patient to the most important person he is ever likely to have dealings with, namely himself.' He added: 'It sounds simple; in fact it is extremely difficult.' More generally, psychoanalysis claims that no one knows him or herself very far, that we are all inclined to narcissistic over-evaluation of ourselves, are all by nature mixtures of love and hate, and that we develop in fits and starts. This means that, as we often have to function in the dark, and as we have to come to terms with changes in outlook and mentality, we may all have alternative versions of ourselves that we might, or might not, inhabit. To grow, we have to be, more or less, born again.

In the normal course of life we all make transitions, from infancy to being a toddler, from a two-year-old to a five-year-old, from childhood to adolescence, and on to adulthood, middle age, old age and death. These changes are stormy or calm, jerky or smooth. The changes brought about by psycho-analysis, too, may be experienced in either way. But there is always an element of disturbance, I think, always a questioning and disruption of some cherished beliefs and habits.

The question is: it this process evolution or revolution? Of two excellent books on the development of science, one – by Albert Einstein and Leopold Infeld – is called *The Evolution of Physics*, the other, by Thomas Kuhn, *The Structure of Scientific Revolutions*. The latter title emphasises the abruptness of change, the former its continuity.

Einstein and Infeld write:

> The solution of the gravitational problem in the general theory of relativity must differ from the Newtonian one. The laws of gravitation must, just as all laws of nature, be formulated for all possible co-ordinate systems, whereas the laws of classical mechanics, as formulated by Newton, are valid only in inertial co-ordinate systems.

In other words, Newton's discoveries are valid for the movements of matter within the gravitational system that applies on or near the surface of the earth. The new theory includes the old one as a particular case. Einstein's discoveries of the importance of relativity stand on Newton's shoulders – although they show the latter to be limited, they explain why and how far they are valid within a particular coordinate system.

The other title, that of Kuhn, emphasises the jumps that occur when at a critical point scientists overthrow the assumptions underlying the paradigms of their field. Such leaps occur, Kuhn persuasively argues, when scientists find themselves having to make constant adjustments and special pleading to allow for incongruities in working out the consequences of the existing explanatory paradigms, even though such paradigms have long been fruitful both in developing theory and in guiding research.

Both terms, 'revolution' and 'evolution', are revealing descriptions of the same facts. It is a matter of which elements are stressed. Einstein revolutionised physics; but it was also an evolution out of what went before.

19

MASKS AND COSTUMES

What a piece of work is a man.

William Shakespeare

How then can you create a narrative of your own life? Janet Frame compares the process to finding a bunch of old rags, and trying to make a dress. A party dress, I'd say: something fit to be seen in. Something to go out in and face the world.

Hilary Mantel

With desire infiltrating the picture, our excitement, our confidence, our applause . . . might get hollowed out, and, like all of our finery that evening, be exposed . . . as features of a manic kind of costume.

Donald Moss

———

Fabrication

A patient once said to me, 'My wife tells bare-faced lies. But I lie in how I am. And that is much worse.' John Ruskin had a similar thought: 'The essence of lying is self-deception, not in words; a lie may be told by silence, by equivocation, by the accenting of a syllable, by a glance of the eye attaching a peculiar significance to a sentence; and all these lies are worse and baser . . . than a lie plainly worded.'

We all find and create costumes in which to dress ourselves up, to cover our nakedness, vulnerability and aloneness. We paper over cracks that in some cases are crevasses. We 'pretend' – etymologically, we 'stretch something (such as a mask, screen or costume) in front of ourselves.'

Some people come across as more inauthentic than others. A few are out-and-out deceivers, people with fronts that are deliberately false, conmen, their lies plainly worded as well as acted.

In the world of sport, no one went further in this direction than Lance Armstrong, the cyclist. Unable to accept defeat, he fought his way back, as a twenty-five-year-old, from advanced, metastatic testicular cancer, diagnosed by his urologist as almost certainly fatal. Eighteen months later, free of cancer, he started his foundation, which subsequently raised large sums of money to assist other survivors. His compulsion to be the best at any price led not only to a systematic and sophisticated use of illegal performance-enhancing drugs over many years, but also, I surmise, to the conviction that he wasn't *really* guilty; that he was, rather, successful not only on the bike, but also in creating a fiction that persuaded virtually the whole world that any suspicion of his amazing transformations in stamina and performance was malign. Although he told the world that 'we're all the authors of our own life story', and that 'you should go out there and write the best damn story you can', almost everyone, star-struck by this secular saint, was seduced by the hero-who-overcame-cancer fairy-tale, and by his intimidating threats of expensive retaliation in the courts. As one writer put it, 'The best place to hide is right out in front, in plain sight, in yellow.' Until, that is, 2012, when a US Anti-Doping Agency investigation concluded that he was guilty of being the ring-leader of the 'biggest doping programme sport has ever seen'.

A Manic Kind of Costume

Since Freud, none of us should be entirely secure in our identities. Psychoanalysis (along with other forms of individual and social psychology) teaches us that borders between the conscious self and the unconscious, between self and other, 'civilised' and uncivilised, between races and between people with different sexualities, the borders of sanity and madness, of morality and immorality, are more porous and less absolute than was commonly maintained. How much do we hide our true identities 'right out in front, in yellow'? Is our masculinity no more than 'drag'? And how precarious are these psychological clothes that reassure us of our stability as part of the 'we' of the various groupings we identify with?

Donald Moss, an American psychoanalyst, recounts Kafka's short story, 'Report to an Academy'. Many years ago, an ape was brought in chains from Africa to Europe. Somehow, it got itself educated, and has become prominent in a profession. The ape is invited to report on his remarkable life to the members of the academy. The evening is a splendid occasion, for which all are dressed in their finest evening clothes. It is a celebration of 'the convergence of our compassion with his genius'.

After the ape's moment of triumph and apparent acceptance by the great and the good, they – 'we' – are relieved that the ape returns home to his live-in concubine, his alter ego, the female chimpanzee with the 'insane look of the bewildered half-broken animal'. Our hypocrisy is deep-seated. We cannot allow this other really to be one of ourselves, one of the 'civilised'. Kafka writes:

> We almost identify with him, and we almost love him. 'Almost' because when it comes down to it, we cannot really identify with this ape, and . . . neither can we love him . . . [There is an] apparently irreducible gap . . . We not only put him there [i.e. on the other side of the boundary] but also keep him there . . . With this desire to 'keep him there' infiltrating the picture . . . our applause is hollowed out . . . and, like all our finery that evening is exposed as a manic kind of costume.

Later in the same paper, Moss describes with admirable honesty a moment when his own security was shaken by a patient he was seeing in consultation, who was within a hair's breadth of hitting him and then left the session in fury and hatred, screaming 'Faggot!' Moss was terrified, and then furious. He was also left 'emotionally uncertain about where on the "masculine" ground I was standing'.

But he had an even more shocking reaction and revelation that evening, coming home on the subway:

> Waiting for the same train . . . stood a man who I was certain was gay. He was small and delicate. I looked closely

at him, more closely than I usually would. I then felt the force of the word *faggot* practically roaring in my mind. The word that had just that morning targeted me was this time targeting *him* . . . For a moment I wanted to really hurt this man . . . to hit him, scare him, get rid of him, to get rid of all of them.

Moss realised how 'slight the difference' was between his patient and himself (as between the ape and the academy members). His professional analytic demeanour, his security as a heterosexual man, his steady sanity – all had been thrown into doubt and confusion in the aftermath of the near-assault. On the subway platform, the scenario had been reversed; violently excluded earlier in the day, now, on the platform, *he* was the violent hater and excluder.

We are not exactly like the emperor with no clothes, but we are not far off. We too, the great and the good, are liable to be reduced to the ape who, removing his dinner jacket after the academy event, goes home to meet, and mate with, his chimpanzee.

'Apparel Oft Proclaims the Man'

Hamlet has just discovered that his old fellow-students are spying on him, an additional reason for his bleak view of human nature:

> What a piece of work is a man! How noble in reason! How infinite in faculty! In form and moving how express and admirable! In action how like an angel! In apprehension how like a god! The beauty of the world, the paragon of animals . . . And yet to me, what is this quintessence of dust? Man delights not me, no, nor woman neither, though by your smiling you seem to say so.

Clothes often make a declaration about the self. They – we – may be a piece of work in a different sense.

In Thomas Mann's 1901 novel *Buddenbrooks*, one feature of his chilling picture of the decline of Thomas Buddenbrook, the head of the once-great family firm of grain importers, is his fastidiousness. He has become 'parsimonious about anything except for his own wardrobe'. His constant attention to personal cleanliness and his immaculate clothing has become his obsession, aimed at 'making him feel at easy and ready to meet the world, much like an actor who has prepared every brush-stroke of his make-up before stepping out on stage . . .'

> His whole life had become a single production, down to the smallest, most workaday detail . . . that constantly engaged and devoured all his energies. He completely lacked any ardent interest that might have occupied his mind. His interior life was impoverished, had undergone a deterioration so severe that it was like the almost constant burden of some vague grief. And bound up with it all was a grim determination to present himself at his best, to conceal his frailties by any means possible, and to keep up appearances. It had all contributed to making his existence what it was: artificial, self-conscious and forced, – until every word, every gesture, the slightest deed in the presence of others had become a taxing and gruelling part in a play.

Exhausted by the effort of all this, by the constant need to keep his face muscles firm and resolute-looking, Thomas Buddenbrook has taken on the pallor of a sick man. When sitting quietly, alone, weariness and disgust would rise up inside him, clouding his eyes, robbing him of control over his posture and the muscles in his face. And then just one wish would possess him: to give way to dull despair, to steal away and lay his head on a cool pillow at home.

Mann shows us both the defence – the 'make-up', the acting – and that which it covers: Thomas's inner impoverishment, deterioration and despair.

The philosopher John Wisdom writes about a woman's sudden revelation that an item of apparel – a glamorous hat she has been trying on – does *not*, after all, 'proclaim the woman': 'She is studying it in the mirror. There's a pause and then a friend says "My dear, the Taj Mahal". Instantly the look of indecision leaves the face in the mirror. All along she has known there was something wrong with the hat, now she sees what it is.'

The comment about the Taj Mahal, Wisdom adds, is 'not a prosaic assertion of similarity – the hat is not *like* the Taj Mahal'; it is a more poetic expression of a grandeur that reveals that 'the hat has become a monument and too magnificent by half'. In this case, the friend acts as an informal therapist, whose perception gels with the woman's misgivings. Instantaneously, she sees how she has been tempted towards donning a persona that she does not really want, and that does not suit her.

Uniforms

Literal uniforms have an ordinary positive role; they declare our rights and responsibilities. In hospitals, nurses are instantly recognisable as such. The judge's wig announces to all his authority. Police and military uniforms disclose not only role but also rank, thus showing levels of responsibility. Playing a role does not necessarily mean falsehood or hypocrisy. Rowan Williams said about the rituals involved in being Archbishop of Canterbury, 'This is what I have to do to keep this community fulfilling its purpose.'

Indeed, self-presentation is an essential part of life. As children, we naturally take our parents and others as models of how to do things, how to be. Later, in all fields of activity we follow a range of exemplars. We imitate our peers, as well as our elders and betters, or perhaps more accurately we enter into their gestures and style. We often learn by taking in a general sense of someone's way of being: in tennis, as we have seen, Timothy Gallwey invited his novice pupil, Paul, to 'get a *visual image* of the basic forehand' rather than learn technique consciously, piece by piece. We 'become' our mentors, and our successors become us.

Moreover, we all need some defences, and it is often only by means of unbalanced or even deformed emotion that we bolster and energise ourselves. To galvanise ourselves into action, we may need to be a touch manic; taking on difficult challenges may make use of a degree of omnipotence.

Nevertheless, fierce conviction may lift us above *merely* putting on a show. Rodney Marsh, Australia wicketkeeper and one-time captain of Western Australia, tells of a one-day match between his side and Queensland in 1976, at that time the two best teams in Australia. Halfway through, Western Australia, all out for 77, were, to any neutral observer, in a hopeless position. Marsh gave a brief motivating talk to his players: 'Let's at least put up a show for the home crowd.' At this point his main bowler, Dennis Lillee, burst in angrily. 'Put up a show? We're going to win.' Lillee then struck several blows with the ball, getting out Queensland's best player, Viv Richards, for 0, and three others cheaply. Western Australia won by fifteen runs.

Conviction may not always trump realism, but it may motivate people to the best possible chance of success. What does realistically underpin such commitment is the knowledge that we *might* end up winning, that we will have given our best towards it, and that we are then entitled to hold our heads up in defeat. A psychoanalyst colleague, Rob Hale, made a further point: Marsh invited a 'show', that is, a performance, for the supporters. Lillee rebutted him, saying in effect 'no, we're going to *really* play, play cricket, *not just put on a show, we're not doing it for anyone else.*' Actors sometimes, old troupers as they are, have to rely on technique and 'putting on a show' to get by when they are not in the mood, not on top form; at other times they feel as if they are the character. Lillee wanted the team to *be* the part.

The Actor – Putting on a Show

In a scathing article on Stefan Zweig, a writer who was in vogue in the 1920s and 30s, critic Michael Hofmann writes that Zweig 'just tastes fake'. Even his suicide note, he suggests, was designed to make an impression:

> A note which, like most of what he wrote, is so smooth and mannerly and somehow machined – actually more like an Oscar acceptance-speech than a suicide note – that one feels the irritable rise of boredom halfway through it, and the sense that *he doesn't mean it*, his heart isn't in it (not even in his suicide).

Writing, like other activities, may become *mere* performance and pretence, an Oscar speech. I am reminded of a friend's description of a recent highly acclaimed theatrical tour de force as a 'pseudo-mystical wank'. A poor piece of theatre, but an impressive ejaculation.

In his short story 'Who Am I This Time?' Kurt Vonnegut presents Harry Nash, a shy, retiring clerk in a hardware store. When onstage, however, he is 'never Harry'; he throws himself into the character he embodies. Playing parts like Marlon Brando's Stanley in A *Streetcar Named Desire,* he is suddenly 'huge and handsome, conceited and cruel'. He has 'added fifty pounds to his weight and four inches to his height'. 'The minute he didn't have a part to play, he disappeared into some hiding place where he couldn't be seen . . . He would put on his coat and tie, and become the pale hardware store clerk again.'

Harry becomes a person only when provided with a script. He has an impact on others, turning fellow-actors into facsimiles of the other characters, so that for instance, one woman feels like 'a drunk and faded Southern belle'. And Helene, the newcomer, who was so bottled up before, a 'walking ice-box', is rapidly transformed into a passionate lover.

The story ends with Helene using lines from *Romeo and Juliet* to seduce Harry into marriage. Once she can get him to read Romeo's lines, in response to her Juliet-lines, the feelings come alive in both of them just as when they are on stage. Their marriage is a succession of enacted dramas. 'They seem very happy, although they're kind of strange from time to time, depending on which play they're reading to each other at the time.' Helene's summary of her situation is: 'Wouldn't you say I was the luckiest girl in town?'

Vonnegut offers one or two telling hints about how Harry might have come to be so empty, yet so able to be filled with life in his assumed parts: 'The trouble with Harry was he'd been left on the doorstep of the Unitarian Church when he was a baby, and he never did find out who his parents were.'

He had, we presume, no internal parents either, with whom to identify and to struggle. He was a nobody, except when in

277

role. At one point he 'hid in the [library's] reference room, passing the time looking at flags of different countries in the front of the dictionary' – a brilliant touch, suggesting Harry's need for labels or signs of identity, something he lacks except when inhabiting a fictional persona. Who needs to be himself when, hiding behind a mask, he can *be* someone else, putting their flag on his masthead?

Montaigne recounts a story not unlike Vonnegut's, from Plutarch, about the dangers of removing a person's self-aggrandising way of perceiving the world. Lykas has led a peaceful, well-regulated daily life. But while holding down a job and doing his duty to familiars and strangers alike, he has the conviction that everything he sees and does is taking place on a stage as a theatrical performance. When a doctor cures him of this delusion, Lykas becomes so miserable that he sues the doctor for robbing him of his only pleasure in life.

Like Lykas's doctor, should we take the view that all such transformations of the world and one's own desires are intrinsically pathological, and that they should therefore be rooted out? The issue of whether to interfere in another's 'agreeable' delusions is at times an ethical dilemma for psychoanalysts and others, a dilemma that may become particularly acute if the deluded person becomes seriously or even fatally ill. Is truth always helpful? When should we let sleeping dogs lie? Will we too be sued for our successes?

Norman, a middle-class man from the West of England, had had a rough upbringing – his mother was an alcoholic, vicious when drunk, his father an old-fashioned parent with a cruel streak. Pocket money had to be earned by doing maths questions – a penny for each correct answer. Father charged his son petrol money to get to school. He beat the boy with a strap.

In his mid-teens, Norman began to transform himself. He conveyed superiority. When a cousin two years older than himself got into Oxford, he was patronising, almost avuncular, in the letter he wrote to their grandmother: 'Louise has done *so* well. I never expected it of her. I always imagined I would be the first in the family to go to Oxbridge.' Becoming 'cultured' to the point of pomposity, pronouncing on French cheeses and fine wines, he found or created a part to inhabit. His regional brogue was overlaid with a pukka BBC accent – a readily detectable layering. He was self-centred in his conversation and choice of topics. He was late even for important events like funerals and weddings. He came across as inauthentic.

Norman's sister was troubled by his selfishness, especially when he avoided the painful tasks of looking after their dying mother, and left her all the problems associated with the will after their mother died. But his partner and the wider family (including many cousins of about the same age, all living near each other) tolerated his eccentricities and affectations fondly, with a sort of sideways smile, as if saying to each other, 'There goes Norman again'. They were not put out by his pretentiousness. Rather they felt protective of him, aware of its roots in his insecurity. They seemed able to see the pained child just beneath the surface. They also recognised that the new identity he had managed to construct was essential in enabling him to thrive. From this relatively safe vantage point he became able to talk with insight about his childhood. Things might have turned out so much worse.

Were this man to go into analysis, his analyst might face an ethical problem: how much to deconstruct the reconstructed Norman? How much to interpret, and possibly contribute to the removal of, his props? The answer would, of course, have to come from within the analysis, from clues the patient would give about his readiness to go through a second disassembling of his identity.

Norman's sister – who had cause for her acerbity – apart, his family seem to have behaved with tact and empathy in relation to the metaphorical clothes he put on. They did not take the moral high ground.

Captured by these kinds of self-serving or self-protective scenarios, we all risk clogging up our mental space, wasting our energies and dissipating our form. Yet, as Hilary Mantel writes in the paragraph I quoted at the start of this chapter: 'When you were a child you had to create yourself from whatever was to hand. You had to construct yourself and make yourself into a person, fitting somehow into a niche that in your family had always been vacant . . . How then can you create a narrative of your own life?'

It's quite an achievement to make a party dress out of a pile of rags.

PART VIII: RADICAL CHANGE

20

DOING THE NEEDFUL

Each unhappy family is unhappy in its own way.
                                        Leo Tolstoy

———

Just as there are innumerable ways of falling ill, so there are of losing form.

Appropriate treatments are equally varied. As with illness, it would be foolish to expect a common cure for them all. Doing medicine without an attempt at diagnosis would be irrational and unethical. There is no one-size-fits-all remedy.

One way to begin to think about reliable solutions for loss of form is to follow the diagnosis between too much horse and too much snaffle, too little control and too little spontaneity. By 'diagnosis' I don't mean only long-term classificatory differentiation; I am thinking of moment-to-moment assessments. What is the current hot point, the main issue, just now?

Ian Botham

Captaining Ian Botham called at times for giving him his head, encouraging the instinctual horse to let go all inhibitions, and at others for reining him in. He was a brilliant

all-rounder, with an all-out attacking attitude whether batting or bowling – he usually believed that he should have
even more close catchers, and fewer fielders saving singles or
boundaries. He was full of enthusiasm for the game and the
team. I was his first England captain. Like any hot-blooded
young man, he would bridle at authority figures, including of
course me, at times, but he was big enough to think further.
However different we were in personality, we got on well. He
helped me be more lively and energetic, and I helped him,
I think, to use his talents fully.

On rare occasions, though, Botham 'lost it' as a bowler. At
Perth in 1978, puffing out his chest in his efforts to bounce
out specialist batsman Peter Toohey, he 'fed' Toohey's pull and
hook shots, contributing to Australia's partial recovery from
128 for eight in a low-scoring game. I quickly took him off
despite his urgent demands to be given the use of the second
new ball so that he could really hurl himself at the insolent
Australian who had had the temerity to hook him. Here was
an example of a curb being used for damage limitation; I had
to disregard his inevitable, but also short-lived, feeling of being
badly done by.

In 1981, I was chosen – by a whisker, I learned much later
– to take over from Botham when he had resigned as captain of England after a difficult year in charge, involving no
less than nine Test matches against the powerful West Indies
and three against Australia, the next strongest team. (When
he and the team were up against it in the Caribbean I had
sent him a letter of advice: he should try captaining England
against somebody else.)

The next match was at Headingley. After Australia won
the toss and batted, it was evident to me from his first few
balls that Ian was running in more slowly than when I had

last played with him almost a year before. He was also stepping in towards the stumps just before delivering the ball, and there was an exaggerated twist in his action. He had developed these complications – almost affectations – in order to try to make the ball swing, but in the process had lost much of what had made him so penetrative: the Botham I knew had been direct and forthright, anything but finicky or fussy. I took him off after three overs. When, predictably, he complained that he couldn't bowl in such short spells, I retorted that I couldn't keep him on if he bowled medium-paced half-volleys. I nicknamed him the 'Sidestep Queen', thereby provoking him and spurring him on. His recently acquired snaffle needed to be removed, the rambunctious horse revived, his earthy energy restored. Botham quickly recovered much of his old form as a bowler, taking six wickets in that Australian first innings.

When he went in to bat in our first innings we were already in a dire position at 87 for five in reply to Australia's 401 for nine declared. Early on, he played an ambitious attacking shot off a ball from Dennis Lillee that reared up past his gloves. He looked up to the players' balcony – not far away, in those days, from the Headingley pitch. I grinned and gestured to him to keep on going for his shots. Botham was at his best as a hitter, and was in general better off playing without inhibition. On that particular pitch, with the ball deviating off the seam and bouncing unevenly, it would have been foolish for him to attempt a careful, defensive approach. Released from the strain of captaincy, given his head by me, he swung his arms and freed his hands to wonderful effect, scoring 50 and 149 not out in his two innings. We were extremely fortunate to win the match, and Botham would no doubt agree that he personally needed a good deal of luck to score all those runs. But for him to play that way was nevertheless his – and our – best chance. This was an occasion when fortune favoured the bold.

These were differential diagnoses, and different treatments. As a bowler in the 1981 match, the sidestep curb had to go. At Perth the prescription had been different: apply snaffle. When batting at Headingley, I gave him licence to set curbs aside and go for the bowling like the proverbial village blacksmith. In my view, Botham had found it hard to captain himself, to know when to bowl and when not, and in what manner to bowl and to bat. But none of his unproductive choices – sidestep, a feeling of insult requiring retaliation, a temptation to bat with solemnity – had entered deeply into his sense of what he had to do. My ripostes, ideas and actions were effective largely because he was open to suggestion. Sometimes modest nudges or rebukes remove obstacles and restore basic strengths.

When Doug Insole told Derek Randall off for impetuosity, the player's first response was, as we saw, insouciant: 'That's the way I play,' he said. 'In that case', Insole came back, 'you should think about the way you play' – that is, Randall should not assume that because to him it felt 'natural', even imperative, to hook balls as soon as he came in, he should give free rein to this impulse. He needed to impose restraint on himself. As a result of listening to Insole, his form was recalibrated. The need for basic discipline in sport (as in other activities) is obvious; a coach's job is to get this across without undermining the player's expressiveness and special qualities.

I remember at the end of one county season telling a young batsman that in my view his technique was not sound enough for when the going got hard, that his natural eye, wrist and flair would not be sufficient to get him to the standard required in top-level cricket; he needed to work on his technique over the winter. The outcome? His priorities were elsewhere; or perhaps he thought I was talking rubbish. He faded out of professional cricket into some other way of living his life.

On the Rock Face

In all areas of life, we need both security and challenge, safety and adventure.

To develop skills and find form, to grow up, takes courage and self-reliance. A powerful argument for embracing risk was made by climber Andy Kirkpatrick about taking his thirteen-year-old daughter, Ella, with him to climb El Capitan in Yosemite. The largest ledge on this climb, which would take five days, is the size of a shoe. The rock face is so steep that climbers are forced to sleep suspended from it in hammocks. Kirkpatrick regarded the expedition as a continuation of his role as a parent – preparing his daughter for life.

Kirkpatrick argued that our society has become far too safety-conscious. Many opportunities for children to prove themselves have been legislated against. Every stranger is a

potential threat. They mustn't play British Bulldogs, a rough game I loved as a boy. Risk aversion, according to Kirkpatrick, bricks us up in fear. It even plays a part in mental illness, and certainly fits into, and tends to create, a blame culture.

Kirkpatrick claimed that children need to define themselves against their parents, and will always find ways of doing so. This is part of the underlying reason for the rites of passage that societies have over millennia prescribed for their adolescents. If positive activities are banned or discouraged by anxious adults, children will turn to more destructive outlets and rebellions, not only to the old ones (sex, drugs and alcohol) but also to newer ones – those to be found, for instance, on the dark internet.

Kirkpatrick himself began climbing as soon as he could walk. He and his friends climbed all over the flats where they lived in Hull, 'hanging by their fingertips from balconies'. They swam in the docks. He offered his children a similar model. When they fell, got cuts, bruises and stitches, he never rushed to pick them up. Children are waterproof, he said, and they bounce. Giving in to fear robs you of what you really want to do, like swimming in a cold stream or asking a girl to dance.

As for Ella's climb, he had no doubt she could do it, and she knew that he believed in her. The real question for him was: how could he *not* share this with her, how could he not give her the opportunity to prove to herself that she was brave enough? On the rock, she had her life and her future in her own hands. She climbed without complaint, crying only once, when she dropped her iPod. He spoke of her tenacity, resilience and grace. There was risk, of course; but objectively, he said, the hazard was less than when cycling to school.

Kirkpatrick put his finger on one source of the anxious protection so often imposed on children: parents don't (or don't only) want them to grow up, to grow away from themselves.

On the climb she had been his equal, not a child receiving special treatment. He lost the child, and saw before him, with him, ahead of him, at the top of El Capitan, an assured young woman.

Now, two years on, she had something that many of her peers, watched over by more sheltering parents, lack. He saw in her a fearlessness, confidence and maturity that sets her apart. She has no need, he said, to define herself by negative behaviour.

A Secure Base

We all need to face El Capitans, however modest our equivalents are. Too much emphasis on safety results in a nanny state. Initiative is stunted, and with it achievement and maturity. However, at the same time, we need to take seriously, and find ways of opposing, reckless and provocative risk-taking. Admiring as I do Ella and her father, I also wonder how Mrs Kirkpatrick felt during that expedition.

As Joseph Conrad wrote: 'Few men realise that their life, the very essence of their character, their capabilities and audacities, are only the expression of their belief in the safety of their surroundings.' In developmental terms, the toddler needs the security of the breast, and of the mother and other caregivers – a 'secure base', as psychoanalyst and pioneer of Attachment Theory, John Bowlby, put it, from which to explore.

Gradually the child ranges further, and for longer, from mother's proximity, but parents continually make assessments about the degree of independence appropriate. When and how high should the girl climb trees, risking a fall? When to leave the boy to pick himself up and try again? When should we allow our son or daughter to cross a busy street by themselves? Or go to their first night club? We try to find a balance between restriction and freedom, between proper limits and protection on one side, and self-motivation and freedom to choose on the other. We (try to) bring up our children to be their own persons, to make as many of their own decisions as possible, not to be versions of ourselves or of the people we wish we had become.

There is a constant tension between foolhardiness and over-caution. Not all risky ventures are as successful as Ella Kirkpatrick's, or her father's. And not everyone is suited to being a pioneer, or a high-level, ambitious leader. The Roman historian Tacitus tersely described the Emperor Galba as 'capable of being Emperor – had he not become Emperor'.

Nor is it the case that *anything* is possible. Deranged opponents of ageism regard age as irrelevant in job or training applications, as if being seventy-five years old should be no drawback to being accepted for a long professional training. Such politically correct responses deny realities such as the lack of time available for development and for productive work in the field, and the increasing risks of incompetence and decline. I am reminded of the one-legged man applying for the role of Tarzan in the great revue from the late 1950s, *Beyond the Fringe*.

Recipes? Or Broader Values?

We seek help in how to live, how to be at our best. Often we think that what we need is a reliable recipe for an end product that is already known. There is a huge appetite for self-help books that appeal to basic wish-fulfilment; how to become a chief executive, say, or a Premier League footballer.

We are encouraged to believe that such aspirations are feasible if only we could find the right prescription and then follow it. At a prize-giving at my school, the speaker, who was, I think, the head of the Scout movement, urged us all to be leaders.

Next day, my teacher, Rev. C. J. Ellingham, writing his weekly skit for the Greek class in motley as well as proper Greek, had a boy noted for asking difficult questions. Query: 'But if everyone is a leader, who will be there to be led?'

I side with Ellingham. In my view, it is by reflecting on and reframing our goals, not by finding simple routes to already established goals, that we are most likely to find new levels of form. We often have to modify our wishes and our thinking, to see things from different angles. We may for example need to remind ourselves of the value of the (apparently) humdrum. Life would be intolerable if emotions had to be continuously ratcheted up to the level of a first date with a desirable girl, or the last day of a tense Test match. Ordinary companionship, uneventful but reliable, may be deeply reassuring. It is one reason why people keep pets.

Moreover, the strenuous and inevitable setbacks of any life-project are tolerable, even satisfying, when we feel the work is contributing to something bigger, of value to ourselves and others, so that what would otherwise be only burdensome or boring is given meaning in a wider context. The pointless gains point. We often need to enlarge our appreciation of our everyday encounters and activities. But this does not always come easily; it takes work and thought.

Routine work may be lifted and boredom relieved. Mihaly Csikszentmihalyi describes how factory worker Rico Medellin transformed his conveyor-belt job by turning it into a competition with himself, performing tasks at speed and beating his own records. Moreover, Medellin saw the limitations of this, and was planning to qualify himself through study and qualifications for a more challenging and rewarding job.

In 1974, soon after the publication of his first 'Inner Game' book, Timothy Gallwey was asked by the board of the American telecommunications company AT&T to help change their corporate culture in order to prepare it for its imminent transition from its established status as a monopolistic utility to being market-driven, in open competition with others. The board was keen to make use of the principles of his book, albeit using the workforce rather than themselves as guinea pigs.

Gallwey initiated a pilot project. The overriding value in the company culture, he learned, was security, achievable by a narrow version of loyalty: 'If we come to work on time . . . and keep our noses clean, we are part of the family, and will have a job for life.' This mentality favoured 'membership individuals'; it also elicited such an orientation. In the telephone company's new environment, things would have to change. The awareness of the looming challenge had led to turmoil among the telephone operators, who were at the sharp end of the new emphasis on customer satisfaction. They were unhappy, nervous about insecurity and the increased responsibility that change would entail.

Gallwey quickly realised that the most interesting aspect of the operators' work was the 'voice of the customer, and the responding voice of the operator'. He asked, 'What can be learned by listening to the customer's voice?' He suggested that they might find their job more interesting if they listened in a non-judgmental way to each caller's tone of voice. Then they could, he suggested, monitor also their own responses.

Listening along these lines not only made the work more interesting; the operators 'no longer took their irritation to heart'. Like Wilfred Bion, who once said that it was 'fascinating how boring a particular patient was', the operators became engrossed in the tetchiness, rudeness or friendliness of their clients. They rated them according to these parameters. They became interested too in their own responses. What's more, it

dawned on them that they could use these new skills of obser-
vation not only at work but also in listening to and interacting
with their own families, partners and friends.

From the viewpoint of what it meant financially for the company, the discussions led to more courtesy with no reduction
in speed; the operators were not *trying* to be more courteous,
they simply *became* more courteous as they felt less threatened
and their curiosity grew. What's more, boredom went down by
40 per cent; enjoyment up by 30 per cent. The operators were
more in control of their work and the environment.

Monotony may be transformed, too, by aesthetic responses.
A street-cleaner's work is transfigured, at least momentarily,
through his aesthetic response to the light, to the beauty of the
buildings, or to the texture and shape of a kerbstone and its join
with the paving stones. A young child is more enchanted by a
sweet wrapper picked up in the gutter of a Paris street than by
anything to be found in the Louvre. A four-year-old boy finds
the deep sound of the voice of a very old woman with short hair
fascinating; after carefully studying her face for some minutes
at a respectful distance, and listening intently, he announces
solemnly: 'That man has a funny voice.'

The child-poet or child-philosopher raises the ordinary
into the extraordinary, and it is a mark of adults who live to
the full that they have not lost this capacity. The philosopher
John Wisdom, then in his mid-sixties, rounding a building in
California, encountered a group of kite-flyers. He peered up into
the bright sky, cupping his eyes with his hands, and said in a tone
of utter absorption and amazement, 'Look how *high* they are!'

During my last three or four years as a professional cricketer
I was in analysis; when I became over-anxious about things
going wrong on the cricket field, my analyst would remind
me that I wasn't the only person in the team responsible for

how things turned out; the winning and losing was the responsibility of us all. Thus she challenged my omnipotence and restored my sense of being part of a team. My problems could be shared, some with the analyst, others with the players.

Such a sense of solidarity lifts our work level. When starting my day of analytic work, I have often been strengthened in my resolve by finding myself calling to mind my colleagues in their consulting rooms, all of us engaged in the same kind of endeavour. I feel less on my own, and more capable of being on form.

A person may reconcile himself to boredom, and feel less bored, by not losing touch with the fact that his having work keeps his family in food and clothing. His ability to bear them in mind carries him through the tedium. He is able to look forward to good times, at home and at work, rather than expecting, and finding, only disappointment or bitterness. He does not forget that his conveyor-belt shift will come to an end. He is able to use the mental space his job affords him to enjoy and elaborate thoughts and plans relating to his emotional life. Like the Bushman tracking the kudu, he holds in mind his family and their need for meat. This altruistic attitude, part of the motivation for earning a living, helps the hunter stick at the chase despite exhaustion and thirst.

Tom Cartwright, who during his playing career for Warwickshire worked during the winters in a car factory, told me after his move to play for Somerset and live in the small rural town of Wells, that he missed the lively debates and arguments on the factory floor in Coventry, about work conditions, politics, sport, philosophy and so on. He also felt the Somerset team were too forelock-touching in their class attitudes. For him, worker solidarity and passion were life-enhancing ingredients in his daily chores.

When it comes to hard, repetitive work, one advantage of communist regimes, at least in their more optimistic and less paranoid early phases, was the conviction that labour was dignified by being shared by all and in the interests of all. This feeling of being in it together occurs especially at times of national catastrophe or danger, when each individual's work is valued as part of a coherent effort. In such frames of mind, work becomes less laborious, however hard it is. We also work better.

Such solidarity of aspiration binds together those who have been imprisoned in their fight for a fairer world. On Robben Island, Nelson Mandela and his fellow-prisoners in the liberation struggle turned their incarceration and forced labour in the stone quarries into what became known as Mandela University. They taught each other what they knew, discussing and studying topics from homosexuality to Xhosa, from non-racialism to Afrikaans. They sang. They befriended the warders, both because they relied on them for permission to talk and debate, and because they never knew who might become radicalised. 'There were', Mandela later said, 'unforgettable occasions when that frustrating monotony was broken, and the entire world ushered into the cell.'

In 1975 he wrote to his wife, 'At least, if for nothing else, the cell gives you the opportunity to look daily into your entire conduct, to overcome the bad and develop whatever is good in you. Never forget that a saint is a sinner who keeps on trying.' When he left prison Mandela emphasised reconciliation and unity.

Seeing otherwise dull work as coming under the aegis of service to God, or as an opportunity to identify with God's service to man, is another such route. In *War and Peace*, the saintly Platon Karataev, Pierre's fellow-prisoner on the forced march under the retreating French army, shares what little food he has, and sees suffering as something to be taken for granted and endured. He experiences life directly, with gratitude and joy. His take on life is spiritual. Pierre is deeply affected, even transformed, by his new friend.

Cooperation and Negotiation

We all need support at times, in some cases, sustained, sensitive and reliable support, both firm and kindly.

Psychoanalysis is one source of such attention. Film producer Tony Garnett describes his analysis with Charles Rycroft. He writes: 'when I repeatedly directed my displaced violent emotions onto my analyst, he [Rycroft] just sailed on, never rising to the bait, never retaliating, always in a quiet good humour, always listening and remembering.' The result was that Garnett was gradually able to 'adjust [his] fantasies in the light of repeated examination'. He seems to have managed to undo some of what Gloucester in *King Lear* calls the 'wrong imaginations' that had deformed his emotional life.

Benign changes do happen. The ability to find mental space, tell our stories and then reflect, may enable us to review and reshape our visceral responses and our reactive defences and priorities, thus becoming liberated, more truthful, and more emotionally accepting of ourselves and (as in Garnett's case) our families.

Within the self too we need to be able to find helpful resources. We can do this when we have a sense of similarly kind and firm internal attitudes to ourselves. Psychoanalysts refer to these inner attitudes as 'good objects'. To speak of different selves or agencies within the self, analogical to social or familial life, is a kind of fiction. But the terminology feels apt. It is *as if* there are more selves than one, each interacting with the other(s). The individual person is a kind of team or group, cooperative or in conflict, housing different figures, realistic and otherwise, all with roots in our early life. Just as any of these agencies of the self, the spontaneous id (seat of instinctual and passionate desires) the controlling superego or the negotiating ego – the horse, the snaffle or the rider – may be distorted and destructive, they may also be healthy and in relative concord with each other. Ian McEwan's 'inner parliament' may function as a dictatorship by one side or the other, as a civil war or as a subtle form of trickery; it may alternatively be a robustly honest partnership and debating chamber, in which each member respects the others. The 'good object' may act as a kind of holding environment, in which these processes may be experienced and worked through; it may also be an internal figure, with whom we relate more directly.

Psychoanalysis offers a chance of radical change in the internal world, with consequences for interpersonal relations. As happens between opposing negotiators at successful peace talks, the selves become more familiar with each other, more capable of tolerance and cooperation. Then emotions that have become deformed by denial and by shame are in some instances re-formed (or reformed); the 'wrong imaginations' that have overridden one's better side and better impulses are less in charge. Destructive tendencies are given house-room, but become, for the most part, less rampant or pervasive. In a successful analysis, these tendencies are more and more held under the aegis of a kinder self.

Often the issue is – which self is in charge?

21

CAN QUICK FIXES STICK?

Bowl as fast and straight as you can.

Bob Willis's team-mates

*I hope my remarks will shed some darkness on the
subject.*

Hans Loewald

At the still point of the turning world.

T. S. Eliot

———

When sportsmen 'lose it', becoming depressed, or over-anxious,
or simply off form for a period, they naturally want a quick fix.
Players fear that decline is terminal. Sporting lifespans are
short, and there are always promising rivals eager to take one's
place. Injury can set one back irrecoverably. Sentiment does
not go far in sport: there is no guarantee of getting a lost place
back, and people demand immediate results.

Immediately before the match against Australia at
Headingley in 1981, in which Bob Willis bowled England to
an improbable, fortunate and remarkable victory by a mere
eighteen runs, taking eight wickets for 43 in the final innings
to dismiss Australia for 111, it appeared likely that he was near

the end of his international career. He had been unwell with a persistent chest problem, and had lost form. He had recently developed a habit of overstepping the bowling mark, bowling no-balls; this was a symptom of, and had added to, his loss of rhythm. He had also lost his spearhead role with the new ball, which had been taken over by the young Graham Dilley. Bob did not relish this 'demotion', and was unsure whether to bowl flat out in an effort to regain it, or to accept the new role by reducing his speed and aiming to be a more controlled, medium-fast bowler.

On the evening before his extraordinary spell, a few players were having a drink in the bar. In effect we said to him, 'Bowl as fast and straight as you can tomorrow, Goose. Don't worry about no-balls, and don't try anything fancy. The pitch is uneven; with your height and speed if you get it right they won't be able to play you.'

Next day he did, and they weren't. He appeared to be in even more of a trance than usual, a man possessed. He was a gambler going for broke.

One ingredient in this last-ditch shift in attitude was anger. Bob was furious, with the press, with the selectors (who had initially left him out of the side for this match), perhaps with me (one of the selectors), probably also with himself. He was able to gather together this aggression and take it out on the opposition. My impression was that his 'I'll show them' attitude, combined with 'what do I have to lose?' contributed to a relaxed but productive intensity. The severe, self-critical side of his personality was pushed into the background. Perhaps our words were a helpful nudge, reminding him of how hard he was to bat against, especially in the prevailing conditions. It was the start of a renewed England career as the main strike bowler. This quick fix stuck.

Another factor in short-term transitions to being in form, or even in the zone, is having our confidence boosted. Playing for Middlesex immediately after having been selected for England for the first time, I felt as if I was taller and bigger at the crease when batting – my one memory of that match is of imperiously hooking Surrey's Robin Jackman for four. Sometimes pride makes us play with more authority. Walking tall we grow in mental stature. (Unfortunately, this enhanced sense of authority at the crease was limited. Andy Roberts and friends were a different kettle of fish bowling for West Indies in the Test match a few days later.)

At the same time there is the risk that such pride, where external approbation reinforces self-respect, shifts into arrogance and carelessness. Fred Titmus, the Middlesex and England all-rounder, used to say that it was easier to get to the top than to stay there. Success, and the ensuing self-importance, may lead us to become caricatures of ourselves. We begin taking ourselves and our task too seriously, or we become complacent, not taking it seriously enough. One patient forcefully countered any tendency that I might have to bask in an overblown image of myself from the cricketing press, and (as he imagined) from other patients. He reminded me, with asperity, not to become smug.

Teams too, and larger organisations, may fail to maintain their level of concentration, but they may also, with the right reminders, emerge from the doldrums. In 1980, when I was captain of Middlesex, having won the first eleven completed matches of the season, we abruptly lost the next four. Having talked to the each player individually, I called a team meeting. After many earnest, sound points had been made, some of them by me, I invited one of the more junior players, Roland Butcher, to repeat what he had said to me in our earlier one-to-one. Butcher spoke along these lines:

'In the last few games, everyone's conversation is about how many trophies we'll end up having on our mantelpieces at the end of the season.' (There were four to play for.) 'Whereas before we were more intense, more aware that every ball, every over, counted, now it's as if we only have to turn up on the ground to win. We are preoccupied with outcomes, and we talk about the next match more than the current one. We have ceased to approach each ball, over or session, as unique challenges.'

Feeling in our pulses the truth of his remarks, we were jolted into a different orientation. We rediscovered our capacity for full engagement with the task, and for monitoring ourselves. Butcher's comments, which had the reflective neutrality of a good psychoanalytic interpretation, were I believe instrumental in the team's ending the season winning two of the four trophies – a big achievement.

Sudden relaxation may also help. If we are liable to be tense, diversion may lead to a remarkable ease of play. But we may also make the wrong deductions from it. I once scored 157 for Cambridge against Gloucestershire immediately after an all-night party. I was totally relaxed, and played at my best. Very likely the party helped me unwind – though no doubt in spite of the wine and the lack of sleep, not because of it. It was a dangerous precedent, especially if, tempted to the fallacy of *post hoc ergo propter hoc* ('after it therefore because of it'), I turned what was primarily a chance succession of events – drink plus little sleep followed by success – into a constant conjunction. More often than not, one does better on an early night and no (or not much) alcohol. Sportsmen are notoriously superstitious about such sequences: some batsmen won't change the socks they have worn while scoring a hundred. However, the point remains: though some of the ingredients are dangerous bedfellows, being more relaxed sometimes provides a quick fix, or even raises us to a higher level.

Restoration, or transformation, of form is at other times the outcome not of the sidelining of a demanding superego, but of buckling down doggedly. We dig in. As writers or artists we stick with the empty page or canvas in front of us, the anxiety inside us. We keep at it, revising or painting over the poor stuff we turn out, believing (or hoping) that in the end something worthwhile will appear. As batsmen, sometimes we are best off battling it out, waiting patiently for things to get easier. I remember the innings of 148 not out by Robin Smith, South Africa-born England player, against West Indies in 1991 at Lord's. At the start he looked vulnerable against three of the greatest fast bowlers, Malcolm Marshall, Curtley Ambrose and Courtney Walsh. Eventually a rare, inexperienced bowler appeared – Ian Allen, from Windward Islands, playing the first of his two Test matches. Smith scored three boundaries off one over, and he was away, unshackled. Nothing could stop him except the fall of England's remaining wickets at the other end. Smith's was a good example of a positive attitude; he held on to his sense of his own ability through the protracted struggle against a hostile and accurate attack. He did not give up, nor did he become rooted in a merely defensive orientation. By the end of his innings he was playing with freedom and control. Smith was not out of form at any stage of this innings. At the start he was, rather, on the verge of being outgunned, outplayed.

Do they Last? Quick Fixes, Deep Problems

So what makes these recoveries reliable? When does a small nudge lead to lasting good form? Willis was rejuvenated and restored. Butcher's insight prompted attitudes that had a long-term beneficial effect on the team.

There seem to be two ways of accounting for the solidity of these changes. One is that they were both recoveries of lost patterns of already achieved excellence. Willis was able to shake off the problems that were blocking his established mental and emotional approach to his task. He also rediscovered his old grooved technique, which needed little further work of adjustment or learning. The Middlesex team in 1980 recovered its early-season concentration and attention to the present.

Second, in both cases William James's notion of 'unconscious incubation' was relevant. Change often happens when the person (or group) is on the point of reaching the new understanding for himself. The leaning wall falls at the touch of a finger. The right word at the right time not only sets us free, the improvement is also sustainable.

Psychoanalysts may use their understanding to promote change by short-term interventions, as Donald Winnicott did, 'meeting *social need and pressure on clinics*'. In other words, the method and understanding can be applied in short-term work, at least in some cases. Winnicott's example was his 'therapeutic consultations' with children, whom he might see only once. By 'exploitation of the first interview,' he writes, 'I am able to meet the challenge of a proportion of child psychiatry cases.' In these contexts, his aim was to release as much momentum as possible on the side of growth from as small an intervention as possible; to help initiate 'changes which indicate a loosening of the knot in the developmental process'. Again, such loosening may only be possible where development has been happening, but something has blocked it. The mooring hawser is in place and can bear the boat's weight: clear the snag and it will do its job.

Cognitive behavioural therapy (CBT) and other short-term treatments may be helpful, too, especially in dealing with a particular symptom. But quick fixes, along with the opportunity and will to work at them, are not always possible or sustainable. Technique and attitude have not in such cases been securely established and then briefly lost. There are deeper problems of one kind or another. Psychoanalysis, in its full form, aims to go as far as possible towards self-knowledge and honesty, almost (an important qualification, this 'almost') without concern for its cost in terms of time and emotion. It aims not so much at a fix as an *un*fixing combined with a new construction. And if we are to address, and gradually modify, underlying personal difficulties, and also integrate the changes into our complex personalities, a radical treatment is often called for.

Psychoanalyst Fakhry Davids implicitly makes this point when he asks how it is that, despite being decent and fair-minded in their regular dealings with others, so many ordinary people are liable to support racist, xenophobic or fundamentalist attitudes and policies. His answer is that there is an underlying paranoid structure in us all which, particularly in situations of neglect, stress or insecurity, unscrupulous or extremist persuaders are able to tap into. Addressing and modifying the 'racist within' takes more time-consuming, deep and across-the-board work than adjusting behaviour in good enough times.

One cannot mend a torn ligament with sticking plaster. Psychological problems often have deeper roots. When long-established patterns of coping break down, people need time to re-establish themselves on a sounder basis; time that most sportsmen don't have. I have occasionally treated sportsmen in short-term work. The task is different from more thorough-going, more long-term and open-ended psychotherapeutic work, when there is the opportunity to go into the difficulties of psychological change. (I have sometimes been unsure about how far we've managed to go.)

Outcome research has not often been applied to psycho-analytic therapy. However, a recent long-term study of depression, undertaken by psychoanalyst David Taylor and others at the Tavistock Clinic, London, patients diagnosed with severe depression were allocated randomly to one of three treatment types – short-term analytic therapy, medication or CBT. When assessed a few months after treatment ended, the three different treatments produced more or less equal improvements; most patients in each sample were classified as only slightly or moderately depressed. When follow-ups were done after two years, however, those who had undergone the analytic therapy were demonstrably in a better state than the others. 'End-of-treatment evaluations or short follow-ups may miss the emergence of delayed therapeutic benefit.'

Sometimes, fortunately, as with Bob Willis, change happens quickly, for the better, and lasts for a long time. A person becomes freer, less timid or anxious, and the improvements hold. Sometimes not.

Mindfulness

Might mindfulness be comparable to psychoanalysis as a method for personal change? It was popular during the 1960s and 70s, in the 'turn on, tune in, drop out' mentality of the counter-culture that burgeoned as part of the opposition to the Vietnam War. In its recent revival, it has become mainstream, being prescribed for thousands of patients and many conditions, notably depression, anxiety and stress. Psychosis, eating disorders and multiple sclerosis have been cited as illnesses that mindfulness can help with. In 2004, NICE, the NHS's quality standards and rationing body, was sufficiently convinced of its benefits to rule that mindfulness-based CBT was cost-effective. In 2007, the same body decided that it could be prescribed for people with three or more episodes of depression. There is evidence that it is effective too for chronic conditions such as ME. Informally, millions have downloaded mindfulness apps like Headspace. Adherents claim that mindfulness reduces anxiety, enhances appreciation and frees up energy for living.

There are many variations of mindfulness, ranging from lifestyle kitsch to a substantial form of meditation undertaken over time that enables significant changes in quality of life. One central feature is its focus on being fully in the present. Those practising it are encouraged to notice the shapes, outlines and details, the smells, sounds, tastes and feel of the world around them, and to become more aware of their own body states, sensations, feelings, emotions and thoughts. One aim of mindfulness is to see the familiar afresh.

The subject is encouraged not to rush off from having an experience to categorising and evaluating it, or to action. At least for the moment, he is invited to suspend judgment and self-criticism, to accept things as they are. A yoga teacher I went to briefly would intone, in a kindly sing-song voice rather like someone reassuring a child, 'Simply watch.' We are to become receptive, by dint of learning to concentrate in this particular way, without furrowed brow, or pressure to label, or anxious guilt. If our attention wanders in such directions, or to more practical things, we are asked to notice this, and then gently bring our attention back to the present. The space between experience and reaction is enlarged.

We are to observe our trains of thought. Our attention here too is to be non-judgmental, to ignore familiar evaluations of what is 'worth' looking at or considering. The idea is that the self should not get in the way of seeing the world, nor should the world preclude our seeing ourselves. Such an approach involves a willingness to give up presuppositions and pigeon-holing. Meditation – serious mindfulness – may interrupt, and in its own quiet way interrogate, our autopilots.

Mindfulness and meditation reverse, for the moment, the results of grooving, which we considered in Chapter 7. There is a link here with the appreciation of art; in both areas we are less committed than usual to thought as a means to an end, or as preparation for, or rehearsal of, purposive activity. We let go temporarily our concern with the pragmatism of everyday life. (One book on climbing is called *Conquistadors of the Useless*.) We are invited to focus on the apparently non-urgent in order to be open to whatever is there; for instance, we may be asked to concentrate on our breathing as a support for clearing the mind of the splatter of thought, much of it anxious and following old, laid-down patterns. Rather than urging ourselves on to think purposively, we come to notice how thoughts arise and fall away.

Similarly, one of Timothy Gallwey's useful tricks of coaching, which entails focusing on the seam of a tennis ball, keeps at a distance the judgmental and paranoid part of the mind that sees the ball coming over the net towards us as a threat. Giving up the anxiety linked to fear of failure, we experience more tranquillity. For a sportsman, this may lead to improved play.

Mindfulness is to be contrasted with mindlessness or distraction, with its rush, anxiety, busyness, multi-tasking, evasion. John Inverarity once said that concentration is not a matter of intensity. It is a calmly alert and attentive state, without 'noise' or 'clutter'. When we are concentrating, irrelevant thoughts or distractions, whether from outside or from self-consciousness or a severe superego, become less intrusive.

These practices may also be contrasted with acquisitiveness ('Getting and spending we lay waste our powers', wrote William Wordsworth). We begin to notice what we have, rather than hurrying on to the next task, or yearning for what we lack, or trying to grab hold of ideas and possess them for ever. As William Blake wrote:

He who binds to himself a joy
Does the winged life destroy;
But he who kisses the joy as it flies
Lives in Eternity's sunrise.

We allow space for emotions rather than being caught up in them. We can 'walk round our depression'. We learn to let go of pressures put on us by others to react in certain prescribed ways. During these experiences we need others less, though over time we may become more aware of our authentic needs and dependency.

As dusk falls during Uttarayan, the winter kite-flying festival in Gujarat, an entrancing phase begins. Chinese lanterns – large balloon-like baskets made of paper, with lights in little cradles underneath – scud on the breeze above the city rooftops, which are thronged with people. Later, in complete darkness, a big kite is sent up, its string secured. One by one, thin candles are lit inside small lanterns, each of which is tied to the kite-string at intervals, creating a necklace of lights curving up towards the kite itself, high in the air. The skill and work that is put into this from one point of view pointless activity epitomises art and play, and creates something not only beautiful but also suggestive – of the aspiration and evanescence of fragile selves, perhaps. Buddhists emphasise the lack of a solid, permanent self; I would suggest that through meditation one may get a sense of a self slenderly held together.

Mindfulness and Psychoanalysis

Mindfulness may be used superficially, as a magical source of tranquillity and calm, a process in which all negativity is banished or placed at too comfortable a distance from our observing selves. Such states are suggestive of retreats from reality, holidays from difficulty. We need such times out; we certainly need to slow down. But we also need to wrestle with the demons, the negative, anti-life forces in ourselves – forces which psychoanalysis tackles and challenges the patient to tackle, inviting us to experience our hatred and envy along with our love and generosity.

Mindfulness is also the basis of Zen Buddhist meditation practices. These constitute a textured method with a long history, imbued with a deep philosophy of life. It leads to radical change in those who engage fully with it, undoing long-held patterns of thinking and feeling that led to tension, anxiety, depression, mania. Zen meditation does not claim to offer *techniques* for change, but rather invites an attitude of complete openness.

I am struck by the similarities between this kind of approach and aspects of psychoanalysis, especially when mindfulness accepts some analytic ideas about resistance to change and the 'hidden reefs' that obstruct change. So how does mindfulness compare with psychoanalysis?

The invitation to be mindful is not unlike the psychoanalytic invitation to free associate. In psychoanalysis too value is placed on having an experience and not running away from it. The wish for precipitate action, or the rush to judgment, impedes or precludes us from living in the moment. In psychoanalysis too we may come to notice from self-observation, as well as from the analyst, or by inference, habitual compulsive and destructive modes of thought and feeling. We may, for example, start to rant, or obsessively make lists, or seek out fights with others, or become triumphant and all-knowing, or obsessed with sexual fantasies. All this is recognised in mindfulness practice as described by Rob Nairn, previously a professor in criminology, now a lecturer and teacher on Buddhism and meditation.

Both meditation and psychoanalysis encourage the kind of benign split that Juliet Stevenson noted when she is in good form on the stage, between being a character within the play and being the professional actress observing the whole scene. In analysis, as in mindfulness practice, we hope to find or create a space in ourselves between the self that is having the thoughts and desires and the self that is observing them. Edward Dusinberre, leader of the Takacs String Quartet, writes of needing a cool head along with a hot heart when playing Beethoven. We have to occupy a third place from which we observe, coolly, the self and its interactions, without denying the self's (hot) feelings. While both psychoanalysis and mindfulness emphasise being aware of our present mind-states as they happen, as they arise and fall away, both recognise, too, in this emphasis, that the present may have too much power. We may feel that our current state is permanent and is all there is. One week we feel we will forever be depressed, next week there is nothing but excitement. It is a sign of healing when a patient brings closer together such opposite states, seeing each foreshadowed in the other.

But the sense of being benignly listened to is only one aspect of the experience of being in psychoanalysis. Psychoanalysts don't stop at this hospitable receptivity. Their interpretations of what they hear and observe will interfere with the patient's gratifying sense that, being encouraged to say what he likes, and being listened to intently, he is loved unconditionally. The interpreting psychoanalyst is rather like a father interrupting his child's blissful cuddle with the mother – and not necessarily out of jealousy. In such circumstances there is likely to be strong resistance to hearing unpalatable truths about ourselves. We not only want to know, we want not to know. When someone meditates, too, he will be reluctant to face such unpalatable truths. But he does not have the equivalent of an analyst; he is on his own.

As psychoanalysts we expect and accept tension, anxiety, in our patients and in ourselves. Sometimes our interpretations contribute to such states. We do not in all situations encourage relaxation and calm. We may believe that the patient, in worrying about things that don't really matter, or that he can't do much about, is making a mountain out of a molehill, that he is getting caught up in things that don't belong to him. Such an insight for the patient may ease anxiety, and free him from a burden created by his own self-importance. This would be a familiar idea to Nairn. But on other occasions the analyst may, in a different way from mindfulness practice, suggest rather that the patient is making a molehill out of a mountain, that he is, for example, underplaying the degree of anger that he (really) feels about someone blocking his view at the theatre, about someone depriving him of easy access to a desired person or scene.

I think there are two differences here. One is that mindfulness, as I see it, is over-attached to detachment. Having seen that at times our attachments, to ways of thinking and to other people, are pathologically distorted and exaggerated, so that we are caught up with them in self-centred ways, Nairn then generalises from this. There seems to be no room for the opposite problem, that of the schizoid person, who cuts off from emotional contact.

The second difference lies in the solitude of the meditating person. Lacking a mentor or therapist, he has all the problems of self-analysis – can he really check himself when he gets onto false tracks, or deceives himself? Whereas, in analysis, there is an analyst to interpret the patient's urgent selfishness, his cruelty or jealousy, his terrors, his shame, his doubt. Taking up such emotions is bound to increase anxiety, at least in the short term. The American psychoanalyst Hans Loewald once began a talk by saying that he 'hoped his remarks would shed some darkness on the subject'. This productive destabilisation occurs in literature, and theatre; playwright Howard Barker asks us to 'overcome the urge to do things in unison . . . to hum banal tunes together . . . I seek to render a scene more complex, ambiguous and unstable.'

Nairn is well aware of the possibilities of self-deception in meditation, and he addresses them. One route of derailment is subtle suppression, which may produce a form of calm which 'lasts for the period of the meditation, but does not lead to true tranquillity, and certainly prevents insight'. He speaks of the difficulty we may find in accepting how we are. 'One of the greatest strangers in the world is this one in the heart . . . We are travelling through life with a stranger who at some level is trying to communicate with us, yet we want to know only a very limited aspect of that communication.' Moreover, we engage in surveillance of ourselves by a part-self that, like Freud's pleasure-ego, 'wants to have only pleasant thoughts and feelings . . . That's its agenda,' Nairn writes.

We fall into conditioned reflexes, that is; we carry around with us basic assumptions built up from the past, which prevent us from seeing things as they are. We egocentrically grasp at and identify with these conditioned reactions. Our minds may be rigid and closed, even paranoid, without our noticing this. The 'hidden reefs of meditation' include expectations, assumptions and goals. All lead not only to blindness, but also to guilt and a sense of failure. In order to recognise these 'hidden reefs', Nairn introduces an 'increasingly interactive component into my retreats. I encouraged group sharing among meditators in a carefully regulated atmosphere.'

However, there is nothing in mindfulness comparable to the use and interpretation of the transference in its moment-to-moment, chameleon-like transitions. Transference is the transferring or displacing of old templates onto the analyst. Psychoanalysis fosters and focuses on the emergence of these patterns in relation to the analyst and the consulting room. As Freud writes:

> We soon perceive that the transference is itself only a repetition, and the repetition is a transference of the forgotten past not only on to the doctor [i.e. the analyst] but also on to all the other aspects of the current situation . . . We have learnt that the patient . . . repeats all his symptoms in the course of the treatment . . . We have made it clear to ourselves . . . that we must treat his illness, not as an event of the past, but as a present-day force.

Part of Freud's genius was to enlist in – and on the side of – the treatment, the compulsion to repeat. The term 'repetition compulsion' needs to be supplemented by a further term, perhaps 'developmental repetition' (a term suggested by the leadership consultant Gabriella Braun), to indicate ways in which repetition is enlisted (as by Freud) in the process of therapeutic change. A theme in music comes back time and again in various forms. Musicians speak of 'development sections', in which possibilities inherent in the theme are worked out. In the last of the thirty sections that make up Bach's 'Goldberg Variations', we hear again the original theme, exactly as it was at the beginning, but transformed and enriched by its developmental journey. It is as if the simple jewel is now encircled with the ghosts of chains of associations and reworkings that we have encountered on the journey. Something similar happens in personal development.

In analysis, once we have been able to hear and bear unflattering comments and ideas about ourselves, we have to work them through, a process akin to mourning, in that many examples of the old pattern, many different forms that a pathological syndrome takes, need to be recognised and reckoned with. Meditation too gives an opportunity for this gritty work, though again the practitioner is largely on his own with it.

The Buddhist temples and stupas in Myanmar, like other Buddhist monuments, illustrate dispassionate detachment. Typically, the devotee enters the darkness of the interior from the bright sunlight outside. He gradually gets used to the dim light. There is a walkway around a central core. At each of four faces of the core there is an image of the Buddha. Though the faces differ in their depicted activity, posture and mood – there are seated, lying, standing, laughing Buddhas – in most of them there is a serene interiority of expression, a half-smile akin to that of some Archaic Greek sculptures. These images remind me of the 'still small voice within' of Christian doctrine. They point towards one great aim in life, to reach from the whirl of life and its emotional ups and downs to a state in which one is calm, accepting, able simply to watch oneself and the world. T. S. Eliot wrote:

> At the still point of the turning world. Neither flesh
>   nor fleshless;
> Neither from nor towards; at the still point,
>   there the dance is,
> But neither arrest nor movement. And do not
>   call it fixity,
> Where past and future are gathered. Neither
>   movement from nor towards,
> Neither ascent nor decline. Except for the point,
>   the still point,
> there would be no dance, and there is only the dance.

Buddhism, through mindfulness, puts stillness at the heart of its value system as the highest point of aspiration. The aim is

to find a retreat within the self; not a withdrawn psychic retreat to which we escape from reality, but a place to be in touch with ourselves and the world around us, while at the same time being detached. A patient once said to me, shortly before finishing her analysis, that now, at times, she felt in the centre of herself. She felt less 'edgy', I inferred, than she had often been.

I have a somewhat different view from this Buddhist goal. I see it rather as one aspiration among many. Let us indeed hope we can develop such capacities. We all aim at the poise of the kestrel in its hover (an image of Marion Milner's), neither abstractly calculating nor driven off course by any wind. But not at the expense of the whirl of life, of also living nearer the edge of Eliot's wheel. To be too much in such a place of stillness would be to resemble a photographer who stays always behind his lens, always watching. It would be to remain perpetually in the third position in life, rather than being one of the passionate couple. I see psychoanalysis, and my own value system, as aiming to embrace both the intensity of passionate involvement and the detachment of the Enlightened: and to be free to move between the two positions. We need both – the stillness and the dance – to be fully alive.

22

THE HARDEST THING OF ALL

The hardest thing of all to see is what is really there.

J. A. Baker

A flash of the obvious.

Wilfred Bion

The aspects of things that are most important for us are hidden because of their simplicity and familiarity. One is unable to notice something – because it is always before one's eyes.

Ludwig Wittgenstein

———

The philosopher Ludwig Wittgenstein, in his posthumously published book, *The Philosophical Investigations*, asks what happens when, having seen the famous duck-rabbit 'illusion' as a duck, one then sees it also as a rabbit. The world has not been altered, there are no new lines on the page. There is nothing, one might say, different in the picture when the viewer sees both creatures from what there was when he saw a duck only. Nothing has changed, yet the world is different. Now, the person can't see the picture only as a duck, or indeed only as a rabbit – though nor can he see it as both simultaneously. But before he saw the rabbit, he was not deluded or mistaken, he

315

simply saw less richly what was in front of him. He may have had his eyes opened to the rabbit by someone tracing its outlines in the picture, saying 'Look, here is the head, these the ears, the rabbit is looking to the right. Can you see it now?' Or he just saw it, maybe with an involuntary exclamation.

Welche Thiere gleichen einander am meisten?

Kaninchen und Ente.

In order for someone to be on form as a batsman he needs to be able to see the ball accurately. He has to make many quick and sure judgments, about length, direction, pace, bounce, the nature of the pitch, the placing of the field and so on. When out of form, he is tentative, his footwork is uncertain, his body tense. He is neither nimble at the crease nor is his head steady.

Similarly, a psychoanalyst has to 'read' the patient, has to be able to 'see' or sense or infer his mood, his beliefs, including some unconscious beliefs. If he reports the session to colleagues, it may turn out that he has been for various reasons unable to identify patterns that they point out, and which now he too can 'see'. Often the shortcoming is to do with being fixed on one version, unable to see more than one side of an issue. We are blind to a version that later we judge to have at least as much force as what we were able to perceive. We have been 'one-eyed'. The duck-rabbit offers an analogy for some forms of blindness or limitation in seeing, and the overcoming of that inability in a new configuration. Comprehending others and ourselves is often a matter of both/and, rather than either/or.

There is a story told about the poet and writer C. S. Lewis. He and friends were walking along a familiar path by the River Cam, in Cambridge; one of the party said how wonderful it was to see the ducks as they always were. Lewis riposted, 'You are not seeing the same old ducks, you are seeing *these* ducks in *these* conditions for the very first time.' As Auden said of Freud: 'All he did was to remember like the old and be honest like children.'

On one hand, we need to see afresh, without prejudice, like a child. My editor tells me that, in getting to grips with the aesthetics of a prospective book cover, he will turn it upside down so as to get a better sense of the design. On the other hand, many things cannot be taken in by an observer who does not have the perceptive eye of the expert who has seen it all before. Birdwatchers, the author Robert Macfarlane writes, 'speak of the "jizz" of the bird, to mean the sum of characteristics – shape, plumage, posture, call, habitat – that allow its instant identification from a general impression. A bird's jizz is its gist and vibe: the aggregation of its particulars into a compound signature of life.' Years ago, I referred a man to an older colleague, H. J. Home, who lived in Norfolk. He met the man, and sent me a postcard. 'I like the jig' – a dialect form of *jizz*, I assume – 'of the bird,' he wrote. We have to be able to read the 'compound signature' of a person and his life. If I'm presented with a sentence in Russian script, I cannot reproduce it; in a sense I haven't seen it. I have only to glance at its English translation, and I could easily reproduce the shapes. 'The hardest thing of all to see' – seeing what is really there – requires both familiarity and unfamiliarity, two different takes.

To return to Auden on Freud's capacity to see: I assume he had in mind someone like the child in 'The Emperor's New Clothes', the fairy tale in which all the adults praise the Emperor's fine new outfit, until the child says, 'But he has no clothes on at all!' I see two versions of this collective, adult denial. One is the more obvious reading, that they pretend, from hypocrisy, fear or a wish to fit in; the second is that their error is not a plain lie, but a delusion, in which they are convinced that the Emperor is indeed wearing a fine new suit. In the first case, the child tells truth to powerful dissembling adults, in the second he is addressing people suffering from a group hallucination, similar to that of the girls who, in Arthur Miller's play *The Crucible*, testify to having seen people 'consorting with the devil'.

Both/and. A friend was having lunch in a restaurant with his mother. At the next table sat a bearded man in his sixties or older, his trousers ripped and his zip half undone, his jacket creased, greasy hair combed awkwardly flat. He had made the best of a bad job in making himself appear respectable. There was a faint smell of urine. He was looking at the menu. After a few minutes the manager came up and said to him, 'The last time you were here you left without paying.' The man muttered something, shifting in his seat. The manager continued, 'I'm afraid you will have to leave. Or pay in advance.' The man fished in his pockets and brought out a credit card, which, not surprisingly, failed. The man was about to leave when my friend's mother said, 'I'll pay for his lunch.' The manager said, 'He does this everywhere, you know.' The man said, 'Thank you. You're a good egg.'

He ordered calamari, a glass of wine and dessert. He ate with relish, almost licking the plate. He thanked his 'hosts' again, and left. The point is: my friend and his mother both knew well that he was a conman, but they also saw, and took seriously, that he was hungry. Like the analyst, they needed two hands to hold the 'patient', one for his vulnerability, the other for his defensive and tricky attitudes and actions. In this instance, they prioritised the vulnerability. They felt it was £29 well spent. But they were well aware of the other side.

Hidden in Plain Sight

The rabbit is at first hidden, hidden in plain sight. There exists a different sort of blindness in which it is not simply that we fail to see something that is in front of our eyes, but rather that, misreading or misperceiving, we distort it.

In 1978, when I was captain of the England team in Australia, we played a match against Western Australia at Perth. We had rested quick bowlers Bob Willis and Chris Old. The pitch was fast, uneven and bouncy. The scores in the match reflected this: England XI 144 and 126, Western Australia 52 and 78. After the match John Inverarity, the captain of the home side, said, in a matter-of-fact way, as if it were plain to any fool, that our best bowler was Mike Hendrick, who had taken five for 11 and three for 23 in the match. This comment opened my eyes. In selecting Hendrick for the tour, we had been inclined to think of him as a bowler unlikely to make the Test side. He was not an out-and-out fast bowler, nor was he a big swinger of the ball – two styles of bowling that tend to have more success in Australian conditions. Hendrick relied rather on pinpoint accuracy, and in English conditions made the ball move off the seam, sometimes alarmingly. Our preconceived idea was that he might be mainly a defensive bowler in Australia. We had not selected him for the first Test in Brisbane, which we had just won.

Until that moment, I had thought of his bowling figures in the recent match as an exception owing to the freakishly uneven pitch. Inverarity's passing remark made me look at the facts again, and put myself in the shoes of the opposition batsmen. As well as being a perfect foil to Willis and Botham, both of whom could be expensive with their attacking mindsets, Hendrick would, I saw, be a handful in most of the conditions we had been playing in. And he was at the top of his form. As a result of this new view of familiar facts, we picked Hendrick for the next Test, on the same ground, a few days later, and he played in the remaining five Test matches with conspicuous success, taking nineteen wickets at 15.73 apiece and conceding only just over two runs per eight-ball over.

As an analyst I have at times missed patients' partially disguised expressions of feeling. With one patient I underestimated the strength of her feelings towards me in our first few encounters. In retrospect, I realise that, like many other patients, she had high, even fantastic, hopes of transfiguration by this mysterious treatment called 'psychoanalysis', and that in this frame of mind she was, during the honeymoon phase, preoccupied with me and the process. She was ready to fall in love. I now see the poems and notes she wrote at that time – which she alluded to only in passing, and vaguely – as undeclared, or disguisedly declared, love letters to me. However, her fall-back position, that it was safer not to risk attachment and subsequent abandonment, led her to keep her feelings mainly in the dark.

Towards the end of this first period, after an interpretation by me of her loneliness over one weekend, she conveyed to me how inadequate my words were. I spoke, she implied, as if it were an ordinary adult separation; for her it was more like the longing and despair produced in a child by its mother being away too long. I believe it was a mistake on my part not to pick up on these hints, and that this was part of what led her to feel that I, like her parents years before, was not open to her love, that I was in a sense rejecting her overtures. I think she was bound to feel disappointment and anger in her analysis; but my failure to see the intensity of this attachment made it harder to track the subsequent disillusionment.

I remember too a patient who surprised me in the opposite direction. Her general attitude to me was positive. She was friendly and warm, and keen to learn. Then she brought a dream in which my wife fell into a swimming pool and was rescued by the patient. I missed the rather obvious possibility that the patient may have wished to push her in. If she had been more generally hostile, I would probably not have failed to notice this expression of jealousy, followed by a compensatory wish to save my wife.

A Doctor's Nose

So we may fail to see the rabbit; we may also distort what is in front of us. A third failure may be described as a failure to intuit, to smell something out. In the old, pre-technology days of medicine, doctors would both literally use the smell of a patient or his urine as an important diagnostic method, and metaphorically sniff out diseases by professional intuition. In these days of tests and measurements, the doctor's 'nose' has been downgraded. A consultant anaesthetist told me that it is shameful in his profession to admit to such presentiments. However, in his view, there is a place for this old-fashioned, less narrowly focused, less 'scientific' attention.

The same anaesthetist speaks of periods during long operations where he has a merely background role. He sits to one side in the operating theatre, keeping an eye on things from a distance, occasionally wandering off to a side room for a cup of tea, while the surgeons and nurses go about their business.

During this unpressured time, he occasionally gets an intuition that something is wrong. These feelings are based on clues that he has not consciously articulated. It is important for him to give them house-room. He is like the hunters and trackers who, author Louis Liebenberg writes, feeling a 'burning sensation in the middle of their foreheads above their eyes, know their quarry is just ahead of them. . . . [Some hunters] claim that they can . . . "feel" the near-presence of their quarry in this way even before they find the spoor.' Liebenberg continues: 'We are constantly bombarded by a multitude of stimuli to which we cannot attend . . . By means of peripheral perception we are able to register stimuli that we do not know we perceive.'

Such skills are suspect in the medical world, as my anaesthetist friend says, and even risk becoming defunct. Experts no longer trust themselves, or others, to detect the jizz of the bird. And yet intelligence moves from logic to instinct. By all means take the blood, do the scan; but experts should not ignore misgivings and suspicions. Novelist Samuel Butler wrote: 'A misgiving is a warning from God, which should be attended to as a man values his soul.'

What Gets in the Way?

So, one reason for our various 'blindnesses' is the interference caused by our assumptions. We cling to what we think we have established as a general fact. We have a narrative ready to hand. I had an almost fixed idea that Mike Hendrick would be less penetrative in Australia than in England. In Bombay in 1980, for a Test match against India, on a ground that was new to us, we expected to find a pitch that helped spinners. In fact, it had a good covering of grass. Because of my expectations I could not see what was in front of my eyes, could not, for a while, believe my eyes. We almost picked three spinners for a match in which the two who did play – Derek Underwood and John Emburey – bowled a mere seven overs between them, and all the wickets were taken by faster bowlers, no fewer than thirteen of them by Ian Botham. My 'glasses' were brown-tinted. My reactions were conditioned by the past, and by my expectations. I could scarcely see what was in front of my eyes.

It is hard to see beyond the customary. Psychiatrist and psychoanalyst Tom Main, director of the Cassel Hospital from the 1940s to the 1960s, describes how, early in this period, orthodox nursing and medical values prescribed that in-patients should always stay in the hospital over weekends. A pioneering member of the nursing staff had the insight and courage to question this habit, and the Cassel made arrangements for some patients, especially when approaching the time of their return home or their re-entry into society, to leave the hospital at weekends. The advantages of this seem obvious: the patient would get used to life outside the institution, so that discharge would be less of a shock to him and his family; the venture would, moreover, challenge mindsets of dependence fostered by in-patient life. Over the next few years, however, this practice became a new orthodoxy, so that everyone went home for weekends, and it became unthinkable for any patient to stay. Thus traditions change, and the requirement and capacity to think, to make differentiations and difficult decisions case by case, are set aside in favour of rule-based, routinised responses. Man once again becomes made for the Sabbath rather than the Sabbath for Man.

Tie Me to the Mast: What Can't Be Borne

In some of the scenarios described in this chapter so far, a person with fewer expectations or assumptions might with relative ease have seen more of the reality than the actual participants. There are of course also situations where uncertainty is inevitable.

We may for instance be unsure how a patient will react to our putting into words what we have observed about him. He may find it humiliating, or outrageous. It may be a priority for him to make the analyst suffer the feeling of being rejected, rather than face his own needs, including the need not to see, so he projects his painful or guilty feelings, and remains in control of the situation.

Psychoanalytic theory makes the difficulty of such situations understandable. If, as we believe, the unconscious – ideas, emotions, dispositions – is partly constituted by what we've repressed or disowned, there will have been persuasive reasons for the initial disowning. It is inevitable therefore that there will be hostility and resistance to their uncovering. Facing up to disturbing feelings often takes courage and persistence from both parties.

If the analyst is able to free *himself* from the indecision resulting from such pressures, as well as from vulnerabilities in himself, to face the reality of the situation, and then to speak truthfully, modestly and directly, he may be surprised by the openness of the patient's response. Such moments of simplicity and plainness may be turning points towards growth.

However, it is also important to be aware of the limitations of such a robust approach. The analytic couple may have to settle for modest gains – temporarily, or in some cases permanently. A colleague once told me that he had in his practice two men, both psychotic, who he knew would be in treatment with him until he or they died or became incapacitated. He would never be able to confront them with their repudiated thoughts and feelings, but he could help them articulate their visions of the world. He felt that this kept them alive and able to function as well as was possible.

There are temptations and intrusions into the mind that are too hot to handle. Then the only recourse is to steer clear of them. This course of action is paralleled in patients who are compelled, sometimes at inconvenience to themselves, to avoid geographical locations that have unbearable associations for them.

Addicts may have to realise that their vulnerability is part of them and won't go away. The fundamental principle of organisations like Narcotics Anonymous (NA) or Alcoholics Anonymous (AA), in which recovering addicts work together through mutual self-help, is that every participant has to admit not only that drugs have been controlling him (which is characteristically denied), but also that he has an addictive personality, so that addiction to drugs, say, or alcohol, is for him a disease without a cure. This means that he has to commit to lifelong abstention. He cannot 'take or leave' alcohol, or drugs. He cannot be satisfied with a single drink. Once 'clean', he has to stay clean. 'Easy the descent to hell', Virgil wrote.

NA lays down steps for addicts on the path towards rehabilitation. They have to own up to their addiction. They are asked to write statements spelling out in detail ways in which they have been tempted, and the often terrible consequences. They have to recognise the harm their addiction has done others, especially those close to them, and begin to come clean about it all, in detail, making reparation where possible. Another fundamental principle is that they all need others to help them. As individuals grow more solid in their resolve, they become mentors to more recent drug users.

In order to keep himself from being seduced by those famous *femmes fatales* the Sirens, who lured sailors to their doom on the rocks with their enchanting music and voices, Odysseus ordered his crew to plug their ears with beeswax, and to tie him to the mast. Aware of his own, and his crew's, weakness and vulnerability, he knew they all needed external constraints. When he heard the singing, he begged to be released, but the sailors, keeping their nerve, tied the ropes tighter.

In everyday life we may have to keep ourselves busy – *occupational* therapy, in a sense. Think of the dictum 'the Devil makes work for idle hands' – a precept that encourages us to keep ourselves and our hormone-ridden adolescent children occupied, hands engaged on constructive tasks.

The siren voices are, as Odysseus knew, extremely powerful. A drug user, for instance, has available, if he follows his own siren voices, a means of almost instantaneously lifting himself out of boredom, despair, anxiety and so on. With dealers lurking on the street corner, and money in his pocket, drugs offer him the quickest of quick fixes. And the lift may be fantastic. One ex-user told me that there is nothing to compare with a heroin high. So, one aspect of 'treatment' or healing is to let go and mourn this loss. He also has to face, with help, the terrible, 'cold turkey' experiences of withdrawal.

Siren voices are the devil speaking. And the devil is cunning. He can speak to us *sotto voce*, as it were, without our knowing, even or perhaps especially when we are most fierce in our repudiation. Moralistic denunciations may be secret modes of temptation, routes to backsliding. Denouncing the lure may induce the very activity it proscribes.

Shakespeare's Sonnet 129 – the opening line of which is 'The expense of Spirit in a waste of shame is lust in action' – exemplifies compulsion in the sexual life. It speaks of the 'swallowed bait on purpose laid to make the taker mad', and the disgust that immediately follows. It ends:

All this the world well knows, yet none knows well
To shun the heaven that leads men to this hell.

And it is not only sex: we may know that we are desperately in love with a woman who is absolutely not the right person for us. We may even know it and yet carry on! Lifelong bonds may be entered into, not out of love but as a result of a desperate infatuation.

A patient, Stephen, had two dreams, separated by more than a year of analysis. In the first he dreamed that a group of strangers had entered his house, and he had let them come upstairs with him. He knew they were dubious, even nefarious characters, but for some reason he could not refuse them entry or tell them to go. The atmosphere in the dream became more and more sinister. He woke in fear and trembling.

The second dream was also located in his home. He was sitting in his lounge looking out. Suddenly he saw two ethnically different men climbing over his back fence. They looked ferocious and predatory. He was convinced they were intent on breaking in. He rushed to his back door, reached it just before the would-be intruders, slammed it shut and locked it. He breathed a sigh of relief.

We came to see the dreams as related. In the earlier dream he had allowed dangerous others, or perhaps even dangerous and foreign elements within himself, entry into his mind; in the later one, he was able to keep them out. He was not yet able, however, to allow them entry in order to get to know them, he was not yet sufficiently self-confident that he would be strong enough not to succumb to their bad influence.

In the first dream, Stephen was naively vulnerable to a takeover by the bad influences of his own self-destructive parts. By the time of the second he was more aware of the dangers;

by rushing to slam the door shut, he did the equivalent of getting himself tied to the mast. There was work to be done before he could allow them in without too much danger of being lured into destructive action by them and their 'poisoned bait'.

By the time of this second dream, then, he was in the position of the analyst imagined by Freud, who deals with his patient's declaration of love by urging her to suppress or renounce her erotic emotions. This is, Freud writes,

> not an analytic way of dealing with them, but a senseless one. It would be just as though, after summoning up a spirit from the underworld by cunning spells, one were to send him down again without having asked him a single question. One would have brought the repressed into consciousness, only to repress it once more in a fright.

For my patient, Stephen, this 'not asking the spirit a single question' was not a senseless policy, but a necessary precaution.

Availability To Interpretation

Here are four prerequisites in a patient for the analyst's interpretations to have traction.

First, there has to be some degree of self-dissatisfaction, or at least a sense that things could be better. Indeed a good deal of the work of analytic therapy consists in increasing patients' awareness of their own needs and shortcomings. We analysts problematise what may have been dismissed by the patient as ordinary, or good enough. Our job may be seen as not only 'comforting the troubled', but also as 'troubling the (too) comfortable'. We shed a little darkness on the situation.

Second, there needs to be the stamina and energy to follow through (Freud called this 'working through'). The impact needs to go deep enough to outweigh the patient's inevitable tendencies to revert to default positions and let it all drop. Like analysts, patients need stamina and continuing curiosity.

The third thing that has to be in place for change to occur is the presence of sufficient therapeutic alliance, such that part of the patient trusts the analyst enough to talk and listen to him. Such alliances can't be taken for granted, nor are they to be induced by seduction. A good working alliance is earned, and reinforced, only by attention, empathy, courage and tact – one might almost say 'love' – on the side of the analyst. The trusting relationship has to become strong enough to accommodate and allow mistrust and other forms of hostility. The possibilities of beneficial change will often hinge on the relative strengths of the two forces – alliance on one side, suspicion on the other.

Fourth, there needs to be, in the patient, some willingness to countenance the shock of the new, of the unexpected. Many interpretations carry conviction because the patient is already on the brink of reaching this point himself, when the most therapeutic approach by the analyst may be to be prepared to come second and allow the idea to come from the patient. But at times a good interpretation will shock the patient to the core, mobilising powerful resistance and, occasionally, a recognition of the truth, and of the work that needs to be done.

23

AT LEAST BUY A TICKET

The best lack all conviction while the worst are full of passionate intensity.

W. B. Yeats

Kennedy was fanatical on only one subject: his opposition to fanatics, foreign as well as domestic, Negro as well as white, on the Left as well as the Right.

Ted Sorensen

I minded that I did not mind
That the matter did not matter any more
But I do know that it is
Out of the gaps
That new things grow.

Marion Milner

————

Passionate Action, Sceptical Reflection

Socrates stood back from and questioned radically what constituted a good life. He also lived out his moral values to the full. He held in balance, and was capable of, detachment *and* attachment, doubt *and* conviction. He combined radical questioning of concepts like courage and virtue with living his practical

life according to strong moral convictions as ordinarily understood. His intellectual doubts, together with his view that our
most damaging ignorance is of how ignorant we are, did not
preclude him from total commitment in battle. When he was
found guilty by the court in Athens of importing strange divinities of his own while refusing to recognise the gods prescribed
by the state, and of corrupting the young, he, like his accusers,
was permitted to propose a sentence. The prosecutors asked for
his death. Socrates audaciously, provocatively, even suicidally,
proposed that he should be dined at the state's expense for the
rest of his life. And his courage in facing his own death was,
according to Plato, exemplary, even saintly.

On every level we often have to make decisions and take
courses of action when we don't, and can't, know for sure
which path is the more promising. Taking either path means
not taking the other one. Yet we have to give up one course or
the other. Taking neither course is being rooted to the spot, or
oscillating between the two, which is another choice. When,
in Kafka's story 'The Burrow', the small rodent leaves his burrow, he watches the entrance to check whether any predatory
creature has found him out. He imagines becoming a predator himself, and fears he might well give away the secret of
the entrance to his home; but going inside and staying there
means not knowing if his entrance has been discovered. I picture the rodent lurking at the entrance, oscillating between the
two options, in the worst of both worlds.

On the same topic: baseball's sage of malapropisms, Yogi
Berra, said: 'When you come to a fork in the road, take it.'

Like Kafka's rodent, most of us are more indecisive than
Socrates, especially when we can't argue our way to a single
conclusion. Despite – or because of – the sack of grain
to one side of its head and the bowl of water to the other,

Buridan's ass (in the paradox named after the fourteenth-century French philosopher), equally hungry and thirsty, and having no reason to turn to the left rather than the right or vice versa, dies of hunger and thirst. A Wittgensteinian philosophy student asked the question: 'Why does a swallow land on this particular bit of telephone wire rather than any other?' And received the Wittgensteinian answer: 'It has to land somewhere, dammit.'

Inability to choose may also result from our refusal to give up a desired course of action. We can't let things go and then face the fact that we are likely to miss them and have to mourn them. We want it all; we can't have it all, so we allow ourselves nothing.

Commitment Despite the Odds

Similarly, commitment is needed even, perhaps especially, when we know the odds are against us. It is possible to be realistic about our how small our chances are and yet fight for the outcome, entering into the almost hopeless contest with whole-hearted vigour and even optimism. Can we show our best form in such circumstances? In fact there are two ways of doing this. One is to deny the reality of the probable outcome. The other is to face it and still give our best.

We have seen (in Chapter 19) how Dennis Lillee's angry conviction, against all odds, made possible Western Australia's victory against Queensland in 1976. Productively denying the inevitability of defeat, he lifted himself and the team. Psychiatrist and psychoanalyst John Bowlby once remarked: 'It is a good thing for children to believe in themselves more than is realistic.' A degree of over-confidence enables us to try things out, rather than squirm back irresolutely into our burrow.

Recognising the odds against us does not mean that we should obsess morosely about them. When the Spartan enemy were about to make a landing at Sphacteria in 425 BC, the Athenian general addressed his troops along the following lines:

> Soldiers, all of us are together in this. I don't want any of you in our present awkward position to try to show off his intelligence by making a precise calculation of the dangers that surround us. Instead we must make straight for the enemy, and not pause to discuss the matter, confident in our hearts that these dangers too can be surmounted.

The general asks for simple resolution and an overall confidence. He does not deny the awkwardness of the present position, but nor does he want 'precise calculation' of danger. This reminds me of Edward Dusinberre and the Takacs Quartet: when one of the quartet has an idea of how to play a particular passage that the other three don't agree with, it is often best, he argues, to try the suggestion out with all the energy and commitment each can muster, rather than debate the potential drawbacks in advance or sabotage the idea by refusing to go for it with full effort in the try-out.

It is not necessarily true that 'the best lack all conviction'. In fact we need what John Keats called 'negative capability'. In a letter to his brothers, George and Thomas, dated 21 December 1817, Keats used the phrase for the only time. He wrote:

> Several things dove-tailed in my mind, and at once it struck me what quality went to form a Man of Achievement, especially in Literature, and which Shakespeare possessed so enormously – I mean Negative Capability, that is, when a

man is capable of being in uncertainties, mysteries, doubts, without any irritable reaching after fact and reason.

We need this, and then need still to be able to commit.

Worms of Doubt

When it is not an obstacle to wholeheartedness, doubt can be fruitful in enabling us to think again or look for evidence. There are worms of doubt making the earth fertile, as well as moths of doubt shredding the fabric of life. Despite the uncertainties of his job, Henry Marsh speaks of 'fierce concentration' as a neurosurgeon. When it came to it, doubt did not render Socrates impotent or paralysed.

Ted Sorensen was John F. Kennedy's close advisor and speechwriter. As well as commenting on Kennedy's fanatical opposition to fanatics, he tells us that the president set up regular meetings of advisors, the specific purpose of which was to criticise current and proposed policies: 'He was in charge and liked hearing alternatives, and [having] assumptions challenged, before he made up his mind.' The president was also well aware of the luxury of the critic as contrasted with the burdens of the decision-maker: 'The Joint Chiefs of Staff advise you the way a man advises another about whether he should marry a girl. He doesn't have to live with her.'

There is a Jewish story about a man who complained non-stop to God about his bad luck in life. 'Just let me win the lottery,' he kept pleading. At last God, fed up with his kvetching, retorted: 'Do me a favour. At least buy a ticket.' We have to enter the lottery of life with commitment.

A key factor in a good life is making the best of both good and bad jobs. We may be dealt a bad hand of cards, but as Aldous Huxley put it, 'Experience is not what happens to a man. It is what he does with what happens to him.' What he does with it to some extent influences not only how *it* turns out, but also the nature of the cards dealt henceforth, of what 'happens' next. Some people invite negativity, others create atmospheres of joint resolution and cheerfulness.

Panic

Form also requires the capacity to stay in the arena, at one's post (whatever it is), through periods of time when we are too frightened or disturbed to be able to think. In *The Long Week-End*, Wilfred Bion describes his utter disorientation and terror as, aged nineteen or twenty, he sat in a small tin can called a tank, of which he was called the commander, on the Western Front, for eighteen months from early 1917, waiting to be burned alive. Much later, reflection on those wartime experiences of sheer terror may have helped him tolerate periods of incapacity and confusion of a less life-threatening but nevertheless potentially devastating order when treating psychotic patients in the consulting room. He writes about making his way along duckboards to see if his sunken tank is salvageable. He has been warned not to stray off the duckboards. He realises that the sounds he hears are men drowning in the mud. Five decades later he still hears in his consulting room warning voices telling him "'Don't go off the beaten track. Don't do as the psychoanalysts do. Leave your mind alone. Don't go down to the Unconscious, Daddy." How wise! How very wise!'

These 'warning voices' belonged to both the sufferers on his couch and to himself. Aware of them, Bion nevertheless had the courage to risk the psychological mud.

Trauma in some cases strengthens and deepens those who survive it and, though tormented by it, manage to integrate it. Bion was awarded the DSO and the Legion of Honour for his bravery at Cambrai. His own verdict on this was: 'Even after Cambrai . . . I felt [my crew] looked at me as if to say, "What, you? Recommended for a VC?" . . . I might with equal relevance have been recommended for a court martial. It depended on the direction which one took when one ran away.'

I suspect, however, that he stayed put long enough in those horrendous circumstances; if he did run away, at crucial times he ran towards the enemy. Courage can be a matter of running shrewdly or of staying put blindly.

At a comparatively trivial level, on the cricket field at Lahore in 1978, I experienced a moment of terror when I was supposed to be a cool commander. We had been warned that there was civic unrest, of a political kind, in the city; there might be some sort of a crowd demonstration. Before play, I told our team to watch me if there was any trouble while we were fielding; I would indicate what we should do. One afternoon, perhaps further stirred by the dull cricket, several thousand people suddenly and unpredictably burst over the boundary, rushing towards the centre of the ground. For all my wise words, I turned and ran. We all ran, fleeing to the safety of the pavilion. The police had disappeared.

In fact, it soon transpired that the frustration was not directed against us. The crowd milled around for a while. One man got near the England dressing room and shouted, 'We are sorry you. Police behaviour very bad.' After a short break, the game resumed. But the moment was shocking to me, the panic visceral. I was unable to 'stay at my post', and without doubt, the direction in which I ran was away from the action.

There are cases in battle when a courageous soldier turns the tide by picking up the standard and rallying the troops. Battles literal and metaphorical hinge on such individual courage and resourcefulness.

Pasquinelli: the role of failure

In his introduction to the book he edited on artificial intelligence, Matteo Pasquinelli argues that turmoil, and the capacity to learn from it, is a central feature of the human mind. This idea was, he writes, inherent in what originally drove pioneers in their search to create artificial intelligence machines. Linking their rationale to earlier views on the nature of mind, he speaks approvingly of accounts of the Age of Enlightenment as being driven 'not by plain confidence in reason . . . Rather, it was obsessed with error, and considered human knowledge to be basically an *aberration* . . . No paradigm of cognition and computation can be assessed without the recognition of the *epistemic abnormal* and the role of noetic failure.'

Pasquinelli writes for a better-informed audience than me. I worry about erroneously taking partially understood bits and pieces from him, but take comfort from his idea that, if we are to go beyond our current states of ignorance, we must risk error. I find his ideas fascinating not so much in relation to artificial intelligence itself as in his suggestions about how ordinary human skills evolve. Pasquinelli links being on form with our usual condition – disruption, error and trauma. It may be part of our intelligent adaptation not only to confront and recover from catastrophes (on small and large scales) but to set ourselves potentially traumatic tasks, beyond the level of our capacity to perform them, beyond even our capacity to know in advance what it would be like to perform them. Without such daring, human thinking and achievement would not have progressed as it has, and will not continue to do so. Pasquinelli may well be right that we need to embrace the forces of negativity, even destructiveness, in ourselves, tendencies that challenge – perhaps going so far as to aim to *get rid of* – what we think we know. Certainly we need Kennedy's critical in-group in our own minds.

We should try not to be too panicked by panic. As Bangladeshi novelist Tahmima Anam put it about the alienation from her family that education and a different social environment created in her, she 'had to learn to be comfortable with [her] discomfort'. Pasquinelli writes that 'Augmentation is always a process of alienation of mind from itself.' He offers a new definition of trauma: 'Trauma is not produced by a vivid content or energetic shock, but by the inability to abstract from that memory, that is, the inability to transform a given experience into an abstract link of memory.' Pasquinelli explains an 'abstract link of memory' as a way of making links or connections between 'fragments of knowledge that are not completely known'.

All this suggests interesting analogies with what we aim to do in psychoanalysis. We need to abstract from immediate and sometimes traumatic experience in order to embrace and give thought to new and as yet unknown features of ourselves. This is an important route to self-reconstruction. Psychoanalyst Gabriele Junkers comments that our choice of the profession of psychoanalysis may be 'influenced by early mental suffering that disrupts our "continuity of being"'. And part of our job as analysts is to disrupt old patterns of functioning. One could almost say that the psychoanalytic process creates traumas, in the hope that together with the analyst the patient can 're-orient' his mind. At the same time the patient is often, usually without deliberate intent, disrupting *our* minds, giving us pieces of his own, getting under our skins. We analysts work in the hope of creative and constructive reorganisations. We are, in one metaphor, open to our own rebirth, as well as that of our patients.

As analysts we learn – in part – by getting things wrong, by being disturbed, by re-entering disturbances that we have evaded. We are constantly adjusting our sense of what is going on between our patients and ourselves. (We should not, though, idealise the making of mistakes!)

Moazem, a friend who loves driving and travelling in his car, comments that he 'likes getting lost'; he doesn't *aim* to get lost, but nor does he get distraught, or furious with himself or his navigator, or at the inadequacy of road signs, when he does. Turning mistakes into opportunities for serendipity, he is not fazed by them. Nor does he feel insecure if he can't hold the whole route consciously in his mind. One man I knew was terrified of speaking in public because he could not mentally predict and run through his answer to every possible question in advance. He was intimidated by the idea of being at a loss, with nothing to draw on.

I think that it is often only through losing our way, failure, distress and difficulty, that we emerge into relative health and (a degree of) good form. However we interpret it, there is no story that better expresses the idea that failure may give birth to new life than the one that tells the life and death of Jesus.

One reason for the difficulty in pinning down the nature of good form – and for the impossibility of finding a recipe for it – is that it is not a clear-cut or purely technical matter. Human qualities and attitudes, many of them in conflict with each other, are involved. To say that we have to hold them in balance is partly true. But it is also the case that we have to give house-room to the more primitive or powerful feelings that are of a kind to frighten us all. We – and our patients – may benefit from 'going off the beaten track', putting one foot at least in the mud, despite the risks we fear so much.

Failure is not, though, usually fatal. We may learn from it. As Samuel Beckett famously wrote, 'Ever tried. Ever failed. No matter. Try again. Fail again. Fail better.'

24

THE CHICKADEE BIRD

If we want things to remain the same, everything must change.

Giuseppe di Lampedusa

———

In 2004, the New Zealand rugby team, the All Blacks, who had a win record of 75 per cent over the previous hundred years, embarked on an ambitious project to change the culture of their team. That something had gone wrong had become apparent the previous year. Discipline had declined, they had done less well than expected in the recent World Cup, and some senior players were threatening to leave. The turning point was a 26–40 defeat to South Africa in 2004, which meant that they came last in the Tri-Nations competition, below South Africa and Australia.

They did not seek quick fixes to their problems. Rather, a new management team under Graham Henry, coach since December 2003, set out to rebuild the culture as well as the team. The result? Over the next eleven years a win rate of 85 per cent and two World Cup victories. James Kerr describes all this in his book, *Legacy*.

Humility

The All Blacks were bold. After intense deliberation by a cadre of coaches and players, the team committed itself to the aim of continuous improvement, with core values of humility, excellence and respect. A central element was: 'Better people make better All Blacks.' (I was reminded of Steve Waugh's Australian cricket team, with its similar philosophy.)

The new attitude was illustrated most starkly in the All Blacks' behaviour after matches. After their 42–9 victory against Wales at Dunedin in 2010, for example, there was for a while the usual mess of activity in the 'sheds' – the New Zealand term for a dressing room. Drink flowed, cuts were stitched up, a few forwards shivered in ice-filled rubbish bins. Rap played, followed by reggae. Relatives, journalists, sponsors milled about.

Then things changed. The manager quietly cleared the room. The team and coaches alone remained for a debrief. The players told their stories. After this, the assistant coach, Steve Hanson spoke. 'It was good, but not good enough. Plenty of work to do on the line-out. Let's not get carried away.'

Then something happened that really surprised me: two of the senior players picked up brooms and swept the floor, brushing the mud and discarded bandages into piles in the corner. The idea is: no one looks after the All Blacks; they look after themselves.

Humility: this group of top sportsmen regarded cleaning the dressing room as one way of keeping their feet on the ground. If they made a mess of the room (as in the ordinary course of events – with all the autograph sheets, the signing of souvenirs, bandages and ointments, wrappings, mud, blood, used towels, drink cans – is bound to happen), then it was up to them to restore it to its former state. The same thing happened after every match, including the World Cup final which they won in 2011. Clearly they were determined not to get above themselves.

Rod Marsh said in 2000 that in Australia, international cricketers were still playing in local club matches, despite the million-dollar incomes earned by a few. 'Club cricket is a reflection of life. Just because you're the Australian captain you can't sit on your arse in the dressing room and do nothing. On a Saturday afternoon, if it starts to rain, he helps the rest of the mob put on the canvas [covers]. Your team-mates won't let you get away with it anyway.' But sweeping up? After the biggest matches? That *was* new to me.

For individuals or teams to improve, there has to be a willingness to self-criticise, individually and collectively, whatever happens in terms of results. This requires an atmosphere in which facing one's shortcomings or even one's decline is not viewed as evidence of weakness. The requirement applies in all sorts of activity, including relationships. We are loath to admit vulnerability, fault, failure. What is so striking with these All Blacks is that humility was placed at the top of the list. Outlawing hubris, the pride that comes before a fall, they set themselves resolutely against complacency.

This attitude was not entirely new for the All Blacks. The idea of individual heroes has always been discouraged in New Zealand culture, and particularly in their rugby. Already by the late 1990s, soon after the rugby union revolution that allowed professionalism in the sport, the New Zealand Rugby Football Union had given out a strict set of guidelines for sponsorship: 'No partnership is contemplated if it contradicts the core values of the brand.'

One offer they turned down was a proposal to link the All Blacks with James Bond, with leading player Jonah Lomu as the front man. The image of a glossy, dashing individualist, with star status, was in conflict with the ideals of team spirit embraced by the whole organisation. The old adage 'there is no I in team' was central to this philosophy, including the policy of selecting on the basis of character as well as talent.

Humility in the very best performers is particularly important. The All Blacks would have admired Sachin Tendulkar's attitude after the Chennai Test between India and England in 2008. In the aftermath of the terrible terrorist attack in Mumbai, the game that was to have been played there had been switched to Chennai. It was a remarkable match: India scored 387 for four in the last innings to beat England on a turning pitch, against an attack that included two fine spinners in Graeme Swann and Monty Panesar. Tendulkar scored a not-out century, reaching this landmark with the stroke that also won the match. Shortly after, he was greeted in the middle of the ground by a groundswoman in a red sari, whose job had been to sweep the ends of the dusty pitch at intervals during the match. She approached Tendulkar diffidently, wanting to greet to him and offer *namaste*, salaams. I was struck by the generosity and modesty of his response. He gave her his full attention. Later I said to him that this must have made her day, if not her year. His reply was humble: 'We don't just play for ourselves; we play for India. Thanks to God, I have been able to play for India for twenty years. It is wonderful for the nation to have a victory in such a fine match, after the events in Mumbai.'

In the All Blacks' set-up, it was not only the players who aspired to humility. Coaches realised that their impact might be negative if they pressed too hard to impose themselves. This was epitomised in the way the working week was structured. They would lead the evening review meeting after a match, but gradually over the week they would hand over responsibility and decision-making to the on-field leadership. By the time of the next match, on Saturday, it was down to the players; contrary to tradition, there was no rousing team talk by coaches before the match. Henry himself rated enabling his players to take charge of their own environment as the achievement he was most proud of.

Perhaps the key element in humility is eagerness to learn, including during periods of success. We need to use high performance as a springboard for improvement. Tom Cartwright used to say that you could learn most about batting while going on after scoring a hundred. In the assurance that comes with occupation of the crease and a big score, a batsman can, if open to it, broaden his range and technique as well as reinforce his confidence.

I remember learning to play a new stroke (hitting a slow left-arm bowler over mid-wicket, against the spin) after reaching a century against Yorkshire in 1973. I realised for a while at least that being in peak form is a time not for basking but for developing.

Flatter Hierarchies

Though autocracy increases resentment and forces opposition underground, it is important for teams to know who is in charge, and for the leader to take the responsibility for decisions. In the heat of battle there is no room for Athenian-style democracy. Business leadership guru Tom Peters maintained that good leaders create other good leaders. I agree, but they also need and create good followers, people who are willing to go along with a decision wholeheartedly even if they do not think it the best option; and are willing to continue to support the leader if that policy proves fruitless. This combination of good followers and good leaders is best achieved, I think, by flattening the hierarchy, by encouraging everyone to think about the well-being of the whole group and voice his opinion. You never know where the next good idea will come from. And every player has to be able to take the lead on (and off) the field; at some moments all may depend on the most junior player taking the initiative and carrying others with him. Having the right, even the responsibility, to express one's views may cause difficulties, as in an argumentative family; but there is life and vigour in such groups.

Margaret Heffernan too recognises the importance of responsibility being devolved to people at all levels. She refers to a hospital where a night nurse who found her ward of severely ill patients dangerously understaffed was able, thanks to the culture of the hospital, to contact the CEO in the middle of the night. He came in at dawn and saw to it that the situation was quickly rectified.

Atul Gawande spoke about a hospital in Klagenfurt, Austria, which pioneered the treatment of people frozen in accidents in the Alps, without pulse, respiration or reaction to the light – in fact, brain-dead. After the first successful case, the hospital authorities came to realise that one crucial element in the possibility of further such 'returns from the dead' was ensuring that essential staff were informed and available at short notice:

> And so what they did was they made a checklist and they gave it to the person who had *least* power in the system: the telephone operator. [So] the telephone operator got the call and could activate the checklist . . . [she] could call up the anaesthesiologists and the cardiac surgeon and tell them, 'You need to come in from home now.' The engineer would get the machine ready. Since when they have saved many lives in this way.

But humility is not always what is most required. An incompetent or depressed team needs to build pride and confidence. It may need stubbornness, even a dash of arrogance. (And this makes it plain that advice on how to achieve form depends on where, psychologically, the recipients of advice are. Advising one group to be more humble might be as inappropriate as advising another to be more arrogant.) When England were at a low ebb in the late 1990s, captain Nasser Hussain helped to restore pride by making them more bloody-minded, more difficult to defeat – an important stage in a process of recovery.

Egghead Intellectual Stuff

As a captain myself, I wanted all eleven players (or all sixteen, say, in a squad or touring party) to think like captains, beyond their own personal skills. And I wanted us all to be open to learning. In one of his first games for Middlesex as a seventeen-year-old, Mike Gatting remembers me asking him on the field what he thought we should do next. He was at a loss for words. Apparently I said, 'Well, next time I want to know your thoughts,' which, he recalls, made him feel both flattered and put on his mettle.

But I did not get as far at Middlesex with this kind of approach as I would have liked. Asking a sportsman to become a better person, whatever that might involve, may be felt to be moralistic, even pietistic; an imposition of values on people who simply want to improve as cricketers or rugby players. Some may also prefer to be told what to do, be given instructions, rather than be expected to change by thinking more deeply for themselves. Life is simpler if you 'watch the wall' and do as you're told.

In the 1970s, especially after working in the Adolescent Clinic with its therapeutic meetings aimed at opening up feelings, I tried to bring to the dressing room ideals of greater emotional awareness and honesty about our own and each other's play. As well as support and interest, I encountered resistance and cynicism. I had not taken the time or made sufficient effort to build a consensus of senior players before embarking on a small-scale version of the All Blacks' plan. Perhaps too I conveyed unwillingness to be criticised myself, and I was not confident enough to go the whole way against others' inevitable reluctance. I had also been liable, especially in my early days as captain, to use thought misguidedly, for example looking up how tomorrow's opposition players had got out in the corresponding match a year before – a largely futile exercise.

At the same time, some of the resistance to thinking that I encountered was itself misguided. In 1971, my first year as captain, Middlesex played what was scheduled to be a forty-over match at Ebbw Vale, against Glamorgan. The rain was sweeping down the valleys and the prospects of play were slight. In fact the rain stopped in time for us to play a match of ten overs per side. As we went to the cars to fetch our cricket bags, I said, enthusiastically, 'We'll have to think about this.' The idea that thought might enter into a ten-over match was greeted with derision – another example of what Geoffrey Boycott once alluded to as my 'egghead intellectual stuff'. But it would not be regarded as absurd today, when a great deal of thought goes into twenty-over matches, which may be reduced to a minimum of five each side when conditions have been unfit for play.

For the All Blacks, though, humility kept them grounded. The players were willing to be criticised shortly after victory, an openness rooted in strength and confidence. They knew, as old pros used to remind precocious young cricketers, that 'you're only as good as your next innings'. At the same time, being a part of this elite was a source of great pride. Laurie Mains, ex-All Black and coach, said, 'If they have not pulled the jersey on, they can't actually feel what it is. I only played fifteen games or so, and yet that jersey just did something to me. The day I pulled it on was something I'll never forget.'

The All Blacks have a motto for each wearer: 'Leave the jersey in a better place'. It is a symbol of a great tradition. It represents the legacy that each individual, each generation, inherits and passes on. It stands for excellence; for pride as well as humility. It represents a recognition of belonging, each in one's small but important way, to something bigger than one-self, bigger too than any current team or generation of players.

'Let Him Finish'

If we lose faith in ourselves too easily, however, then our humility becomes weakness and emptiness. In 1968 I was shortlisted for a job as Lecturer in Philosophy at the University of Newcastle upon Tyne. At the interview, I was asked a complicated and (I still think) difficult question by the professor of law, the gist of which was: 'The law states that hearsay is not allowed as evidence except when the report is of the person's own state of mind. Is there a philosophical basis for this legal distinction?'

In response, I was tentatively feeling my way towards an answer when the professor cut in to contradict what I had said (or what he thought I was about to say). At which point, the professor of philosophy, Karl Britton, cut across him sharply with 'Let him finish.' At least one person in the room, then, had confidence that I had something to say, to finish! This gave me confidence. I said my piece and got the job. I was extremely grateful to Britton; without his intervention, I might have taken on the law professor's apparent view of me and humiliated myself. There was a sequel to this episode. Nine years later, at the team meeting before the Centenary Test in Melbourne, Derek Randall, who was diffident in such situations, was hesitantly speaking. Captain Tony Greig intervened – too quickly, according to me – and I was able to say, with Britton inside me, 'Let him finish.'

We need not only the willingness to put the team before ourselves, but also the courage and spirit to stand out against prevailing prejudices. Sometimes this involves dissociating oneself from institutional attitudes and standing by our opinions. We become feeble, even abject, if our humility is extreme.

The need for forcefulness and assertion makes me question whether the All Blacks' attitude might risk inhibiting individuality. Is flair sufficiently prioritised in their value system? In the terms suggested by Pierre Turquet, does the All Blacks' trenchant opposition to 'singletons' encourage players to become 'membership individuals'? After all, as well as cooperation and reciprocation, teams need individual brilliance. Important contributions come from eccentrics or loners, people who don't easily fit in to the 'groupishness' of the team. I am reminded of the brilliant, quirky England wicketkeeper Alan Knott, who was an invaluable member of the team (in Turquet's terms, an 'individual member'), but the last to party or be hearty.

And does the All Blacks' attitude provide sufficient support for the sometimes difficult or provocative 'singletons'? According to James Kerr, they refer to such people as 'dickheads', and are proud of their refusal to have anything to do with them. There are after all inevitable and valuable traits of selfishness in everyone, and a tension between these characteristics and the willingness to make personal sacrifices for the team. Some egos need massaging, others have to be supported through being confronted. Teams at their best are able to carry, for a while, gifted players who are down on their luck and out of form; as often as not it is the gifted players who most need to be reassured, to be reminded of the swings in form and fortune. The best teams neither ignore such players (out of embarrassment) nor embarrass them (by false or excessive encouragement). Geoffrey Boycott went through a bad patch in Australia in 1978–9. He became fixed in the crease, immobile, no longer deft and nimble in his foot movements. He needed regular confirmation of his long-term excellence and a clear appraisal of how he had become stuck. The young Ian Botham was able to offer both, talking to Boycott about the light-footedness of boxers.

The All Blacks rightly saw as an essential part of continuous improvement the need fearlessly to bring in new talent and replace those who are declining. This too is a delicate balance to manage. My question is: does the ethic of continuous improvement risk tipping into a desire for instant change, and may this predominate over the need to keep those who are tried and tested? I remember agonising debates about this, for example in deciding, at a certain point in the mid-1970s, whether John Emburey, the young contender, should replace the older master, Fred Titmus, in the Middlesex team.

The re-formed, reinvented All Blacks teams played in an atmosphere in which being on form was itself re-formed. Brilliant individual performances mattered less than previously. In the new system there would be more emphasis on how each individual linked with others, how he fitted the overall style and plan. There might be issues about how aware a top player was of the states of mind of his less mercurial colleagues. He had to grow from a singleton into an individual member.

Radical Hope from Rock Bottom

The All Blacks are a highly successful team with a lot to be proud of. Their radical change rested on this strong base, though it required a crisis to energise the new resolve, the new beginning.

Equally radical changes sometimes start from hopeless or even catastrophic beginnings. People may have to reach rock bottom before their need for change registers and becomes undeniable, even to themselves. Individuals and teams may be like buildings that can no longer be patched up; dilapidated and neglected, they need a total and often costly overhaul. Sometimes, too, disaster strikes through traumas that are no fault of our own. Either way, we often enter psychoanalytic treatment, or religious belief, or communism, or Alcoholics Anonymous, as a result of shock or near-despair. 'That which does not kill us makes us stronger', Nietzsche wrote and though this can be facile, it is also true.

A whole culture may suffer losses so extreme as to constitute a collapse of their way of life. In *Radical Hope*, Jonathan Lear gives an account of an American Indian tribe, the Crow, which in the nineteenth century suffered the loss of concepts central to their existence. The Crow were a nomadic tribe, hunting

buffalo across the plains. They sided with the United States in their fights with the Sioux, and later accepted being placed in a reservation. The disappearance of the buffalo, together with the restrictions of space and the acceptance of alien laws, meant that their traditional hunter-gatherer existence, with all its paradigms of excellence, its rituals and many modes of belonging – concepts that had held the tribe together and given meaning over millennia – suddenly became extinct. The Crow were deprived of the social as well as the physical environment in which their concept of virtue (especially courage) could be lived out. Lear shows us that some losses – of concepts, activities and identifications – mean that there is no longer any possible place for the traditional ways of belonging to, gaining credit in, or even seeing oneself as a member of, a particular culture. While losses of all kinds call for reorientation through mourning, the rupture in the Crow's sense of identity made their loss even more catastrophic than, say, the traumatic loss of family members in a natural disaster or war. The Crow, like other hunter-gatherers, were deprived of the very possibility of excelling. Lear shows that, when a cultural context ceased to exist, a certain 'form of life' became inconceivable.

Lear goes on to describe ways in which the Crow managed to respond to these major threats to their identity. He relates in particular the dream of a nine-year-old Crow boy called Plenty Coups, in 1855, at a time when the tribe was still vigorous but was threatened with genocide at the hands of their enemies the Sioux, and when the white man was also increasingly becoming a presence. Lear suggests, to my mind plausibly, that the boy dreamed this dream on behalf of the tribe, picking up subliminal and unarticulated anxieties relating to the loss of the buffalo and the culturally damaging 'storm' that was on its way. The dream was as follows:

First, through a hole in the ground, all the buffalo disappeared. Out of that hole came strange spotted bulls and cows that gathered in small groups to eat the grass; they lay down in strange ways, not like buffalo. Second, Plenty Coups was told that the Four Winds were going to cause a terrible storm in the forest, and only one tree would be left standing, the tree of the Chickadee-person. He sees an image of an old man sitting under that lone tree and is told, in the dream, that that person is himself. Finally, he is told to follow the example of the chickadee.

The dream was interpreted by the 'wisest man in the lodge', Yellow Bear. The old man under the lone tree represented the dreamer himself in old age. The spotted cows were the domesticated cattle of the white man. The dream offered a clue to survival and repair, in the form of the chickadee, a bird noted for its wily ways and its capacity to learn from others. Lear suggests that the chickadee can be understood as an indication of a new ego ideal, in the form of a canny openness, an ideal that was inevitably unspecific; an ideal necessary in the new context in which the old forms of courage – in battle and in hunting – would no longer have their traditional lived place.

Thus imagination was given enhanced value by the Crow tribe, first in their attention to the dream, and further in the role given to imagination as a result of so unsaturated an ideal.

The Crow's crisis was similar to, and yet different from, the ordinary crises of growing up. Like the Crow, the child or adolescent has limited capacity to imagine what later stages of development will involve; but unlike the Crow, his elders have themselves been through the developmental phases they are struggling with, so that they and the culture have in place established ways of guiding the young through the inevitable difficulties and crises of these changes. Parents and others are exemplars, for good and ill, of what the young may become.

The situation is similar for a patient in analysis. He has to have some trust in the analyst and in the process, a sense that development is possible, that a new set of values will gradually emerge. He does not yet know what the developed stage will feel like, but at least he may reasonably have confidence that the analyst has some knowledge of what going through his stage of life is like. For the Crow, by contrast, no one in the whole history of the tribe had had similar, relevant experience. No one had had to deal with so wholesale a catastrophe. Like his contemporaries, young Plenty Coups was, as in the dream, the only tree left standing, on his own.

The dream may also have represented the young man's predicament in terms of Oedipal conflicts. We could speculate that the bulls and cows lying down together are the parental couple, weakened by their trauma or in other ways, and therefore unavailable to support him as he grows up into a man. He is thus left alone partly as a result of their weakness, partly too as a result of the force of the terrible storm coming from all points of the compass, including from inside himself and his body.

Destruction of central elements of their cultural and collective life has faced hunter-gatherer tribes across the globe as, one by one, they have been confronted by the immense expansionist power of agriculturists with life structures and attitudes to the land so much in conflict with their own. Many tribes have lost their pride and their identity in the face of such devastation. There have been damaging levels of alcoholism, depression and suicide, especially among the young men, those most undermined and emasculated in the collapse of the millennia-long way of life forged through, and dependent on, prowess in hunting. Plenty Coups' dream underpinned

– within a system in which dreaming and dream interpretation already had a highly regarded place – the valuing of qualities that would stand individuals and the tribe as a whole in good stead during a period of cataclysmic change.

Novelist and essayist Marilynne Robinson writes of a vision of the soul, which is 'wholly realist in acknowledging the great truth of the centrality of human consciousness, wholly open in that it anticipates and *welcomes disruption of present values in the course of finding truer ones*'. I would say that we are never *wholly* realist or *wholly* open to the 'disruption of present values'; but we may be more or less so, and the vision is there as an ideal.

To be open to learning from experience, and thus to reach and maintain peak form, requires, then, both humility and sufficient belief in ourselves. We need both to learn from our successes, and at times to pick ourselves up from the floor, from failure, from trauma, and from psychological or cultural disruption.

In extreme cases, for us to have any form at all requires a kind of rebirth, a revolution and evolution in our values and our evaluation of the resources we have. We have to face unbearable facts with our imagination intact. Constant change is itself disabling, but leaders and ordinary people too need to have some willingness to think radically and to commit to individual and systemic change, even when confronted by ordinary disturbances in their ways of life.

PART IX: DISPATCHES

25

HOW DO I KNOW WHAT I THINK UNTIL I READ WHAT I WRITE

Writing a book is an adventure. To begin with it is a toy and an amusement. Then it becomes a mistress, then it becomes a master, and then it becomes a tyrant. The last phase is that just as you are about to be reconciled to your servitude, you kill the monster and fling him to the public.

Winston Churchill

The whole history of human life could be written on the back of a postage stamp: we are born, we suffer, we die. But these are not the stories that I am inclined to write.

Joseph Conrad

We are more than we are.

Marilynne Robinson

There are stages in writing. As with Winston Churchill, the happiest time for me is early in a project, when the mind begins to think exuberantly around a subject, and, as sometimes happens, ideas come bubbling up. Getting them down in writing without as yet worrying about whether they're relevant, or how they might fit, is stimulating; it's also necessary, a hedge against losing them. At such times I feel alive, fertile, especially when these welcome visitors come in vivid form, with images, which makes me even happier, as then my imagination is working alongside me, cooperative, endowing me with gifts from my unconscious. I may even feel in the zone, on a roll; a dangerous place to be, as you will have found out if you have read this far.

The process has something in common with hitting a few cricket balls in the nets, playing some stroke or other without concern for risk, to get the body and the hands flowing. But this writing malarkey is unlike cricket practice in that the latter is a matter of grooving, whereas writing is to do with letting things emerge.

It is more like free association in psychoanalysis. Freud proposed only one rule for patients – to say what comes into the mind without censorship; without editing, one might put it. Patients surprise themselves, sometimes enjoyably. 'How do I know what I think until I see what I say,' wrote E. M. Forster.

All sorts of attitudes inhibit our freedom in this associating. Some patients clam up because they resent being expected to start the ball (of the session) rolling. They may also fear being inauthentic – saying things just for effect, perhaps – if they express themselves out loud; they may repeatedly tell small lies, either exaggerating or underplaying what they really think. But at times a patient will feel safe enough in the setting to speak with freedom and sincerity to someone construed as listening closely and non-judgmentally.

Freedom of this kind is, though, more an aspiration than an achievement. The philosopher R. C. Collingwood overstates things when he says, 'If art means the expression of emotion, the artist as such must be *absolutely* candid, his speech must be absolutely free. This is not a precept but a statement.'

There is a mystery in this freedom. We cannot tell how, when or why something will occur to us. We may have some understanding of the kinds of conditions that are conducive to moments of expressiveness and creativity, but we certainly can't force them to happen. And in the end, when we make a decision to speak, or for that matter to act, on what basis, really, do we do it? Can we ever be sure? The unconscious is stronger and more prevalent than we give it credit for.

Marilynne Robinson writes about moments of inspiration for the athlete, as well as 'across the range of human skill and effort':

> The subject of Pindar's *Odes* is always the intervention of the divine in lifting an athlete beyond merely human strength or skill, an experience the poet could claim for himself, *mutatis mutandis*. Pindar says, 'one born to prowess/ May be whetted and stirred/ To win huge glory/ If a god be his helper.' Our own athletes may deserve a more respectful hearing when they, like Pindar, attribute a magnificent throw or catch to a moment of divine favor. This . . . feeling that one's own capacities are somehow transcended in one's own person, seems to find no expression among us in terms that can be understood as descriptive rather than as merely pietistic . . . In Pindar's ode, great acts of prowess exalted and sanctified experience on one particular evening 'lit/ By the lovely light of the fair-faced moon.' And they might well do as much for us, since they can only mean that *we are more than we are.*

Absolute freedom is certainly an illusion. For thought to exist, structuring goes on all the time. Wilfred Bion suggests that thinking starts with non-thought, or with 'thoughts without a thinker': with what he calls 'bizarre objects', bits and pieces to be got rid of; moments of anxiety, terror, desire thrown out by the baby. Bion held that thought proper emerges out of these precursors by means of *containment* by the mother or other carer. That is, the mother imagines her way into the baby's state; by really attending to him, she finds out, partly by trial and error, what he really needs – food, a hug, being cleaned or burped, something to soothe pain, whatever. This process of 'reverie' – making thought available to the baby – gives *meaning* to the bizarre objects, conveying, in effect, 'you're hungry so I'll feed you; I suspect that you have stomach ache, I'll soothe you; you're in such a mess, so I'll clean you'. Thus the carer makes increasing sense of these 'proto-thoughts', which are thereby changed, *translated* – etymologically, 'carried across'. Very gradually the infant begins to do the same for himself.

Structuring (containment) goes on all the time. But of course there is *relatively* unstructured thought. With *On Form*, I began to do some more explicit structuring, grouping ideas into provisional sections or 'chapters'. But as yet there was no worry about eventual publication.

Editor as Psychoanalyst

One problem my editor pointed out relates to my capacity to be balanced. Back in 1977, the co-author of my first two cricket books, Dudley Doust, who taught me a lot about writing, wrote about my way of talking: 'It is as though he has been turning over pebbles, searching for the clearest, most unflawed, most precise and above all best balanced opinion to plop into a pool of conversation . . . If he writes an autobiography, its title should be *On the Other Hand*.'

The good side is to be looking at ideas from different angles. But (on the other hand, inevitably) this quality is liable to degenerate into a sort of butterfly thinking, in which I hurry off to an alternative view without staying long enough on any flower or position. I may skate on the surface like a water-strider, weightless, insubstantial, like that 'water-fly' Osric in *Hamlet*. Oscillation and skittering are not balance. I have to resist this tendency.

Doust also contacted one of my supervisors at Cambridge, the by-then retired Professor John Wisdom, to ask him about his old pupil. Wisdom said, kindly, that I 'never set out to demolish another man's argument . . . and always looked for something valuable before making any objections' – a quality less apparent in domestic situations, as my wife will tell you. But if it leads to a lack of trenchancy and forthrightness, that good quality too may be a shortcoming.

My editor jibs against my tendency to turn the book into a quasi-academic critique of the subject. I should get most of what I have to say across by means of stories, fully enough told, with myself in them more, rather than spelling out the arguments as a set of pros and cons. The role of editor, whether another human being or the writer's own internal editing self, includes telling the author home truths. In this, he is not unlike one's psychoanalyst. (I remember saying, on the couch, that I was a late developer. Self-satisfied, I quoted a phrase from a children's book: 'Better late than never, Chippybobby.' The response was dry: 'When are you going to begin?')

One lesson for the writer-me is: this (life) is not a rehearsal. It is all too easy to work blithely on the assumption that I can always revise what I write, that it's forever better to be late than never. I can revise the very words that I am writing now! I don't need to commit to them – they are forever provisional. My grandson, Luka, when about four or five, told me a similar home truth. He remarked one day as I was pushing him on

a swing that he sometimes thought there was a God, sometimes not. I said: 'That's a good position, not unlike my own.'
There were a couple of swings. 'And what's more,' I added, 'you
have plenty of time to make up your mind.' Swing, swing. 'Yes,
Mike,' he said. 'But *you* don't.'

Another exchange with my analyst went something like
this:

Analyst: 'Do you have any further thoughts on what you've just told me?'
  Silence.
  Me: 'No, I don't think I do.'
  Silence.
  Analyst (*sardonically*): 'You surprise me.'

It took me some time to realise that this was not so much
a put-down as a message that my mind was richer than I was,
just then, aware of.

A lot of the process of writing is itself a sort of editing; an
internal, ongoing, silent and more or less automatic editing.
As I worry at the text, something doesn't sound right, the sentence is awkward, the point is lost. Worrying at it – essential
for me, I think – is liable to degenerate into fiddling; I make
one list, then another, and then a list of the lists. On other
occasions, I wobble, like a child learning to ride a bike, and
then correct the handlebars violently. In writing there is nothing bluntly equivalent to falling off the bike, but it is painful,
and gets more painful and burdensome later, when the work
involves realising banality or lazily strung-together ideas, and
I have to throw out whole sections that I have laboured over.

Editing is present from first to last; but the editing angst
grows as the stage of finalising the book approaches.

So: writing, however spontaneous, is and needs to be

accompanied by watching and adjustment. But one needs to watch this too. For monitoring may get in the way of being on form, not only by being too loose, with chaos the result, but also by being too oppressively, tediously correct. In writing as in sport and life in general, there are horses and snaffles.

In the end, like other writers, I have to send the book, like a child, out into the world, trusting it to make its own way. I have to say 'I'm sorry, but this is the best I can do at this time, and I don't have limitless time.'

Digressions

There are diversions, reroutings, in this book. Hopefully, they will have been, as the Michelin Green Guide has it, 'worth the detour'. It was hard to know how many signposts are needed. I didn't want to fuss you, the reader, or treat you condescendingly, but nor did I want to confuse you, or lose you in a maze or a trackless wilderness.

My editor and I discussed the issue of how varied I should be in writing the book. He said we had to start with something down to earth; once I'd won the reader's interest, then I could be more adventurous. He was probably right.

In writing, on one side there is rambling, an 'anything goes' attitude – which is undisciplined, vague, jumping from one thing to another, incoherent; as if, in the words of Allen Ginsberg, 'First thought, best thought'. On the other, what we end up with may be flat, stereotypical, overworked, formalist.

As I say, I worried at the text like a dog at a bone. Did you know that the word 'worry', originally the Old English *wyrgan*, derives from the Proto-Germanic *wurgjan*, meaning 'strangle'? I don't suppose you did, and nor did I, till, worrying at it, I looked up the word in the online etymological dictionary.

Where does one stop the 'blue-sky' thinking? Psychoanalysts

rely greatly on free association. But at times it is anything but free. One patient presented his analyst with long, complicated dreams, to disarm him, and to disempower him by drawing him into clever intellectualisation. Another patient would bring his dreams in written form, say nothing about them till near the end of the session, and then read them out all together as if they belonged to someone else. His aim? I think to escape understanding, and to drown and test his analyst. A third patient dreamed of observing hippopotami hurrying by on a narrow path, and then he himself, the patient, joining in. I interpreted this as his unconscious awareness of how he got caught up in a sort of hectic rush that mimicked free association. I was reminded of the Gadarene swine in St Mark's Gospel hurling themselves over the cliff. A fourth patient presented himself as lazy, in need of special treatment. He was smug about it, speaking about this lazy person as if it had nothing to do with him. He seemed to be asking what I proposed to do about it. To which an appropriate response would be: 'The question is, what are *you* going to do about it?'

We writers too breathlessly proliferate, or rush over the edge. We have verbal diarrhoea. But this insight runs the risk of being countered by another extreme: we had better not run at all. We are constipated! If we don't cross the road we won't get run over; but neither can we get to the other side.

At some point we have to stop ourselves digressing, or stop the patient on the couch. But at which point? When have we, or they, gone far enough? When has a list become a litany, excitement a rant, urgency an intrusive colonising of the listener's mind? When is it one example too many? (Was bringing not two, not three, but *four* patients in my recent paragraph over the top? Would two have sufficed?)

So it's OK to ramble, but not too much, and not always. Sometimes stories or episodes that wander into one's writing are damaging, ruining the sense and the narrative logic. It is like inviting arsonists to move in, as in Max Frisch's play *The Fire Raisers*. They end up burning the house down.

Nevertheless, let's give the last word on digressions to Lawrence Sterne, author of the prodigious (and prodigiously digressive) novel, *Tristram Shandy*:

> Digressions, incontestably, are the sunshine; – they are the life, the soul of reading; – take them out of this book for instance, – you might as well take the book along with them . . . Restore them to the writer; – he steps forth like a bridegroom, – bids All hail; brings in variety, and forbids appetite to fail.

Affiliation Anxiety

A psychoanalyst once referred to consulting rooms as goldfish bowls – meaning, I think, that more things get around about how we work than we imagine. But we would be even more self-conscious if we were doing our work onstage (which is an occasional nightmare of analysts).

By contrast, write a book and you literally go public. In my case, the editing angst grew as the deadlines – two of them – approached and passed.

Psychoanalyst Ronald Britton writes about writers' publication anxiety – the fear of being found out, even savaged, in public. Britton's main focus is on what he calls 'affiliation anxiety': will friends and heroes in our field be scornful, or feel let down? I don't have the same worry about cricket, my psychoanalytic superego being harsher than my cricketing one – though that was not the case when I was playing. I find writing about cricket, if not easier, then less anxiety-making than playing it. But writing about psychoanalysis does arouse affiliation anxiety in me. Will my colleagues think I'm shallow, that I'm offering a lightweight version of psychoanalysis?

In fact, one late decision in the writing of the book was to take out some of the psychoanalytic material with the intention of using some of these deletions as the basis for a second book, in due course (better late than never?), on *The Art of Psychoanalysis*. At first this decision felt like dividing my baby into two, and I wondered if the wisdom of Solomon would have led me to prefer the baby to be kept whole, rather than be born with limbs amputated. But I think it was the right decision. The text is certainly long enough as it now is, and I hope I have left enough in, at least to intrigue you, Reader, about psychoanalysis, and to give a psychoanalytic take on the topic. My editor had already commented that after two years, he had decided that this was not really a book about form after all; rather, its main subject – discovered as we went along – was, he suggested, my psychoanalytic attitude to life, sport and psychoanalysis itself. I hope this overall orientation has not been lost.

Against Finality

In general, I try to keep in mind George Orwell's guidelines for good writing – be simple; avoid technical and Latinate words when English ones will do; guard against confused metaphors; and avoid 'polite' and ready-made phrases of disclaimer and caution.

In his acceptance speech as the recipient of the Orwell Prize in 2015, Rowan Williams argued against *finality* in writing: against a kind of writing that renders dialogue with a reader impossible. He compares such writing to the situation alluded to by an American commander in Vietnam: 'To save the village it became necessary to destroy it . . . [whereas] the good writer attempts to speak in a way that is open to the potential challenge of a reality she or he does not own and control.'

What makes a good writer is in part something that happens off the page. He has, the reader senses, a hinterland; there is more where this comes from. As a result, perhaps we do not entirely lose the thoughts that are discarded from the final version. With Williams himself I sense always a rich background, where truthfulness rather than narcissism prevails. Such a writer comes across as open to his own many selves, some of them unknown to him, and to those of the reader.

This is harder to describe than to detect. There are no simple criteria. Simple prose, as advocated by George Orwell, is not a necessary condition – look at Henry James and Marcel Proust, purveyors of complex thought and ideas in complex language. Perhaps Williams's point relates to authenticity, and to a mindset that is open to other points of view, however much one might disagree with them. There are authors who strike one as fake, somehow always drawing attention to themselves, self-congratulatory; like those ex-players commentating on sport who have a concealed agenda, with a subtext: 'Today's players are less good than in my era!' or 'If someone is good, I feel lessened. Let's make sure no one is!'

All this may be a hostage to fortune, an unconscious admission, or fuel for the hostile reviewer. I hope not.

The Writing Self

Do I become a different person when I write? Proust says:

The best books are written in a sort of foreign language . . .
A book is the product of a different self from the self we
manifest in our habits, in our social life, in our vices. If we
would try to understand that particular self, it is by searching
our own bosoms, and trying to reconstruct it there, that we
may arrive at it.

Is this right? There are echoes here of D. H. Lawrence's
answer to the question 'what is man's soul?' – that it is 'a wide,
dark forest, the wholeness of him'. But Proust's 'particular self'
– how is it to be found? Is it so different, so much more real?
He continues: 'A book is the secretions of our innermost self,
written in solitude and for oneself alone, that one gives to the
public . . . this innermost self which one can only recover by
putting aside the world and the self that frequents that world.'

Similar questions are sometimes raised about psychoanalysts
– are we better in our work selves, less petty, more generous?
And ought we, more than others, to be better, more generous,
in our relationships? We psychoanalysts have our significant
work setting, more specifically local and unchanging than that
of the writer. We are protected, for the fifty-minute hour, from
the immediate pressures and intrusions of life. While engag-
ing in the analytic conversation, I don't answer the door or the
phone, I don't read my emails, I don't try to make a fried egg
for a fractious, hungry child. I don't usually have to take practical action on a difficult issue. (All this I may be called on to do
in everyday life). The analyst is entitled, even duty-bound, to
retain a certain neutrality or abstinence, which, if maintained
in ordinary life, would be insufferably superior or interfering.
But the work is not tame; I can do damage in many ways – for
example, by cowardly avoidance of difficult topics, by over- or
under-emphasis on the patient's destructiveness, or by glorying

in my own cleverness rather than allowing the patient to come to his own ideas.

The 'I' who sits behind my patients is a close relative of the 'I' who sits with my family around the dinner table, or argues about who will do the washing up. Perhaps I should say: the structure of psychoanalysis gives me, as the process of writing did Proust, or even an ordinarily skilled writer, a *chance* to be better, at least in some ways – more thoughtful, more able to stay with my emotions, more empathic, and more aware of the impact of the other on me and vice versa. And sometimes as an analyst I am also more able to stand my ground and hold a person (and myself) to the implications of what they and I say and do.

While at his desk, or musing in his deckchair, the writer too has a certain freedom from the everyday practicalities of life. He can follow his own mind. Like the patient in psycho-analysis, screened from having to act or to take into account the immediate demands of life, he may be able to enter more fully into his imagination. He has licence to follow his intuition, to write without knowing how it will turn out. He may express – ex-press – something of himself, something perhaps that was unknown to him and is now articulated. What he reveals may be not so much the self who acts, or performs, or makes a party dress out of a pile of rags, but the rags themselves, illuminating the areas of darkness that constituted him and led him to his masks and costumes.

Writing in a foreign language – foreign to himself, that is – he may reveal some of the animals in his vast forest.

26

ITHAKA

The ability to be present and absent at the same time.

Stephen Frears

So many go to bed as a human and wake as an insect, not feeling part of the society, not feeling part of the family, not feeling part of themselves.

Abdelkader Benali

———————

In his book *What Does Sport Teach Us About Life*, Ed Smith quotes Stephen Frears, the creative British film director, who talks about his job as

> trying to create a kind of benign dictatorship – though I use the term reluctantly. You are paid to make decisions, you can't avoid that. It's mostly about bringing the best out of other people. And beneath the surface, of course, you are dealing with the actors' unconscious, alongside your own unconscious – all on a day-to-day level.

And then Frears says:

That's the Mike Brearley position . . . [He] had the ability to be present and yet somehow absent at the same time. I recognise something of that in myself . . . What I really admire . . . is the feeling that what they [people in such states] have lost physically they make up for by seeing the whole picture. They grasp the shape of the game, they can somehow stand above it and see it clearly . . . There are periods in your life when you have that clarity. And then the fog descends again. And you don't know why.

At first I didn't know what to make of this comment. I hadn't thought in those terms. Now I have a sense of what Frears is getting at. Leaders need to lead, even dictate (the term he used reluctantly). They need to be in charge. But they – we all – also need to be capable of removing ourselves and our deliberate endeavour sufficiently to allow the world to come to us in a more impressionistic, overall way, so that we 'grasp the shape of the game' before 'the fog descends again'. One way of putting it is that we need to have traditionally feminine as well as traditionally masculine qualities. I suggest there are elements of playfulness in the 'absence', as when the small child is absorbed in drawing (like the six-year-old making a portrait of God). Being on form involves thinking *around* a problem, as well as focusing on a list of pros and cons. At best we are alert to the *emotional* shapes and resonances of things, too, without losing touch with the blunt facts.

This 'absence' allows also, paradoxically, for a more nuanced and simultaneously more metaphorically freighted take on the world. As an artist, Marion Milner looked at and took in the detail, focusing narrowly, with scientific objectivity. But she also looked with a broader gaze, in a way that allowed space for unconscious ideas and connections to flow, that did not 'shut out the overtones and haloes of subjective feeling and subjective seeing'. The creative person picks up on realities and associations beyond the material and the measurable. Milner adds: 'Both ways of looking [are] sterile without each other. In fact one had to stand apart in order to come together again in a restored wholeness of perception.'

The blank page (the one inside our heads as well as that in front of our eyes) is then no longer a threat and a remonstration, but a space that may fill up abundantly, with ideas that need time to flower, to come up – if they do – unbidden, almost automatically, like snowdrops in January. This is not a strategy to rely on, but it should be allowed for. We do well to allow our conscious minds to go missing for a while, having faith that we will be able to conceive.

'Absence' may also be literal. The writer goes off to bed, or on a long walk, and then finds the solution emerging into his mind unsought. The most famous example of conscious absence giving birth unconsciously to presence is the arrival, fully formed, of Samuel Taylor Coleridge's poem 'Kubla Khan' after a three-hour, opium-induced nap. In his preface, Coleridge refers to himself in the third person, as if the writer of the poem had indeed been a different person from his everyday self:

> On awakening he appeared to himself to have a distinct recollection of the whole . . . and instantly and eagerly wrote down the lines that are here preserved. At this moment he was unfortunately called out by a person on business from Porlock, and detained by him above an hour, and on his return to his room, found, to his no small surprise and mortification, that though he still retained some vague and dim recollection of the general purport

of the vision, yet, with the exception of some eight or ten scattered lines and images, all the rest had passed away like the images on the surface of a stream into which a stone had been cast, but, alas! without the after-restoration of the latter.

Coleridge had delayed publication for almost twenty years – perhaps for all this time he harboured hopes of retrieving the lines lost on account of that most damaging intruder in literature, the person on business from Porlock. About the process of 'composition', he writes: 'if that indeed can be called composition in which all the images rose up before him as things, with a parallel production of the correspondent expressions – without any sensation or consciousness of effort'.

One requirement for good writing is to achieve a balance between a capacity to get rid of non sequiturs and tone down excesses in the cool light of day – involving conscious effort – and alongside this a fecundity that admits unexpected and unforeseeable elements. We need inebriation as well as sobriety. We need to be like the tribe that has its debates and makes its decision twice, once drunk, once sober. (In that order, I presume.)

We are attached, even dictatorial. We are also detached, almost absent.

The discovery and recovery of form, then, requires, at times, the 'Ten Tips' type of approach, where the focus is narrow – on the specifics of the task. But this is not enough. It also calls for space for changes of heart, for transformations. There are situations where what is required is practice at one's scales (and more practice, and more) to get them grooved and solid as a basis of technique, and situations where there is little or no emphasis on technique, in which ends are unknown (as Harold

Pinter said about writing his plays) until we get there. We have to give room to intuition, respecting ideas and feelings whose relevance we can't yet see. We may even, in such states, let go of memory or desire, of premeditation.

Many scenarios are mixed. My hands and arms are tense on the bat. A coach may focus either on the technicalities of my grip, or on the prevailing emotional background ('do you think you'll hit the ball harder if you frown?'). Or the emotional trouble may be more episodic and specific, as in the golf example with which I began the book. Though no doubt the collapse of my golf would have been less drastic if my technique had been more reliable and less vulnerable to shock, the precipitating factor in that collapse was clearly emotional – I felt suddenly excluded.

Again, it may not so much be technical advice that we need, as to have our options expanded. I helped Derek Underwood broaden his range with my suggestion that he should consider occasionally bowling over the wicket rather than sticking to his usual method of bowling round the wicket. Or we may need to re-frame our activity, setting it in a larger context. J. S. Bach saw his *St Matthew Passion* as a communal expression of faith in God, of sin and repentance, so that it was of the utmost importance that its performance be regarded as itself a matter of life and death, a matter to give one's all to. Again, the focus widens along with the context.

One thing I've learned in writing this book is that what has to be addressed is deeper than the mechanics of form. There is no simple technique for bringing about transformations. Psychoanalyst Irma Brenman Pick once suggested, in discussing the analysis of a writer, that the analyst treating her should worry less about the actual writing. Instead, if he could help the patient give space to the continuing impact of early traumas, and become more aware of her tendency to mood swings, then 'the writing would take care of itself'. Brenman Pick also said, about psychoanalysis more generally, that we have to know how little we can do, but knowing this makes it possible to do a surprising amount.

We are all ambivalent about change and development. Until we try playing tennis, we don't know what being on (or off) form in tennis entails. We are like young children who, though from early on full of love (and hate), are not yet in a position to know what adult, erotic love is like. When we move up a gear, we enter another stage of potential, not only for form, but for loss of it. If we keep growing, we discover new areas opening up to be explored, with new storms to contend with. We climb a hill only to find unexpected peaks and valleys beyond. There is no 'happy ever after' plateau. The new potential – for falling passionately in love, say, or having a child – creates new problems, new possibilities of hurt and subsequent loss of equilibrium – betrayal, humiliation, jealousy, conflict, failure, loss. Loving another is a hostage to fortune and to our own limitations. Reluctant to face disappointment, we are tempted to regress to default positions. We take one (or more) steps back for two (or fewer) steps forward.

If we start to 'mind the gap' when we are separated from our loved one(s), we feel, naturally, a sense of loss. If we tell ourselves we don't care, this painful feeling can to an extent be obliterated. But if we do open ourselves to, and endure, these painful feelings, life is enriched, fuller. The pain is, after all, witness to the love.

Personal or institutional change takes time. The side of us that is willing to countenance change is bound to have difficulties, shots fired across our internal and external bows. Fixing one thing may throw up new versions of the underlying problem, as when someone who manages to stop smoking finds that now he can't stop eating, and becomes obese – an intrinsic drawback of therapies that aim mainly at the removal of symptoms. If we are to reinforce change, we have to work at it. We have to get beyond the initial manic excitement, epitomised by Archimedes, who, having found a method of determining the volume of an irregularly shaped object, famously jumped out of the bath and ran naked through the streets shouting 'Eureka!'

We may imagine that finding form will be a matter of entering a permanent zone of excellence, a plateau, a sort of heaven of unmitigated and uninterrupted bliss. It is as if a relationship could – should – be all sexual and emotional climax, and is worth nothing if not. If this is our belief, then small, piecemeal improvements will be devalued. With one patient, it became clear that because years had been wasted in addiction and mental illness and a struggle to face life, work and friendships, and he could not get those years back or catch up with his peers, he was repeatedly gripped by the idea that nothing could be repaired. This belief and attitude limited his capacity to change. Each achievement came to feel to him puny and worthless. On top of this, recognition of the difficulties brought on by the illness brings with it guilt and shame at so much waste of life. What's the point in trying?

Here is a general truth: when we are out of form we need to work on ourselves. We have to get ourselves into a better frame of mind in order to think and relate, to work and play, with more freedom. In planes, safety announcements tell us that in the unlikely event of a loss of air pressure, masks will drop from above our heads; we should fix our own masks before attending to the children's. To help others, as well as ourselves, we have to survive, and be in good enough shape.

Give a Man a Fish . . .

There is an ultimate mystery about motivation. Why do I take a particular route at a particular moment? Why do I take it and you don't?

Form often goes beyond being a matter of continuing improvement in a task that is clearly set out and doesn't change. Achieving new levels of form involves a development in what is possible, a change of heart and orientation akin to that achieved in growing up. We develop or move into new forms for our form. (And as in growing up, it is important to keep in touch with earlier states.)

In a BBC Radio 4 talk (the first in a series by European writers in the aftermath of the murder of twelve people in the attack on the offices of the weekly satirical newspaper *Charlie Hebdo* in Paris on 7 January 2015, and the ensuing anti-immigration demonstrations in Germany), novelist Abdelkader Benali spoke of his experience as a child-immigrant. In December 1979, at the age of four, he arrived from Morocco in snow-covered Rotterdam with his mother and sister, to join his father, a butcher. As a child, he was, he tells us, always rushing around 'looking for an exit', until he bumped into a glass pane in a door, and broke it. This was him, 'trying to break out of the mould'.

He speaks of his first day at kindergarten. His mother gave him 'this yellow edible thing that we called a "*plátano*"', a Spanish word, Benali adds, elaborating that the Spanish had colonised the Riff, in northern Morocco, before going back to Iberia, 'leaving behind their buildings, their language and their crimes'. The family never spoke of Morocco. The kindergarten teacher, who was the most beautiful woman he'd ever seen, asked him what he had with him. He told her it was a *plátano*. She laughed and said 'we call it a *bnaan*'. He said, '"no, it's a *plátano*"'. The *plátano* was mine, the *bnaan* was hers.'

When he got home his mother asked him about his day. He told her, "'The *plátano* is a *bnaan*". My mother said "I want you to call it *plátano*. In this house it's a *plátano*". I shouted "Stop it", and started running around the house.'

There were only two books in the Benali home. One was the Koran, the other the Rotterdam telephone directory. He tells a brief story about each. As a small boy, he would phone people at random from the directory, and tell them his name and where he came from. They would say, kindly, that there must have been lots of sand and camels; no, he told them, he came from the mountains, he never saw sand or camels.

The Koran – to the little boy the place where all the dead people were who hadn't left a number – was the basis of his argument with a boy in his class at school, a Jehovah's Witness. Both boys had been forbidden by their families to go on the class's first overnight trip away from Rotterdam: it was not fitting for boys and girls to go away together. Benali recalled a sort of Arsenal v. Chelsea supporters' battle between the two boys about which God was greater, and who was the true prophet, Muhammad or Jesus.

Benali sketches a picture of a hyperactive child breaking things: one who fought his corner for his religion, had a sense that his identity had been stolen, but at the same time made contact with local people and corrected their prejudices. How might this have turned out? He might, he implies, have become any kind of adult – a model citizen, or a violent extremist. One day, however, Benali's life changed:

I stumbled on a book that talked about transformation, talked about being an outsider. The first sentence gripped me instantly. 'One morning, when Gregor Samsa woke from troubled dreams, he found himself transformed in his bed into a horrible insect.' Never before had I read so honestly, so deeply, and so without compromise, about myself, as I did in Kafka's 'Metamorphosis'. I too changed into an insect when I felt so misunderstood by, and was so angry at, a world that seemed to mock my beliefs and my identity. After the anger melted away, nothing was left but shame, shame at not being wanted, at being out of place. Kafka's book gave me a place where I could belong. That place was literature.

Benali started reading the Koran, too. '"He who created man from a blood clot said 'Recite, in the name of the Lord'", which I understood also as "Read". He taught men what they knew not.' Not that this new home in words and books has made his life easy. 'Many times I have shuddered: why step out of my comfort zone, so far from home, reading Joseph Brody, Robert Frost, and Kafka?'

The child running frenetically around the small house had no words for his feelings. But Kafka was a revelation for him. Here was someone who understood what it was like to feel alien and confused. More than this, here was a *writer*, one who found words to shape and transform his anger, and created extended metaphors for states of mind. Kafka, like the Koran, taught him what he knew not, what he hadn't known he didn't know.

Benali also implies that there can be a hair's breadth between our taking one route in life and another. He grew into a different kind of person, going through a personal metamorphosis into understanding and articulation, rather than staying on the old path of reactive, hyperactive rage.

This reminded me of Rowan Williams's *Writing in the Dust*, the small book he wrote in response to the atrocity in New York on 9/11. Williams had been a few blocks away when the planes were flown into the Twin Towers. For him as for many others this murderous event produced first terror, then a wish for revenge. But he did not stop there. He remembered how Jesus, when provocatively challenged to throw the first stone at the woman accused of adultery, took a stick and wrote in the dust. Williams suggests that whatever it was that Jesus wrote or doodled, he thereby created time and the mental space to reach beyond his crude initial feelings (perhaps of condemnation, or of being tempted to comply with those who were trying to catch him out). And the outcome was his magnificent, magnanimous, compassionate, but not exculpatory, response: 'Let him who is without sin cast the first stone.'

Williams's own change of heart took him beyond terror and revenge into a consideration of what might have motivated the terrorists. He was not being defensive, nothing was denied of the initial feelings, or indeed of the condemnation. As in Westerns, the sheriff rightly rides out to track down the perpetrators. And we never eliminate either the old emotions and default positions or the realistic feelings of horror. But we may rebalance them and deepen our responses, working our way towards a more rounded, more compassionate view.

In his influential book on the significance of small-scale economics, *Small is Beautiful*, E. F. Schumacher wrote:

> When we give a man a fish we give him and his family a meal. When we give him a rod we give a capacity to catch fish, for several meals. When we give him training in how to make rods and start a business, we give him a capacity for an expanded way of life and living.

The first is the gift of an item, the last a life-changing capacity. There is a parallel to what is given to a patient by a psychoanalyst's interpretation when it resonates for him. First

– the fish – an understanding of a particular moment of experience. Second, the interpretation, which may give insight to the patient about a pattern in his life, repeated in many situations. And third, the start, when things go well, of the patient's ability to acquire an enlarged capacity for thinking, an 'expanded way of living'. If the analyst has enough depth of mind himself, and the patient is able to take in what is offered, the patient comes to internalise something of that thinking capacity himself.

The shift does not have to be recondite or highly intellectual. Tim Gallwey's telephone operators, as we have seen, did not simply become quicker and more courteous, the goal of the management team. In fact, Gallwey explicitly insisted that goals should not be mentioned in setting up his meetings with the operators. Rather, with his suggestion that they attend to the tone of voice of the hundreds of callers they interacted with each day, and also that they notice their own, he (and they) changed their *frame of mind*. They even exported the new way of listening into their home lives. Their form improved and was transformed through the process. They had moved outside the box.

I don't remember very much of what I was taught at school. But one lesson stuck because the teacher spoke of this kind of deepening of capacity. I remember clearly Stanley Ward, the head of classics, talking about Homer's account of religion. Much of Greek religion in the *Iliad* was at the level, he said, of 'I give prayers and offerings to you to persuade you to give good things to me' – the theme of many prayers to this day. But, he added, there is at one point in the *Iliad* an allusion to a more deeply moral attitude, beyond self-interest. This is the passage where Homer speaks of Sin racing round the world doing harm, while lame Prayer hobbles after trying to put things right. How vivid and true this is! How many of our mistakes, crimes and moral failings are to do with rushing to judgment and to action; and how slowly we come to see the errors of our ways, let alone repent and make reparations.

Kafka's image of alienation offered Benali a new way of dealing with his conflicts. Not only did it give him a resonating image for central aspects of his own predicament, it also gave him, through his identification with the writer, an eagerness to study literature, and a vocation. Even more, he was enabled to grow a new articulation in his own thinking, a new capacity to evoke and create images, stories, and versions of self and other. This amounts to a radically different developmental path. Through literature and his own writing he has found a voice for a changed self. He has not simply improved his form along the old lines. A banana no longer has to be either a *plátano* or a *bnaan*. Nor is this growth a matter of learning a technique, a means to an end. The ends themselves change along with the means.

Mysterious Motivations, and the Illusion of Serene Good Form

Benali recognises the moment when his life took a new course. But why did that moment resonate with him? Why did I take the fork that led to cricket, then philosophy, then cricket again, then psychoanalysis? These choices, like insights, have an element of mystery about them. There are in some lives moments of dreadful choice: life-or-death decisions, between further harrowing treatment for a life-threatening disease or acceptance of dying, taking a path of love or hate, moving towards change or sticking with, and reverting to, more primitive, easier options. There are also everyday versions of such dramas on a small scale. Form, and the form it will take, often takes us by surprise. It is provisional, subject to fluctuations, and in many ways hidden from us before, and sometimes even after, we get there.

Psychoanalysis allows us to explore in our minds all the tempting forks, and, hopefully, enables us to let go and mourn those we choose (and have chosen in the past) not to take, while yet being committed to those we do take. We hold in mind the paths untravelled without letting them preclude commitment. We are more open to our ambivalence, without being disabled by it. The Ten-Tips-for-Being-On-Form self-help book assumes the destination is clear, and that there are discoverable routes to it. My view is that many ends are more open, less fixed, more conflict-ridden. Our beginnings rarely know our ends.

I have been lucky in my life to have had the opportunity to enjoy and be stretched by several careers and serious activities, including this current one: writing. Returning to cricket at the age of twenty-nine, to captain Middlesex, was a risk. I was giving up the security of an academic career – and whenever I came to the end of my cricket career, I would have to make a new choice. Yet in fact my friend Michael Scholar was more nervous for me than I was. At that point I knew what I wanted.

Ithaka

> Hold on to Ithaka in your mind always.
> To return there is your goal.
> But don't hurry to complete the journey.
> Finer that it takes many years,
> so that you drop anchor there as an old man,
> wealthy with all that you've acquired on the journey,
> Not banking on Ithaka to make you rich.

In the famous poem by Greek poet C. P. Cavafy, our destination is reached. But the travelling is at least as important as the arrival. And don't expect Ithaka to answer all your problems! We reach the destination slowly and uncertainly. It is in the going that we have discovered new things, that we have become rich through all we've gained on the way.

I find it hard to end this book, Reader, not knowing if we've arrived in Ithaka, or whether there is even an Ithaka to arrive at. Moreover, I have the inclination to end with a bang not a whimper, with a definitive statement, a last, fast run on the ski-slope, or a happy marriage in which all is solved, not with an invitation to you to be open, or a mere 'goodbye and good luck'. But we know that would be fake. So, if you have got this far, or have dipped into this last page, I have to let you – like the book itself, or like one's children when they leave home – find your own path, with no hard-and-fast signposts, no clear route-planner to a clear destination, no guarantees. I hope you enjoyed the journey, as I have done, and that you feel you gained something on the way, as I certainly did.

From time to time we all, like Odysseus and like my car-driver friend, Moazem, take wrong turnings on our journeys. Though we miss the safety of the already known, this is not all bad. Form and change often grow from loss and difficulty. As Moazem recognised, losing our way is an opportunity for serendipity.

Well, go on, then. Get lost!

SELECTED BIBLIOGRAPHY

1 Getting Out of Bed on the Wrong Side (pages 1–12)

Jonathan Smith, *The Learning Game*. London: Abacus, 2002.

Leo Tolstoy, *Anna Karenina*. London: Everyman's Library, 1992.

Malcolm Gladwell, *Blink: The Power of Thinking without Thinking*. New York: Little Brown, 2005.

D. W. Winnicott, *Therapeutic Consultations in Child Psychiatry*. London: Hogarth and Institute of Psychoanalysis, 1971. (The squiggle game is also described in earlier writings, e.g. in *Collected Papers*, London: Tavistock, 1953.)

Joseph Conrad, *Notes on Life and Letters*. Cambridge: Cambridge University Press, 1921.

J. L. Carr, *A Month in the Country*. Hemel Hempstead: Harvester Press, 1980.

Ovid, *Metamorphoses*. Oxford: Oxford University Press, 2008. (Story of Icarus.)

David Hume, *A Treatise of Human Nature*, 1738. Oxford: Oxford University Press, 2000.

2 Zen and the Art of Batting (pages 13–22)

Alan Paton, *Cry the Beloved Country*. London: Jonathan Cape, 1948.

Mike Brearley, *The Art of Captaincy*. London: Hodder and Stoughton, 1985.

Eugen Herrigel, *Zen in the Art of Archery*. New York: Random House, 1989.

Pat Barker, interview with Alex Clark. *Guardian*, 29 August 2015.

3 On to the Couch (pages 23–33)

Edward St Aubyn, *Some Hope*. London: William Heinemann, 1994.

Anna Freud, quoted in Heinz Kohut, *The Search for the Self*. New York: International Universities Press, 1978.

John Wisdom, *Other Minds*. Oxford: Blackwell, 1952.

John Wisdom, *Philosophy and Psychoanalysis*. Oxford: Blackwell, 1953.

William Shakespeare, *Hamlet*.

James Strachey, 'The Nature of the Therapeutic Action of Psychoanalysis', in *International Journal of Psychoanalysis*, vol. 15, 1934.

Sigmund Freud, 'The Dynamics of Transference'. *Standard Edition*, vol. 12, 1912; London: Hogarth, 1958.

Sigmund Freud, 'Remembering, Repeating and Working-through'. *Standard Edition*, vol. 12, 1914; London: Hogarth, 1958.

4 A Kind of Rapture (pages 34–47)

J. L. Carr, *A Season in Sinji*. London: Alan Ross, 1967.

S. Knight, 'Follow the white ball', interview with Ronnie O'Sullivan. *New Yorker*, 30 March 2015.

C. Foster and D. Foster, *The Great Dance: A Hunter's Story*, Film, 2000.

David Sylvester, *London Recordings*. London: Chatto and Windus, 2003. (On timing and placement.)

Scyld Berry, *Cricket: The Game of Life*. London: Hodder, 2005.

Kenneth Robinson, 'Do Schools Kill Creativity?', TED talk, 2006.

Don DeLillo, 'The Art of Fiction'. Interview with Andy Begley, *The Paris Review*, 1993.

Andy Kirkpatrick, BBC Radio 4 talk on exposing your own child to risk. *Four Thought*, 12 November 2014.

Charles Lindbergh, *The Spirit of St Louis*. New York: Scribner, 1953.

George Orwell, *Burmese Days*, 1931. London: Victor Gollancz, 2005.

D. W. Winnicott, 'True and False Self', in *The Maturational Processes and the Facilitating Environment*. London: Hogarth and Institute of Psychoanalysis, 1982.

Hugh Brody, *The Other Side of Eden*. London: Faber & Faber, 2002.

Joseph Sandler, 'On communication from patient to analyst: not everything is projective identification', in *International Journal of Psychoanalysis*, vol. 74, 1993.

C. S. Lewis, *The Lion, the Witch and the Wardrobe*. London: Geoffrey Bles, 1950.

Doris Kearns Goodwin, *Team of Rivals: The Political Genius of Abraham Lincoln*. New York: Simon & Schuster, 2005, p. 104.

5 Who Cleans Up After the Party? (pages 48–60)

Ayrton Senna in K. Sturm, *Ayrton Senna – Goodbye Champion, Farewell Friend*. Croydon: Motor Racing Publications, 1994.

Edson Arantes do Nascimento (Pelé), *My Life and the Beautiful Game*. New York: Doubleday, 1977.

Hilary Mantel, 'My writing day'. *Guardian*, 16 April 2016.

Andreas Campomar, *Golazo: A History of Latin-American Football*. London: Quercus, 2014.

Joseph Conrad, *The Mirror of the Sea*. London: Methuen, 1906.

R. Crawford, *Young Eliot: From St Louis to The Waste Land*. London: Jonathan Cape, 2015.

David Tuckett, *Minding the Markets*. London: Palgrave, 2011.

Mervyn King, *The End of Alchemy*. London: Little, Brown, 2016.

Tom Main, 'The Ailment', in *The Ailment and other Psychoanalytic Essays*. London: Free Association Books, 1989.

6 Disencumbering Consciousness (pages 61–70)

W. R. Bion, *Learning from Experience*. London: Heinemann, 1962.

Alan Watts, *The Way of Zen*. New York: Pantheon Books, 1957.

George Eliot, *Middlemarch*, 1871. London: Everyman's Library, 1991.

Timothy Gallwey, *The Inner Game of Tennis*. London: Jonathan Cape, 1975.

Daniel Kahneman, *Thinking, Fast and Slow*. New York: Farrar Strauss and Giroux, 2011.

Matthew Syed, *Bounce*. London: Fourth Estate, 2011.

D. W. Winnicott, *Therapeutic Consultations in Child Psychiatry*. London: Hogarth and Institute of Psychoanalysis, 1971.

Sigmund Freud, 'Recommendations on Analytic Technique'. *Standard Edition*, vol. 12, 1912; London: Hogarth, 1958.

7 Practising Your Scales (pages 71–87)

George Grove, *A Dictionary of Music and Musicians*. New York: Macmillan, 1879.

Harold Pinter, *Art, Truth and Politics*. London: Faber & Faber, 2006.

Ken Barrington, *Playing it Straight*. London: Stanley Paul, 1968.

Life, 'Life Report', 25 January 1943.

Frances Cuka and Hannah Gumbrill, interview transcript: Theatre Archive Project. The British Library, http://sounds.bl.uk, 2008.

J. Kahn and D. Watkin, 'Classical Music Looks toward China in Hope'. *New York Times*, 3 April 2007.

Sigmund Freud, 'New Introductory Lectures'. Standard Edition, vol. 22, 1932; London: Hogarth, 1958.

W. H. Auden, *Twelve Songs!*, 1938–8. London: Faber & Faber, 2001.

George Orwell, *Animal Farm*. London: Secker and Warburg, 1945.

Graham Gooch, interview with Jo Harman in *All-Out Cricket*. London, 2013.

R. C. Collingwood, *The Principles of Art*. Oxford: Oxford University Press, 1938.

Alison Gopnik, *The Gardener and the Carpenter*. London: Bodley Head, 2016.

8 'You idiot, Rags!' – Talking to Oneself (pages 88–106)

Yogi Berra, *The Yogi Book*. New York: Workman, 1998.

Paula Heimann, 'On Counter-transference', in *International Journal of Psychoanalysis*, vol. 31, 1950.

Antonio Gramsci, *Letters from Prison*, ed. F. Rosengarten. New York: Columbia University Press, 1994.

Mike Brearley and Dudley Doust, *The Ashes Retained*. London: Hodder and Stoughton, 1979.

Ken Barrington, *Playing it Straight*. London: Stanley Paul, 1968.

John Sutton, 'Batting, Habit and Memory: the Embodied Mind and the Nature of Skill' in *Sport in Society*, vol. 10, 2001.

René Descartes, 'Meditations on First Philosophy', in E. S. Haldane and G. R. T. Ross, *The Philosophical Works of Descartes*. Cambridge: Cambridge University Press, 1967.

Marion Milner, *A Life of One's Own*. London: Chatto and Windus, 1936.

Maurice Merleau-Ponty, *The Phenomenology of Perception*. London: Routledge and Kegan Paul, 1945.

W. R. Bion, 'Notes on Memory and Desire', in *Psychoanalytic Form*, vol. 2, 1967.

9 'We Let Our Cricket Do the Talking' (pages 107–16)

Kazuo Ishiguro, *The Remains of the Day*. London: Faber & Faber, 1989.

Scyld Berry, *Cricket: The Game of Life*. London: Hodder, 2015.

C. L. R. James, *Beyond a Boundary*. London: Hutchinson, 1963. (On Learie Constantine.)

M. K. Gandhi, 'Satyagraha', in *Young India*, 19 January 1920.

Jean-Paul Sartre, *Essays in Existentialism*. New York: Citadel Press, 1993.

V. S. Naipaul, 'On Being a Writer'. *New York Review of Books*, 1987.

10 The Making of a Team (pages 117–35)

D. H. Lawrence, *Studies in Classic American Literature*, 1923. Cambridge: Cambridge University Press, 2003.

Raymond Domenech, *Tout seul*. Paris: Flammarion, 2012.

Leo Tolstoy, *Anna Karenina*, 1877. London: Everyman's Library, 1992.

Jonathan Smith, *The Learning Game*. London: Abacus, 2002.

Ian McEwan, *Solar*. London: Jonathan Cape, 2010.

Chrispher Bollas, *The Christopher Bollas Reader*. Hove: Routledge, 2011.

Becki Lawson, www.nature.com/articles/srep17020.

Atul Gawande, Reith Lectures, BBC Radio 4, 2014.

Margaret Heffernan, *Wilful Blindness*. London: Simon & Schuster, 2012.

George Orwell, *Nineteen Eighty-four*, 1949. London: Penguin, 2004.

Kevin Pietersen, *KP: The Autobiography*. London: Sphere, 2014.

Hillel the Elder, *Ethics of the Elders*.

11 Why Sport? (pages 136–60)

Heinrich Harrer, *The White Spider*, 1958 London: Harper Perennial, 2005.

Jonathan Smith, *The Learning Game*. London: Abacus, 2002.

Johan Huizinga, *Homo Ludens: A Study of the Play-Element in Culture*. Boston: The Beacon Press, 1971.

Julie Stone, 'Tom's Perfect World', in *The Baby as Subject: Clinical Studies in Infant-Parent Therapy*, ed. Campbell Paul and Frances Thomson-Salo. London: Karnac, 2014.

Michael Ignatieff, *Fire and Ashes*. Harvard: Harvard University Press, 2013.

Jonathan Trott, *Unguarded*. London: Sphere, 2016.

'Isaiah Berlin, the Soviet Union and the Captive Nations.' Isaiah Berlin Lecture, Riga, Latvia, 2012. *Isaiah Berlin Virtual Library*.

Steve Waugh, *The Meaning of Luck*. Macquarie Park: Sams Marketing, 2013.

Iris Murdoch, *The Sovereignty of Good*. Abingdon: Routledge, 2001.

Henry James, *The Portrait of a Lady*, 1881. Oxford: OUP, 2009.

12 Seeing the Wood and the Trees (pages 161–87)

(Several of those quoted in the sections on directing and conducting were interviewed for a programme on BBC Radio 4, 2007, or for the prequel, 'The Art of Conducting', 2005.)

Henry Marsh, *Do No Harm: Stories of Life, Death and Brain Surgery*. London: Weidenfeld and Nicolson, 2014.

D. Barrett, *The Committee of Sleep: How Artists, Scientists, and Athletes Use their Dreams for Creative Problem Solving – and How You Can Too*. New York: Random House, 2001.

Wayne Smith, quoted in the *Guardian*, 28 June 2017, in 'Wayne Smith's role in transforming All Blacks culture bears fruit', by Alexander Bisley.

Peter Brook, *The Empty Space*. London: Penguin, 2008.

Georg Wübbolt, 'I am lost to the world', DVD, 2014. (Documentary on Carlos Kleiber.)

Siddhartha Mukherjee, *The Emperor of All Maladies: a Biography of Cancer*. New York: Simon and Schuster, 2010.

13 A Tiny Mistake in the Blink of an Eye (pages 188–96)

Helen Pidd, article in the *Guardian*, 14 August 2016.

14 Freudian Slip (pages 197–214)

John Wisdom, *Other Minds*. Oxford: Blackwell, 1952.

Aristotle, Form and Matter, discussed widely, for instance in *The Physics* 350 BCE, Oxford: OUP, 2008, and *The Metaphysics*, Oxford: OUP, 1924.

David Hume, *A Treatise of Human Nature*, 1738. Oxford: OUP, 2000.

Julian Barnes, *The Noise of Time*. London: Jonathan Cape, 2016.

Jonathan Lear, *A Case for Irony*. Harvard: Harvard University Press, 2014.

Plato, *The Republic*.

Jean-Paul Sartre, *Essays in Existentialism*. New York: Citadel Press, 1965.

Sigmund Freud, 'Remembering, Repeating and Working-through'. *Standard Edition*, vol. 12, 1914; London: Hogarth, 1958.

David Foster Wallace, 'Plain old untrendy troubles and emotions'. Address to graduating class, Kenyon College, 2005, published in the *Guardian*, 20 September 2008.

Benedict de Spinoza, *Ethics*, 1677. London: Penguin, 1996.

Ludwig Wittgenstein, *Philosophical Investigations*. Oxford: Blackwell 1953.

15 Horse or Snaffle? (pages 215–28)

William Shakespeare, *Othello*.

Herman Melville, *Billy Budd, Sailor and Selected Tales*, 1924. Oxford: OUP, 2009.

Michael Eigen, *Reshaping the Self*. Madison: Psychosocial Press, 1995.

Nuno Oliveira, *Reflections on Equestrian Art*. London: J. A. Allen, 1988.

Roy Campbell, 'Some South African Novelists', in *Adamastor*. London: Faber & Faber, 1930.

Anna Freud, *The Ego and the Mechanisms of Defence*. London: Karnac Books, 1992.

V. S. Naipaul, 'On Being a Writer', *New York Review of Books*, 23 April 1987.

Alan Ross, *Cape Summer and the Australians in England*. London: Faber & Faber, 2012.

Jonathan Trott, *Unguarded*. London: Sphere, 2016.

Jean-Paul Sartre, *Sketch for a Theory of the Emotions*. London: Methuen & Co., 1962.

Margaret Heffernan *Wilful Blindness*. London: Simon & Schuster, 2012.

Mihaly Csikszentmihalyi, *Flow*. London: Rider, 2002.

16 Fear of Failure (pages 229–38)

Neville Symington, 'Phantasy Effects that which it represents', in *International Journal of Psychoanalysis*, vol. 66, 1985.

Herman Melville, *Moby-Dick*, 1851. London: Everyman's Library, 1991.

Kathryn Hunter, talk at event in honour of Peter Brook, Victoria & Albert Museum, 2015.

Franz Kafka, *The Burrow*. London: Penguin, 2017.

Adrian Stokes, *A Game that must be Lost: Collected Papers*. Cheadle: Carcanet Press, 1973.

R. Nairn, *Diamond Mind*. Cape Town: Kairon Press, 1998.

Jared Tendler, *The Mental Game of Poker*. US: Jared Tendler LLC, 2011.

17 Fear of Success (pages 239–51)

Sigmund Freud, 'Those wrecked by success'; *Standard Edition* vol. 14, 1916, London: Hogarth, 1958.

William Shakespeare. *Macbeth*.

Henrik Ibsen, *Rosmersholm*, 1886. London: Nick Hern Books, 2002.

Carole Satyamurti, *Mahabharata: A Modern Retelling*. New York: Norton, 2015.

Mike Brearley, *The Art of Captaincy*. London: Hodder and Stoughton, 1985.

Henry James, *The Portrait of a Lady*, 1881. London: Everyman's Library, 1991.

18 Once-born, Twice-born (pages 252–67)

Graham Greene, *Ways of Escape*. London: The Bodley Head, 1980.

Leo Tolstoy, *A Confession*, 1882. London: Penguin, 1987.

William James, *The Varieties of Religious Experience*, 1902. London: Penguin, 1983.

Henry James, *The Europeans*, 1878. London: Penguin, 2007.

Ludwig Wittgenstein, *Tractatus Logico-Philosophicus*, 1921. New York: Cosimo Classics, 2007.

Ludwig Wittgenstein, *Philosophical Investigations*. Oxford: Blackwell, 1953.

Ray Monk, *Wittgenstein: The Duties of Genius*. London: Vintage, 1991.

Douglas Gordon and P. Parreno, *Zidane: A 21st Century Portrait*, film shown at the Edinburgh Festival, 2006.

Jonathan Smith, *The Learning Game*. London: Abacus, 2002.

Timothy Hyman, Introduction to: *Amit Ambalal: the 'Unseen' Drawings and Watercolours*. Ahmedabad: Archer, 2014.

W. R. Bion, *Four Discussions with W.R. Bion*. Scotland: The Clunie Press, 1978.

Albert Einstein and Leopold Infeld, *The Evolution of Physics*. Cambridge: Cambridge University Press, 1938.

Thomas Kuhn, *The Structure of Scientific Revolutions*. Chicago: University of Chicago Press, 2012.

19 Masks and Costumes (pages 268–80)

Hilary Mantel, *Giving up the Ghost*, London: Fourth Estate, 2003.

Donald Moss, 'The insane look of the bewildered half-broken animal', in *Journal of the American Psychoanalytic Association*, 2016.

Stephen Frears, *The Programme*, 2015 – film about Lance Armstrong.

Catherine Shoard, *Guardian* review of Frears' film, 15 September 2015.

Franz Kafka, 'Report to an Academy'. 1917.

Thomas Mann, *Buddenbrooks*, 1901. London: Everyman's Library, 1994.

John Wisdom, *Philosophy and Psychoanalysis*. Oxford: Blackwell, 1953.

Rowan Williams, interviewed by Robert McCrum, the *Observer*, 28 December 2014.

Mike Brearley, *The Art of Captaincy*. London: Hodder and Stoughton, 1985.

Michael Hofmann, *London Review of Books*, 28 January 2010.

Kurt Vonnegut, *Welcome To The Monkey House and Palm Sunday*. London: Vintage, 1994.

20 Doing the Needful (pages 281–95)

John Klauber, *Difficulties in the Analytic Encounter*. London: Karnac Books, 1986.

Mike Brearley and Dudley Doust, *The Ashes Retained*. London: Hodder & Stoughton, 1979.

Mike Brearley, *Phoenix from the Ashes*: London: HarperCollinsWillow, 1983.

Andy Kirkpatrick, BBC Radio 4 talk on exposing your own child to risk. *Four Thought*, 12 November 2014.

Graham Greene, *Ways of Escape*. London: The Bodley Head, 1980.

Joseph Conrad, *Heart of Darkness and Other Tales*, 1889. Oxford: Oxford University Press, 2002.

John Bowlby, *A Secure Base*. London: Routledge, 1988.

Peter Cook et al., *Beyond the Fringe*. DVD.

Mihaly Csikszentmihalyi, *Flow*. London: Rider, 2002.

W. Timothy Gallwey, *The Inner Game of Tennis*. London: Jonathan Cape, 1975.

W. Timothy Gallwey, *The Inner Game of Work*. New York: Random House, 2001.

Nelson Mandela, *Long Walk to Freedom*. London: Abacus: 1995.

Leo Tolstoy, *War and Peace*, 1869. London: Everyman's Library, 2010.

Tony Garnett, *The Day the Music Died*. London: Constable, 2016.

William Shakespeare, *King Lear* (for the phrase 'wrong imaginations': Gloucester, blinded, confronted by the frankly mad King, says 'Better I were distract: /So should my thoughts be sever'd from my griefs, /And woes by wrong imaginations lose /The knowledge of themselves').

Ian McEwan, *Solar*. London: Jonathan Cape, 2010.

21 Can Quick Fixes Stick? (pages 296–314)

Jonathan Lear, introduction to Hans Loewald, *The Essential Loewald*. Hagerstown: University Publishing Group, 2000.

T.S. Eliot, 'Burnt Norton', first of *The Four Quartets*. New York: Harcourt and Brace, 1943.

Mike Brearley, *Phoenix from the Ashes*. London: Hodder and Stoughton, 1982.

Mike Brearley, *The Art of Captaincy*. London: Hodder and Stoughton, 1985.

William James, *The Varieties of Religious Experience*. London: Penguin, 1983.

D. W. Winnicott, *Therapeutic Consultations in Child Psychiatry*. London: Hogarth and Institute of Psychoanalysis, 1971.

Peter Fonagy, David Taylor et al. 'Pragmatic randomized controlled trial of long-term psychoanalytic psychiatry for treatment-resistant depression', in *World Psychiatry*, 14, 2005.

William Blake, *The Complete Poems*. London: Penguin, 1977.

Rob Nairn, *Diamond Mind*. Cape Town: Kairon Press, 1998.

Edward Dusinberre, *Beethoven for a Later Age: the Journey of a String Quartet*. London: Faber & Faber, 2016.

Sigmund Freud, 'Remembering, Repeating and Working-through', in *Standard Edition*, vol. 12, 1914; London: Hogarth, 1958.

Gabriella Braun, *The Counter-Intuitive Leader*, forthcoming.

22 The Hardest Thing of All (pages 315–29)

J. A. Baker, *The Peregrine*. 1967.

W. R. Bion, *Brazilian Lectures*. London: Karnac Books, 1990.

Ludwig Wittgenstein, *Philosophical Investigations*. Oxford: Blackwell, 1953.

W.H. Auden, *A Selection by the Author*. London: Penguin, 1958.

Robert Macfarlane, 'Violent Spring'. The *Guardian*, 15 April 2017.

Hans Christian Andersen, *The Emperor's New Clothes*. London: Penguin, 1995.

Arthur Miller, *The Crucible*, 1953. London: Penguin 2000.

Louis Liebenberg, *The Art of Tracking*. Cape Town: David Philip, 1990.

T. F. Main, 'The Ailment', in *The Ailment and other Psychoanalytic Essays*. London: Free Association Books, 1989.

Virgil, *The Aeneid*. London: Penguin, 2003.

Homer, *The Iliad*. London: Penguin, 2003.

Shakespeare, *The Complete Sonnets and Poems*.

Sigmund Freud, 'Remembering, Repeating and Working-through'. *Standard Edition*, vol. 12, 1914; London: Hogarth, 1958.

23 At Least Buy a Ticket (pages 330–39)

W. B. Yeats, 'The Second Coming', 1922.

Ted Sorensen, *Kennedy: The Classic Biography*. New York: Harper, 1965.

Marion Milner, 'Mind the Gap', in *Between Sessions and Beyond the Couch*, ed Joan Raphael-Leff. Colchester: CPS Psychoanalytic Publications, 2002.

Jonathan Lear, *A Case for Irony*. Harvard: Harvard University Press, 2014. (Re Socrates, doubt and commitment. I owe a lot to Lear for this whole chapter.)

Plato, *The Last Days of Socrates*.

Franz Kafka, *The Burrow*. London: Penguin, 2017.

Aristotle, *On the Heavens*. Warminster: Aris and Phillips, 1995.

Edward Dusinberre, *Beethoven for a Later Age*. London: Faber & Faber, 2016.

Henry Marsh, *Do No Harm*. London: Weidenfeld & Nicolson, 2014.

Aldous Huxley, *Texts and Pretexts: an Anthology with Commentaries*. New York: Harper and Brothers, 1933.

W. F. Bion, *The Long Week-End, 1897–1919*. Karnac Books, 1982.

Matteo Pasquinelli, *Alleys of the Mind: Augmented Intelligence Traumas*. Luneberg: Meson Press, 2015.

Gabriele Junkers, *The Empty Couch: the Taboo of Ageing and Retirement in Psychoanalysis*. London: Routledge, 2013.

Tahmima Anam, *The Bones of Grace*. London: HarperCollins, 2016.

24 The Chickadee Bird (pages 340–55)

Giuseppe di Lampedusa, *The Leopard*. London: Time, 1960.

James Kerr, *Legacy: What the All Blacks Can Teach Us About the Business of Life*. London: Constable, 2013.

C. Gilson, M. Pratt, K. Roberts, E. Weymes, *Peak Performance*. London: HarperCollins, 2000. (For Rod Marsh story, and other details of NZ rugby.)

Margaret Heffernan, *Wilful Blindness*. London: Simon & Schuster, 2012.

Atul Gawande, Reith Lectures, BBC Radio 4, 2014.

William Shakespeare, *Henry IV Part 1*.

Jonathan Lear, *Radical Hope: Ethics in the Face of Cultural Devastation*. Cambridge, MA: Harvard, 2008.

Hugh Brody, *The Other Side of Eden: Hunters, Farmers and the Shaping of the World*. London: Faber & Faber, 2001. (On the expansion of agriculturalists and the impact on hunter-gatherers.)

Marilynne Robinson, *When I Was a Child I Read Books*. London: Virago, 2012.

25 How Do I Know What I Think Until I Read What I Write (pages 356–68)

Winston Churchill, Speech, London, 2 November 1949.

Joseph Conrad, Author's note to *Chance*, 1913. Oxford: Oxford World Classics, 1999.

Marilynne Robinson, *The Givenness of* Things. London: Virago, 2015.

R. G. Collingwood, *The Principles of Art*. Oxford: Clarendon Press, 1947.

W. R. Bion, *Learning from Experience*. London: William Heinemann, 1962.

Laurence Sterne, *The Life and Opinions of Tristram Shandy, Gentleman*. Oxford: OUP, 2009.

Ronald Britton 'Publication Anxiety: Conflict between Communication and Affiliation'. *International Journal of Psychoanalysis*, vol. 75, 1994.

George Orwell, *Politics and the English Language*. London: Penguin, 2013.

Rowan Williams, Acceptance speech, Orwell Prize 2015.

Marcel Proust, *Against Sainte-Beuve*. London: Penguin, 1994.

26 Ithaka (pages 369–83)

Ed Smith, *What Sport Tells Us About Life*. London: Penguin, 2009.

Abdelkader Benali, BBC Radio 4 talk, 2015.

Marion Milner, *A Life of One's Own*. London: Chatto and Windus, 1936.

S. T. Coleridge, Preface to 'Kubla Khan', 1816.

Franz Kafka, *Metamorphosis and Other Stories*. London: Penguin, 2007.

Rowan Williams, *Writing in the Dust*. London: Hodder & Stoughton, 2002.

E. F. Schumacher, *Small is Beautiful: A Study of Economics as if People Mattered*. London: Vintage, 1993.

W. Timothy Gallwey, *The Inner Game of Work*. New York: Random House, 2001.

Homer. *The Iliad*. London: Penguin, 2003.

C. P. Cavafy, 'Ithaka', 1911, trans. Mike Brearley, 2017.

ACKNOWLEDGMENTS

———

One person present at the talk I gave at the London School of Economics in 2012 was Ed Smith, whom I'd known when he captained Middlesex at cricket, and whose book, *What Sport Teaches Us About Life*, I had enjoyed and learned from. Ed took part in the discussion, and afterwards encouraged me to write up my thoughts as a paper. Dinah Wood, theatre editor at Faber & Faber, was shown the paper and suggested this might make a short book (though it has not, I'm afraid, turned into a *short* book). I am grateful to Tim Newton, also present at the talk, for allowing me to write about our contact. I would not normally disclose the identity of anyone I see in a professional capacity, and had no such intentions about this encounter. But in September 2015 I had a second email from him, recalling things that we had discussed that had helped him. He put it so clearly that I wrote to him later to ask if he would mind my describing his experience in the book. I said that if I used it, I would of course not expect to name him, and could if he preferred disguise his identity. He replied that he would be happy for me to do so with or without his name.

There are many others who made contributions by being in the book, quoted or described, named or unnamed. There are my cricketing colleagues and opponents, and there are also my patients, analysts, supervisors and colleagues. There are people who have helped in so many ways, not least my parents and original family. Often one doesn't know who helped whom – how far ideas and new orientations came from oneself, how far from others. I will mention a few people who undoubtedly made a difference to me. First, from the psychoanalytic field: Pearl King, Michael Feldman, Harold Stewart and Irma Brenman Pick. And from philosophy: Renford Bambrough, John Wisdom, Ilham Dilman and Karl Britton. I should also like to mention David Sylvester, David Sheppard, Dudley Doust, Humphrey Walters, Richard Cohen and Martin Smith.

Since starting on this book, I have given talks based on early versions of different chapters to various groups including the 1952 Club, the Sports Forum, the Budleigh Salterton Festival, the BM Institute of Mental Health in Ahmedabad, a Hawks Club dinner, a conference in Paris held by the International Artists' and Managers' Association, and at a Chipping Camden Literary lunch.

The people who helped me most directly were those who read and commented on long drafts of the whole or part of the book. Ted Braun, whom I first met when we were at Cambridge, read a whole early draft perceptively – he very sadly died in March 2017. My agent, Matthew Hamilton (thank you to Daniel Pick and Stephen Grosz for putting me in touch), read the whole thing at least twice, and has throughout made encouraging and strong comments that made a difference to the end outcome. Mischa Gorchov Brearley and Hugh Brody offered insights over large swathes of the book at various stages. Others who read parts and were very helpful included:

Lara Brearley, Mana Sarabhai Brearley, Fae Dussart, Jacobo Quintanilla, Irma Brenman Pick, Mervyn King, Siddarth Wettimuny, Hilary Mantel, J. M. Coetzee, Ed Miliband, Ian Rickson, Amit Ambalal, Kannan Navaratnem, Ed Smith and Michael Scholar.

I am also indebted to the publishers, Little, Brown, and to more people there than I could name. Richard Beswick was encouraging in the early phases. I'm told I'm lucky to get a copy-editor these days, and Steve Gove's comments were perceptive and salutary. Nithya Rae, keeping the book on track for publication, and Grace Vincent, publicising it, have done a lot to finalise and promote the book. But most of all I'd like to thank Andreas Campomar, my editor. There is a story that Freud tells about an atheist insurance agent who was dying. His family were distraught that he refused to see a pastor. As he neared his end, to their surprise and gratification, he not only agreed to see the pastor, but the latter stayed for a long time with him in the sick room. When he left, the outcome was: the dying man remained an atheist, but the pastor left with an insurance policy. For some time I wondered if this might be true with Andreas, that he would leave for a training in psychoanalysis, while I would not finish my book. But this early stage passed. He himself was, as I say in the text, a sort of analyst in his comments on my character as shown in the writing and its shortcomings. I – we, I believe – greatly enjoyed our frequent meetings. In fact, all faults are down to him.

Finally, there has been my family, many of them mentioned above, and especially Mana, patient throughout, as I remained downstairs for longer, leaving even more of the household chores to her. She has been a wonderful support, and we have often discussed issues, passages and ideas relating to the book. Mischa and Lara, as well as their partners Fae and Jaco, have been supportive, encouraging and willing to challenge. And our two older grandchildren, Luka and Alia, who both feature in the book, have been terrific. The third, Maia, has done what she could; at the time of writing this, at four months she offers an intensity of attention and engagement in contact that is an inspiring example of how to live, perhaps of being on form. She reminds me of the laughing Buddhas of Chapter 21.

PICTURE AND TEXT CREDITS

INDEX